Web Development with Bootstrap 4 and Angular 2

Second Edition

Combine the power of Bootstrap 4 and Angular 2 to build cutting-edge web apps that truly stand out from the crowd

Sergey Akopkokhyants
Stephen Radford

BIRMINGHAM - MUMBAI

Web Development with Bootstrap 4 and Angular 2

Second Edition

First published: May 2015

Second edition: November 2016

Production reference: 1221116

Published by Packt Publishing Ltd.
Livery Place
35 Livery Street
Birmingham
B3 2PB, UK.

ISBN 978-1-78588-081-0

www.packtpub.com

Credits

Authors

Sergey Akopkokhyants

Stephen Radford

Reviewer

Eslem Alzate

Commissioning Editor

Wilson D'souza

Acquisition Editor

Smeet Thakkar

Content Development Editor

Onkar Wani

Technical Editor

Shivani K. Mistry

Copy Editor

Safis Editing

Project Coordinator

Ulhas Kambali

Proofreader

Safis Editing

Indexer

Rekha Nair

Graphics

Abhinash Sahu

Production Coordinator

Shraddha Falebhai

About the Authors

Sergey Akopkokhyants is a software architect with more than 20 years of professional experience in designing and developing client and server-side applications. He is also a certified Java developer and project manager. He has general knowledge of many tools, languages, and platforms.

For the last decade, Sergey has been responsible for customizing and producing web-oriented applications for wholesale business management solutions projects for several worldwide mobile communication companies. His responsibilities have included: architecture design and guidance of client software development using Flex, CSS, HTML, JavaScript, TypeScript, and Dart, and client-server integration with Java. He is also the founder and an active contributor to several open source projects on GitHub.

Sergey is passionate about web design and development and likes sharing his expertise with others, helping them to increase their skills and productivity. He is author of the book *Mastering Dart* and also he was one of reviewers of the books *Learning Dart* and *Dart Cookbook*.

> First and foremost, thanks to my family for having the patience with me for taking yet another challenge that decreases the amount of time I can spend with them, especially Lada, my wife, who has taken a big part of that sacrifice, and Alexander, my father, who shares credit for every goal I achieve.

Stephen Radford is a full-stack web and app developer based in the heart of England--Leicester. Originally from Bristol, Stephen moved to Leicester after studying Graphic Design at college to accept a job at one of the UK's largest online marketing companies.

Whilst working at a number of agencies, Stephen developed several side projects, including FTPloy, a SaaS designed to make continuous deployment available to everyone. The project was subsequently a finalist in the .NET Awards Side Project of the Year category.

He and his business partner now run Cocoon, a web development company that builds and maintains web and mobile apps. Cocoon also works closely with a handful of startups and businesses to develop ideas into websites and apps.

About the Reviewer

Eslem Alzate is a self-taught software engineer who started to program at the age of 11. He has multiple certifications from Sena, an associate degree from FP Mislata, and computer science in an open source society.

At the age of 17, he created his own company of software development, making projects for companies and startups, from apps to algorithms for the stock market.

I want to thank the support that my family always gives me, especially my sister, who has always been with me.

www.PacktPub.com

eBooks, discount offers, and more

Did you know that Packt offers eBook versions of every book published, with PDF and ePub files available? You can upgrade to the eBook version at www.PacktPub.com and as a print book customer, you are entitled to a discount on the eBook copy. Get in touch with us at customercare@packtpub.com for more details.

At www.PacktPub.com, you can also read a collection of free technical articles, sign up for a range of free newsletters and receive exclusive discounts and offers on Packt books and eBooks.

https://www.packtpub.com/mapt

Get the most in-demand software skills with Mapt. Mapt gives you full access to all Packt books and video courses, as well as industry-leading tools to help you plan your personal development and advance your career.

Why subscribe?

- Fully searchable across every book published by Packt
- Copy and paste, print, and bookmark content
- On demand and accessible via a web browser

Table of Contents

Preface

This book is about Angular 2 and Bootstrap 4, the two tremendous and most popular names in contemporary web development.

Angular 2 is the successor of AngularJS, but better than the predecessor in many ways. It combines the maximum speed possible on web browsers and scalability when you work with massive data requirements. This makes Angular 2 the first candidate of choice when building new systems or upgrading from the old ones.

Bootstrap 4 is the next evolutionary stage of building responsive, mobile-first web applications. It can easily and efficiently scale a website from mobile to desktop with a single codebase.

If you would like to take advantage of Angular 2 power with Bootstrap 4 flexibility to build robust web-scale or enterprise web applications, you are in the right place.

I had the desire to write a book about Angular 2 and Bootstrap 4 that would make no assumptions about the reader's prior experience and knowledge. My mind was about the book with full of technical details wherever required. Now, the book you are holding in your hands is that desire realized as it is both beginner-friendly and technically deep at the same time. It covers everything a developer requires to get into serious web development using those two fantastic frameworks.

What this book covers

Chapter 1, *Saying Hello!*, guides you through establishing a development environment for the simplest application possible in order to show you how easy it is to get a web application up and running with Angular 2 and Bootstrap 4.

Chapter 2, *Working with Bootstrap Components*, shows how you can start using Bootstrap 4 by showcasing a demo layout page, and how you can explore the framework and customize it to your requirements.

Chapter 3, *Advanced Bootstrap Components and Customization*, explains how to use components such as Jumbotron, Carousel, and spend you along the way through input groups.

Chapter 4, *Creating the Template*, lets you learn how to build a UI template using built-in Angular 2 directives. You'll become familiar with the template syntax, and how to bind properties and events in an HTML page and transform display using pipes.

Chapter 5, *Routing*, helps you understand how router code manages navigation between views when the user performs application tasks. We will take a look at how we can create static routes as well as routes containing parameters and how to configure them.

Chapter 6, *Dependency Injection*, teaches the readers how to decouple the requirements of an application and how to create a consistent source of data as a service.

Chapter 7, *Working with Forms*, shows the readers how to use Angular 2 directives related to form creation and how to use a code-based form component to the HTML form. We will use Bootstrap 4 to enhance the look of the form and to indicate invalid input for our web application.

Chapter 8, *Advanced Components*, describes the lifecycle of components and the methods that can be used at different stages. We will analyze each stage of this cycle and we will learn how to make the most of the hook methods that are triggered when a component moves from one stage to another.

Chapter 9, *Communication and Data Persistence*, explains how to use the built-in HTTP library to work with endpoints. We will learn how to work with Firebase as the persistence layer of the application.

Chapter 10, *Advanced Angular Techniques*, introduces advanced Angular techniques. We will transform our application with help of the Webpack, and we will learn how to install and use the ng2-bootstrap. We will discover the world of Angular CLI and will use AOT to dramatically decrease the size of the code for production.

What you need for this book

Any modern PC with installed Windows, Linux, or Mac OS should be sufficient to run the code samples in the book. All the software used in the book is open source and freely available on the Web:

- `https://git-scm.com`
- `https://nodejs.org`
- `https://www.npmjs.com`
- `http://v4-alpha.getbootstrap.com`

- https://www.ruby-lang.org
- https://firebase.google.com

Who this book is for

Whether you know a little about Bootstrap or Angular or you're a complete beginner, this book will enhance your capabilities in both frameworks and help you build a fully functional web app. A working knowledge of HTML, CSS, and JavaScript is required to fully get to grips with Bootstrap and Angular.

Conventions

In this book, you will find a number of text styles that distinguish between different kinds of information. Here are some examples of these styles and an explanation of their meaning.

Code words in text, database table names, folder names, filenames, file extensions, pathnames, dummy URLs, user input, and Twitter handles are shown as follows: "It supports number, boolean, and string type annotations for the primitive types and any for dynamically-typed structures."

A block of code is set as follows:

```
function add(first: number, second: number): number {
    return first + second;
}
```

When we wish to draw your attention to a particular part of a code block, the relevant lines or items are set in bold:

```
var x = 3;
function random(randomize) {
    if (randomize) {
        // x initialized as reference on function
        var x = Math.random();
        return x;
    }
    return x; // x is not defined
}
random(false); // undefined
```

Any command-line input or output is written as follows:

```
npm config list
```

New terms and **important words** are shown in bold. Words that you see on the screen, for example, in menus or dialog boxes, appear in the text like this: "Clicking the **Next** button moves you to the next screen."

Warnings or important notes appear in a box like this.

Tips and tricks appear like this.

Reader feedback

Feedback from our readers is always welcome. Let us know what you think about this book-what you liked or disliked. Reader feedback is important for us as it helps us develop titles that you will really get the most out of.

To send us general feedback, simply e-mail feedback@packtpub.com, and mention the book's title in the subject of your message.

If there is a topic that you have expertise in and you are interested in either writing or contributing to a book, see our author guide at www.packtpub.com/authors.

Customer support

Now that you are the proud owner of a Packt book, we have a number of things to help you to get the most from your purchase.

Downloading the example code

You can download the example code files for this book from your account at http://www.packtpub.com. If you purchased this book elsewhere, you can visit http://www.packtpub.com/support and register to have the files e-mailed directly to you.

You can download the code files by following these steps:

1. Log in or register to our website using your e-mail address and password.
2. Hover the mouse pointer on the **SUPPORT** tab at the top.
3. Click on **Code Downloads & Errata**.
4. Enter the name of the book in the **Search** box.
5. Select the book for which you're looking to download the code files.
6. Choose from the drop-down menu where you purchased this book from.
7. Click on **Code Download**.

Once the file is downloaded, please make sure that you unzip or extract the folder using the latest version of:

- WinRAR / 7-Zip for Windows
- Zipeg / iZip / UnRarX for Mac
- 7-Zip / PeaZip for Linux

The code bundle for the book is also hosted on GitHub at
`https://github.com/PacktPublishing/Web-Development-with-Bootstrap-4-and-Angular-2-Second-Edition`. We also have other code bundles from our rich catalog of books and videos available at `https://github.com/PacktPublishing/`. Check them out!

Errata

Although we have taken every care to ensure the accuracy of our content, mistakes do happen. If you find a mistake in one of our books-maybe a mistake in the text or the code-we would be grateful if you could report this to us. By doing so, you can save other readers from frustration and help us improve subsequent versions of this book. If you find any errata, please report them by visiting `http://www.packtpub.com/submit-errata`, selecting your book, clicking on the **Errata Submission Form** link, and entering the details of your errata. Once your errata are verified, your submission will be accepted and the errata will be uploaded to our website or added to any list of existing errata under the Errata section of that title.

To view the previously submitted errata, go to `https://www.packtpub.com/books/content/support` and enter the name of the book in the search field. The required information will appear under the **Errata** section.

Piracy

Piracy of copyrighted material on the Internet is an ongoing problem across all media. At Packt, we take the protection of our copyright and licenses very seriously. If you come across any illegal copies of our works in any form on the Internet, please provide us with the location address or website name immediately so that we can pursue a remedy.

Please contact us at copyright@packtpub.com with a link to the suspected pirated material.

We appreciate your help in protecting our authors and our ability to bring you valuable content.

Questions

If you have a problem with any aspect of this book, you can contact us at questions@packtpub.com, and we will do our best to address the problem.

1
Saying Hello!

Let's follow several steps to establish a development environment for the simplest application possible, to show you how easy it is to get a web application up and running with Angular 2 and Bootstrap 4. At the end of the chapter, you will have a solid understanding of:

- How to set up your development environment
- How TypeScript can change your development life
- Core concepts of Angular and Bootstrap
- How to create a simple Angular component with Bootstrap
- How to display some data through it

Setting up a development environment

Let's set up your development environment. This process is one of the most overlooked and often frustrating parts of learning to program because developers don't want to think about it. Developers must know the nuances of how to install and configure many different programs before they start real development. Everyone's computers are different; as a result, the same setup may not work on your computer. We will expose and eliminate all of these problems by defining the various pieces of environment you need to set up.

Defining a shell

The **shell** is a required part of your software development environment. We will use the shell to install software and run commands to build and start the web server to bring life to your web project. If your computer has the Linux operating system installed then you will use a shell called **Terminal**. There are many Linux-based distributions out there that use diverse desktop environments, but most of them use the equivalent keyboard shortcut to open Terminal.

 Use keyboard shortcut *Ctrl + Alt + T* to open Terminal in Ubuntu, Kali, and Linux Mint. If it doesn't work for you, please check the documentation for your version of Linux.

If you have a Mac computer with OS X installed, then you will use the Terminal shell as well.

 Use keyboard shortcut *command + space* to open the **Spotlight**, type Terminal to search and run.

If you have a computer with a Windows operating system installed, you can use the standard **Command Prompt**, but we can do better. In a minute I will show you how can you install Git on your computer, and you will have Git Bash free.

 You can open a Terminal with the `Git Bash` shell program on Windows.

I will use the Bash shell for all exercises in this book whenever I need to work in Terminal.

Installing Node.js

Node.js is technology we will use as a cross-platform runtime environment to run server-side web applications. It is a combination of a native, platform-independent runtime based on Google's V8 JavaScript engine and a huge number of modules written in JavaScript. Node.js ships with different connectors and libraries help you use HTTP, TLS, compression, file system access, raw TCP and UDP, and more. You as a developer can write your own modules on JavaScript and run them inside the Node.js engine. The Node.js runtime makes it easy to build a network event-driven application servers.

The terms *package* and *library* are synonymous in JavaScript so we will use them interchangeably.

Node.js is utilizing the **JavaScript Object Notation (JSON)** format widely in data exchanges between the server and client sides because it is readily expressed in several parse diagrams, notably without the complexities of XML, SOAP, and other data exchange formats.

You can use Node.js for the development of service-oriented applications, doing something different than web servers. One of the most popular service-oriented applications is **node package manager** (**npm**), which we will use to manage library dependencies, deployment systems, and which underlies the many **platform-as-a-service** (**PaaS**) providers for Node.js.

If you do not have Node.js installed on your computer, you should download the pre-build installer from `https://nodejs.org/en/download`, or you can use the unofficial package managers from `https://nodejs.org/en/download/package-manager`. You can start to use Node.js immediately after installation. Open Terminal and type:

```
node --version
```

Node.js will respond with the version number of the installed runtime:

```
v4.4.3
```

Bear in mind that the version of Node.js installed on my computer could be different from yours. If these commands give you a version number, you are ready to go with Node.js development.

Setting up npm

The npm is a package manager for JavaScript. You can use it to find, share, and reuse packages of code from many developers across the world. The number of packages dramatically grows every day and now is more than 250K. The npm is a Node.js package manager and utilizes it to run itself. The npm is included in the setup bundle of Node.js and available just after installation. Open Terminal and type:

```
npm --version
```

The npm must respond on your command with a version number:

```
2.15.1
```

My Node.js comes with that particular version of npm. The npm gets updated quite frequently, so you'll want to move to the latest version with the following command:

```
npm install npm@latest -g
```

You may experience permission problems to search or install packages with npm. If that is the case, I recommend following the instructions from `https://docs.npmjs.com/getting-started/fixing-npm-permissions`and don't use superuser privileges to fix them.

The following command gives us information about Node.js and the npm install:

```
npm config list
```

There are two ways to install npm packages: locally or globally. In cases when you would like to use the package as a tool, it's better install it globally:

```
npm install -g <package_name>
```

If you need to find the folder with globally installed packages you can use the next command:

```
npm config get prefix
```

Installation global packages are important, but best to avoid if not needed. Mostly you will install packages locally.

```
npm i <package_name>
```

You may find locally installed packages in the `node_modules` folder of your project.

Installing Git

If you're not familiar with Git then you're really missing out! Git is a distributed version control system and each Git working directory is a full-fledged repository. It keeps a complete history of changes and has full version tracking capabilities. Each repository is entirely independent of network access or a central server. You can keep Git repositories on your computer and share it with your mates, or you can take advantage of the many online VCS providers. The big guys you should look at closely are GitHub, Bitbucket, and Gitlab.com. Each has its own benefits, depending on your needs and project type.

Mac computers comes with Git already installed into the operating system but usually the version of Git is not the same as the latest one. You can update or install Git on your computer via a set of pre-build installers available on the official website `https://git-scm.com/downloads`. After installation, you can open Terminal and type:

```
git -version
```

Git must respond with a version number:

```
git version 2.8.1.windows.1
```

As I said, for developers who use computers with an installed Windows operation system, you now have Git Bash free on your system.

Code editor

You can imagine how many programs for code editing exist, but we will talk today only about the free, open source, runs everywhere Visual Studio Code from Microsoft. You can use any program you prefer for development, but I will be using only Visual Studio code in our future exercises, so please install it from `http://code.visualstudio.com/Download`.

A TypeScript crash course

TypeScript is an open source programming language developed and maintained by Microsoft. Its initial public release was in October 2012 and was presented by Anders Hejlsberg, the lead architect of C# and creator of Delphi and Turbo Pascal.

TypeScript is a typed superset of JavaScript that compiles to plain JavaScript. Any existing JavaScript is also valid TypeScript. It gives you type checking, explicit interfaces, and easier module exports. For now, it includes **ES5**, **ES2015**, **ES2016**, and, in fact, it's a little like getting some of tomorrow's ECMAScripts early so that we can play with some of those features today.

Here is the relationship between ECMAScripts and TypeScript:

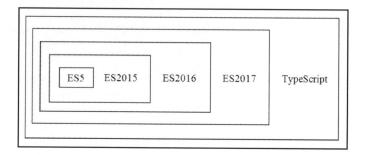

Writing code using TypeScript is relatively straightforward if you already have a background in the JavaScript language. Try the TypeScript playground `http://www.typesc riptlang.org/play` to play with IntelliSense, find references, and so on, directly from your browser.

Types

TypeScript provides a static type checking operation that allows many bugs in the development cycle to be caught early. TypeScript enables type checking at compile time via type annotations. Types in TypeScript are always optional, so you can ignore them if you prefer the regular dynamic typing of JavaScript. It supports `number`, `boolean`, and `string` type annotations for primitive types and `any` for dynamically-typed structures. In the following example, I added type annotations to `return` and parameters for `function`:

```
function add(first: number, second: number): number {
  return first + second;
}
```

In one moment of compilation, a TypeScript compiler can generate a declaration file which contains only signatures of the exported types. The resulting declaration file with the extension `.d.ts` along with a JavaScript library or module can be consumed later by a third-party developer. You can find a vast collection of declaration files for many popular JavaScript libraries at:

- The **DefinitelyTyped** (`https://github.com/DefinitelyTyped/DefinitelyType d`)
- The **Typings** registry (`https://github.com/typings/registry`)

Arrow function

Functions in JavaScript are first class citizens, which means they can be passed around like any other values:

```
var result = [1, 2, 3]
  .reduce(function (total, current) {
    return total + current;
  }, 0); // 6
```

The first parameter in `reduce` is an anonymous function. Anonymous functions are very useful in many scenarios but too verbose. TypeScript introduced new, less verbose syntax to define anonymous functions called **arrow function** syntax:

```
var result = [1, 2, 3]
    .reduce( (total, current) => {
      return total + current;
    }, 0); // 6
```

Or event less:

```
var result = [1, 2, 3]
    .reduce( (total, current) => total + current, 0); // 6
```

When defining parameters, you can even omit parentheses if the parameters are just a single identifier. So the regular `map` method of array:

```
var result = [1, 2, 3].map(function (x) {
    return x * x
});
```

Could be much more concise:

```
var result = [1, 2, 3].map(x => x * x);
```

Both syntaxes `(x) => x * x` and `x => x * x` are allowed.

Another important feature of arrow function is that it doesn't shadow `this` and pick it up from the lexical scope. Let's assume we have a constructor function `Counter` which increments the value of an internal variable `age` in timeout and prints it out:

```
function Counter() {
    this.age = 30;
    setTimeout(() => {
      this.age += 1;
      console.log(this.age);
    }, 100);
}
new Counter(); // 31
```

As result of using the arrow function, the `age` from the scope of `Counter` is available inside the callback function of `setTimeout`. Here is the converted to JavaScript ECMAScript 5 code:

```
function Counter() {
    var _this = this;
    this.age = 30;
```

```
    setTimeout(function () {
        _this.age += 1;
        console.log(_this.age);
    }, 100);
}
```

The following variables are all lexical inside arrow functions:

- `arguments`
- `super`
- `this`
- `new.target`

Block scope variables

All variables in ES5 declared with a `var` statement are function-scoped, and their scope belongs to enclosing functions. The result of the following code can be confusing because it returns `undefined`:

```
var x = 3;
function random(randomize) {
    if (randomize) {
        // x initialized as reference on function
        var x = Math.random();
        return x;
    }
    return x; // x is not defined
}
random(false); // undefined
```

The `x` is an inner variable of the `random` function and does not have any relation to the variable defined on the first line. The result of calling the `random` function at the last line returned `undefined`, because the JavaScript interprets the code in `random` function like that:

```
function random(randomize) {
    var x; // x is undefined
    if (randomize) {
        // x initialized as reference on function
        x = Math.random();
        return x;
    }
    return x; // x is not defined
}
```

This confusing code can be fixed in TypeScript with new block-scope variable declarations:

- The `let` is a block-scope version of `var`
- The `const` is similar `let` but allows initialize variable only once

The TypeScript compiler throws more errors with new block-scope variable declarations and prevents writing complicated and damaged code. Let's change `var` to `let` in the previous example:

```
let x = 3;
function random(randomize) {
    if (randomize) {
        let x = Math.random();
        return x;
    }
    return x;
}
random(false); // 3
```

And now our code works as expected.

 I recommend using `const` and `let` to make the code cleaner and safer.

Template literals

If we need string interpolation, we usually combine the values of variables and string fragments such as:

```
let out: string = '(' + x + ', ' + y + ')';
```

The TypeScript supports template literals–string literals allowing embedded expressions. You can use the string interpolation features of the template literals out of the box:

```
let out: string = `(${x}, ${y})`;
```

If you need multiline string, the template literals can help again:

```
Let x = 1, y = 2;
let out: string = `
Coordinates
 x: ${x},
 y: ${y}`;
```

```
console.log(out);
```

The last line prints results as follow:

```
Coordinates
  x: 1,
  y: 2
```

 I recommend using template literals as a safer way of string interpolation.

The for-of loop

We usually use `for` statement or `forEach` method of `Array` to iterate over elements in JavaScript ES5:

```
let arr = [1, 2, 3];
// The for statement usage
for (let i = 0; i < arr.length; i++) {
    let element = arr[i];
    console.log(element);
}
// The usage of forEach method
arr.forEach(element => console.log(element));
```

Each of these methods has its benefit:

- We can interrupt the `for` statement via `break` or`continue`
- The `forEach` method is less verbose

The TypeScript has `for-of` loop as a combination of both of them:

```
const arr = [1, 2, 3];
for (const element of arr) {
    console.log(element);
}
```

The `for-of` loop supports `break` and `continue` and can use the `index` and `value` of each array via new `Array` method `entries`:

```
const arr = [1, 2, 3];
for (const [index, element] of arr.entries()) {
    console.log(`${index}: ${element}`);
```

```
  }
```

Default value, optional and rest parameters

We quite often need to check the input parameters of functions and assign default values to them:

```
function square(x, y) {
  x = x || 0;
  y = y || 0;
  return x * y;
}
let result = square(4, 5); // Out 20
```

The TypeScript has syntax to handle default values of parameters to make previous functions shorter and safer:

```
function square(x: number = 0, y: number = 0) {
  return x * y;
}
let result = square(4, 5); // Out 20
```

 A default value of a parameter is assigned only by its undefined value.

Each parameter of a function in JavaScript ES5 is optional, so an omitted one equals undefined. To make it strict, TypeScript expects a question mark at the end of parameters we want to be optional. We can mark the last parameter of the square function as optional and call the function with one or two parameters:

```
function square(x: number = 0, y?: number) {
  if (y) {
    return x * y;
  } else {
    return x * x;
  }
}
let result = square(4); // Out 16
let result = square(4, 5); // Out 20
```

Any optional parameters must follow the required parameters.

In some scenarios, we need to work with multiple parameters as a group, or we may not know how many parameters a function takes. The JavaScript ES5 provides the `arguments` variable in the scope of functions to work with them. In TypeScript, we can use a formal variable to keep the rest of the parameters. The compiler builds an array of the arguments passed in with the name given after the ellipses so that we can use it in our function:

```
function print(name: number, ...restOfName: number[]) {
  return name + " " + restOfName.join(" ");
}
let name = print("Joseph", "Samuel", "Lucas");
// Out: Joseph Samuel Lucas
```

Interfaces

The interface is the way of defining contracts inside and outside the code of your project. We use the interface in TypeScript only to describe a type and the shape of data to help us keep our code error-free. In comparison with many other languages, the TypeScript compiler doesn't generate any code for the interface so that it has not runtime cost. The TypeScript defines interfaces via the interface keyword. Let's define a type `Greetable`:

```
interface Greetable {
  greetings(message: string): void;
}
```

It has a member function called `greetings` that takes a string argument. Here is how we can use it as a type of parameter:

```
function hello(greeter: Greetable) {
  greeter.greetings('Hi there');
}
```

Classes

JavaScript has a prototype-based, object-oriented programming model. We can instantiate objects using the object literal syntax or constructor function. Its prototype-based inheritance is implemented on prototype chains. If you come from an object-oriented approach, you may feel uncomfortable when you try to create classes and inheritance based on prototypes. TypeScript allows for writing code based on an object-oriented class-based approach. The compiler translates the class down to JavaScript and works across all major web browsers and platforms. Here is the class `Greeter`. It has a property called `greeting`, a `constructor`, and a method `greet`:

```
class Greeter {
  greeting: string;
  constructor(message: string) {
    this.greeting = message;
  }
  greet() {
    return "Hello, " + this.greeting;
  }
}
```

To refer to any member of the class we prepend `this`. To create an instance of the class we use the `new` keyword:

```
let greeter = new Greeter("world");
```

We can extend an existing class to create new ones via inheritance:

```
class EmailGreeter extends Greeter {
  private email: string;
  constructor(emailAddr: string, message: string) {
    super(message);
    this.email = emailAddr;
  }
  mailto() {
    return "mailto:${this.email}?subject=${this.greet()}";
  }
}
```

In the class `EmailGreeter`, we demonstrate several features of inheritance in TypeScript:

- We use `extends` to create a subclass
- We must call `super` in the first line of the constructor to pass values into base class
- We call the `greet` method of the base class to create a subject for `mailto`

The TypeScript classes support public, protected, and private modifiers to access the members that we declared throughout our programs. Each member of the class is public by default. There are not a requirement to labeled all public members with that keyword but you may mark them explicitly. Use protected modifier if you need to restrict access to members of the class from outside, but bear in mind that they are still available from deriving classes. You can mark the constructor as protected so that we cannot instantiate the class but we can extend it. The private modifier restricts access to member only on the class level.

If you look at constructors of EmailGreeter, we had to declare a private member email and a constructor parameter emailAddr. Instead, we can use parameter properties to let us create and initialize a member in one place:

```
class EmailGreeter extends Greeter {
  constructor(private email: string, message: string) {
    super(message);
  }
  mailto() {
    return "mailto:${this.email}?subject=${this.greet()}";
  }
}
```

You can use any modifier in parameter properties.

Use parameter properties to consolidate the declaration and assignment in one place.

TypeScript supports getters and setters to organize intercepting access to members of an object. We can change the original Greeter class with the following code:

```
class Greeter {
  private _greeting: string;
  get greeting(): string {
    return this._greeting;
  }
  set greeting(value: string) {
    this._greeting = value || "";
  }
  constructor(message: string) {
    this.greeting = message;
  }
  greet() {
    return "Hello, " + this.greeting;
  }
```

}

We check the `value` parameter inside the setter of `greeting` and modify it if necessary to empty string before assigning it to the private member.

TypeScript supports class members via the static modifier as well. Here the class `Types` contains only static members:

```
class Types {
    static GENERIC: string = "";
    static EMAIL: string = "email";
}
```

We can access those values through prepending the name of the class:

```
console.log(Types.GENERIC);
```

TypeScript gives us supreme flexibility via abstract classes. We cannot create instances of them, but we can use them to organize base classes from which each distinct class may be derived. We can convert the `greeting` class into abstract with just one keyword:

```
abstract class BaseGreeter {
    private _greeting: string;
    get greeting(): string {
        return this._greeting;
    }
    set greeting(value: string) {
        this._greeting = value || "";
    }
    abstract greet();
}
```

The method `greet` is marked as `abstract`. It doesn't contain an implementation and must be implemented in derived classes.

Modules

When we are writing the code, we usually divide it into functions and the blocks inside those functions. The size of a program can increase very quickly, and individual functions start to blend into the background. We can make such a program more readable if we split them into large units of an organization like modules. At the beginning of writing a program, you may not know how to structure it, and you can use structureless principles. When your code becomes stable you can put pieces of functionality into separate modules to make them easy to track, update, and share. We store modules of TypeScript in files, exactly one module per file and one file per module.

The JavaScript ES5 doesn't have built-in support for modules and we used AMD or CommonJS syntax to work with them. TypeScript supports the concept of modules.

How do the scope and module depend on each other? The global scope of JavaScript doesn't have access to the scope of executing modules. It creates its own scope for each individual execution module, so everything declared inside the module is not visible from outside. We need to explicitly export them to make them visible and import them to consume them. The relationship between modules is defined at the file level regarding exports and imports. Any file defines a top-level `export` or `import` and is considered a module. Here is a `string-validator.ts` file which contains the exported declaration:

```
export interface StringValidator {
   isAcceptable(s: string): boolean;
}
```

I have created another file `zip-validator.ts` with several members, but exported only one of them to hide another one from outside:

```
const numberRegexp = /^[0-9]+$/;
export class ZipCodeValidator implements StringValidator {
   isAcceptable(s: string) {
      return s.length === 5 && numberRegexp.test(s);
   }
}
```

You can re-export declarations if your module extends other modules. Here `validators.ts` contains a module, wraps other validator modules, and combines all their exports in one place:

```
export * from "./string-validator";
export * from "./zip-validator";
```

Now we can import validator modules using one of the import forms. Here is a single export from a module:

```
import { StringValidator } from "./validators";
let strValidator = new StringValidator();
```

To prevent a naming conflict we can rename an imported declaration:

```
import { ZipCodeValidator as ZCV } from "./validators";
let zipValidator = new ZCV();
```

Finally, we can import an entire module into a single variable, and use it to access module exports:

```
import * as validator from "./validators";
```

```
let strValidator = new validator.StringValidator();
let zipValidator = new validator.ZipCodeValidator();
```

Generics

The authors of TypeScript put maximal effort into helping us to write reusable code. One of the tools that helps us to create code that can work with a variety of types rather than a single one is **generics**. The benefits of generics include:

- Allows you to write code/use methods which are type-safe. An `Array<string>` is guaranteed to be an array of strings.
- The compiler can perform a compile-time check on code for type safety. Any attempt to assign the `number` into an array of strings causes an error.
- Faster than using `any` type to avoid casting into a required reference type.
- Allows you to write code which is applicable to many types with the same underlying behavior.

Here is the class I have created to show you how useful generics can be:

```
class Box<T> {
    private _value : T;
    set value(val : T) {
        this._value = val;
    }
    get value() : T {
        return this._value;
    }
}
```

This class keeps the single value of a particular type. To set or return it we can use corresponding getter and setter methods:

```
var box1 = new Box<string>();
box1.setValue("Hello World");
console.log(box1.getValue());
var box2 = new Box<number>();
box2.setValue(1);
console.log(box2.getValue());
var box3 = new Box<boolean>();
box3.setValue(true);
console.log(box3.getValue());
// Out: Hello World
// Out: 1
// Out: true
```

What are promises?

A promise represents the final result of an asynchronous operation. There are a number of libraries that support the use of promises in TypeScript. But before starting to talk about this, let's talk a bit about the browser environment which executes your JavaScript code.

Event loop

Each browser tab has an event loop and uses different tasks to coordinate events, user interactions, running scripts, rendering, networking, and so on. It has one or more queues to keep an ordered list of tasks. Other processes run around the event loop and communicate with it by adding tasks to its queue such as:

- The timer waits after a given period and then adds a task to the queue
- We can call a `requestAnimationFrame` function to coordinate DOM updates
- DOM elements can call event handlers
- The browser can request the parsing of an HTML page
- JavaScript can load an external program and perform computation on it

Many of the items in the list above are JavaScript code. They are usually small enough, but if we run any long-running computation it could block execution of other tasks, and as a result it freezes the user interface. To avoid blocking the event loop we can:

- Use the **web worker API** to execute a long-running computation in a different process of the browser
- Do not wait for the result of a long-running computation synchronously and allow the task to inform us about results via events or callbacks asynchronously

Asynchronous results via events

The following code uses an event-driven approach to convince us and adds event listeners to execute small code snippets inside:

```
var request = new XMLHttpRequest();
request.open('GET', url);

request.onload = () => {
    if (req.status == 200) {
        processData(request.response);
    } else {
```

```
            console.log('ERROR', request.statusText);
        }
    };

    request.onerror = () => {
        console.log('Network Error');
    };

    request.send(); // Add request to task queue
```

The method `send` in the last line of code just adds another task to the queue. This approach is useful if you receive results multiple times, but this code is quite verbose for a single result.

Asynchronous results via callbacks

To manage asynchronous results via callbacks, we need to pass a callback function as a parameter into asynchronous function calls:

```
    readFileFunctional('myfile.txt', { encoding: 'utf8' },
        (text) => { // success
            console.log(text);
        },
        (error) => { // failure
            // ...
        }
    );
```

This approach is very easy to understand, but it has its disadvantages:

- It mixes up input and output parameters
- It is complicated to handle errors especially in the code combined many callbacks
- It is more complicated to return result from combined asynchronous functions

Asynchronous results via promises

As I mentioned earlier, the promise represents the final result of an asynchronous operation happening in the future. Promises have the following advantages:

- You write cleaner code without callback parameters
- You do not adapt the code of the underlying architecture for delivery results
- Your code handles errors with ease

A promise may be in one of the following states:

- **Pending state**: The asynchronous operation hasn't completed yet
- **Resolved state**: The asynchronous operation has completed and the promise has a value

- **Rejected state**: The asynchronous operation failed and the promise has a reason which indicates why it failed

The promise becomes immutable after resolving or rejecting.

Usually, you write the code to return the promise from functions or methods:

```
function readFile(filename, encode){
  return new Promise((resolve, reject) => {
    fs.readFile(filename, enccode, (error, result) => {
      if (error) {
        reject(error);
      } else {
        resolve(result);
      }
    });
  });
}
```

We use the `new` keyword with a function constructor to create the promise. We add a factory function with two parameters into the constructor, which does the actual work. Both parameters are callback functions. Once the operation has successfully completed the factory function calls the first callback with the result. If the operation fails it calls the second function with the reason.

The returned promise has several methods such as `.then` and `.catch` to inform us of the result of the execution so that we can act accordingly:

```
function readJSON(filename){
  return readFile(filename, 'utf8').then((result) => {
  console.log(result);
  }, (error) => {
  console.log(error);
  });
}
```

We can call another operation returns promise to quickly transform the result of original one:

```
function readJSON(filename){
```

```
return readFile(filename, 'utf8').then((result) => {
  return JSON.parse(result);
}, (error) => {
  console.log(error);
}
}
```

Angular 2 concepts

The **Angular 2** is a development platform for building web, mobile, and desktop applications. It is based on web standards to make web development simpler and more efficient, and entirely different from the Angular JS 1.x. The architecture of Angular 2 builds on top of the web component standard so that we can define custom HTML selectors and program behavior for them. The Angular team develops Angular 2 to use in the ECMAScript 2015, TypeScript, and Dart languages.

Building blocks of Angular 2

Any web application built on Angular 2 consist of:

- HTML templates with Angular-specific markup
- Directives and components managing the HTML templates
- Services containing application logic
- Special bootstrap function which helps to load and start the Angular application

Module

The Angular 2 application is an assembly of many modules. Angular 2 itself is a set of modules with names beginning with the @angular prefix, combined into libraries:

- The @angular/core is the primary Angular 2 library and contains all core public APIs
- The @angular/common is the library which restricts APIs to reusable components, directives, and form building
- The @angular/router is the library that supports navigation
- The @angular/http is the library that helps us work asynchronously via HTTP

Metadata

Metadata is information we can attach to underlying definitions via TypeScript decorators to tell Angular how to modify them. Decorators play a significant role in Angular 2.

Directives

Directives are the fundamental building block of Angular 2 and allows you to connect behavior to an element in the DOM. There are three kinds of directive:

- Attribute directives
- Structural directives
- Components

A directive is a class with an assigned `@Directive` decorator.

Attribute directives

The attribute directive usually changes the appearance or behavior of an element. We can change several styles, or use it to render text bold or italic by binding it to a property.

Structural directives

The structural directive changes the DOM layout by adding and removing other elements.

Component

The component is a directive with a template. Every component is made up of two parts:

- The class, where we define the application logic
- The view, which is controlled by the component and interacts with it through an API of properties and methods

A component is a class with the assigned `@Component` decorator.

Template

The component uses the template to render the view. It is regular HTML with custom defined selectors and Angular-specific markups.

Data binding

The Angular 2 supports *data binding* to update parts of the template via the properties or methods of a component. The *binding markup* is part of data binding; we use it on the template to connect both sides.

Service

Angular 2 has no definition of a service. Any value, function, or feature can be a service, but usually it is a class created for a distinct purpose with an assigned `@Injectable` decorator.

Dependency injection

Dependency injection is a design pattern that helps configure objects by an external entity and resolve dependencies between them. All elements in the loosely coupled system know little or nothing about definitions of each other. We can replace almost any element with alternative implementation without breaking the whole system.

SystemJS loader and JSPM package manager

We have discussed TypeScript modules, so it's time to talk about tools we can use for loading modules in our scripts.

SystemJS Loader

SystemJS is a universal dynamic module loader. It hosts the source code on GitHub at the following address `https://github.com/systemjs/systemjs`. It can load modules in the web browser and Node.js in the following formats:

- ECMAScript 2015 (ES6) or TypeScript
- AMD
- CommonJS
- Global scripts

SystemJS loads modules with an exact circle reference, binding support, and assets through the module naming system such as CSS, JSON, or images. Developers can easily extend the functionality of the loader via plugins.

We can add SystemJS loader to our future project:

- Via direct link to a **Content Delivery Network (CDN)**
- By installing via npm manager

In both scenarios, we include a reference to the SystemJS library in our code and configure it via the `config` method:

```
<!DOCTYPE html>
<html>
  <head>
    <script src="https://jspm.io/system.js"></script>
    <script src="https://jspm.io/system.js"></script>

    <script>
      System.config({
      packages: {
      './': {
      defaultExtension: false
          }
        }
      });
    </script>

    <script>
    System.import('./app.js');
    </script>
  </head>
<body>
    <div id="main"></div>
```

```
    </body>
  </html>
```

We will speak about installation via npm manager a bit later in this chapter.

JSPM package manager

The developers of the SystemJS followed the single-responsibility principle and implemented a loader for doing only one thing: loading the modules. To make modules available in your project, we need to use the package manager. We spoke about the npm package manager at the beginning, so now we will talk about the JSPM package manager sitting on top of SystemJS. It can:

- Download modules from any registry such as npm and GitHub
- Compile modules into simple, layered, and self-executing bundles with a single command

The JSPM package manager looks like an npm package manager, but it puts the browser loader first. It helps you organize a seamless workflow for installing and using libraries in the browser with minimum effort.

Writing your first application

Now, when we have everything in place, it's time to create our first project, which is actually an npm module. Open Terminal and create the folder `hello-world`. I intentionally follow the npm package naming conventions:

- The package name length should be greater than zero and cannot exceed 214
- All the characters in the package name must be lowercase
- The package name can consist of/include hyphens
- The package name must contain any URL-safe characters (since the name ends up being part of a URL)
- The package name should not start with dot or underscore letters
- The package name should not contain any leading or trailing spaces
- The package name cannot be the same as a `node.js/io.js` core module or a reserved/blacklisted name like `http`, stream, `node_modules`, and so on.

Move the folder in and run the command:

```
npm init
```

npm will ask you several questions to create a `package.json` file. This file keeps important information about your package in JSON format:

- Project information like name, version, author, and license
- Set of packages the project depends on
- Set of pre-configured commands to build and test the project

Here is how `package.js` could look:

```
{
  "name": "hello-world",
  "version": "1.0.0",
  "description": "The Hello World",
  "author": " Put Your Name Here",
  "license": "MIT"
  "scripts": {
    "test": "echo "Error: no test specified" && exit 1"
  }
}
```

We are ready to configure our project.

TypeScript compile configuration

Run the Visual Studio code and open the project folder. We need to create a configuration file which guides the TypeScript compiler on where to find the source folder and required libraries and how to compile the project. From the **File** menu create `tsconfig.json` file, and copy/paste the following:

```
{
  "compilerOptions": {
    "target": "es5",
    "module": "commonjs",
    "moduleResolution": "node",
    "sourceMap": true,
    "emitDecoratorMetadata": true,
    "experimentalDecorators": true,
    "removeComments": false,
    "noImplicitAny": false
  },
  "exclude": [
```

```
        "node_modules",
        "typings/main",
        "typings/main.d.ts"
    ]
}
```

Let's look closer at the `compilerOptions`:

- The `target` option specifies the ECMAScript version such `es3`, `es5`, or `es6`.
- The `module` option specifies the module code generator from one of these: `none`, `commojs`, `amd`, `system`, `umd`, `es6`, or `es2015`.
- The `moduleResolution` option determines how modules get resolved. Use `node` for `Node.js/io.js` style resolution or `classic`.
- The `sourceMap` flag tells the compiler to generate a corresponding `map` file.

- The `emitDecoratorMetadata` emits the design-type metadata for decorated declarations in source.
- The `experimentalDecorator` enables experimental support for ES7 decorators such iterators, generators and array comprehensions.
- The `removeComments` removes all comments except copyright header comments beginning with `/*!`.
- The `noImplicitAny` raises an error on expressions and declarations with an implied `any` type.

You can find the full list of compiler options here: `https://www.typescriptlang.org/docs/handbook/compiler-options.html`.

The TypeScript compiler needs type definition files of JavaScript libraries from `node_modules` of our project because it doesn't recognize them natively. We help it with `typings.json` file. You should create the file and copy/paste the following:

```
{
    "ambientDependencies": {
        "es6-shim": "registry:dt/es6-shim#0.31.2+20160317120654"
    }
}
```

We should provide enough information to typings tool to get any typings file:

- The registry dt is located in the DefinitelyTyped source. This value could be npm, git

- The package name in `DefinitelyTyped` source is the `es6-shim`
- We are looking for the version `0.31.2` updated `2016.03.17 12:06:54`

Task automation and dependency resolution

Now, it's time to add the libraries into the `package.json` file that the application requires. Please update it accordingly:

```
{
    "name": "hello-world",
    "version": "1.0.0",
    "description": "The Hello World",
    "author": "Put Your Name Here",
    "license": "MIT",
    "scripts": {
        "start": "tsc && concurrently "npm run tsc:w" "npm run lite" ",
        "lite": "lite-server",
        "postinstall": "typings install",
        "tsc": "tsc",
        "tsc:w": "tsc -w",
        "typings": "typings"
    },
    "dependencies": {
        "@angular/common":   "~2.0.1",
        "@angular/compiler":   "~2.0.1",
        "@angular/core":   "~2.0.1",
        "@angular/http":   "~2.0.1",
        "@angular/platform-browser":   "~2.0.1",
        "@angular/platform-browser-dynamic":   "~2.0.1",
        "@angular/router":   "~3.0.1",
        "@angular/upgrade":   "~2.0.1",

        "systemjs": "0.19.39",
        "core-js": "^2.4.1",
        "reflect-metadata": "^0.1.8",
        "rxjs": "5.0.0-beta.12",
        "zone.js": "^0.6.25",

        "angular-in-memory-web-api": "~0.1.1",
        "bootstrap": "4.0.0-alpha.4"
    },
    "devDependencies": {
        "concurrently": "^3.0.0",
        "lite-server": "^2.2.2",
        "typescript": "^2.0.3",
```

```
    "typings":"^1.4.0"
  }
}
```

Our configuration includes `scripts` to handle common development tasks such:

- The `postinstall` script runs after the package is installed
- The `start` script runs by the npm `start` command
- The arbitrary scripts `lite`, `tsc`, `tsc:w`, and `typings` are executed by the npm `run <script>`.

You can find more documentation on the following web page: `https://docs.npmjs.com/misc/scripts`.

After finishing the configuration let's run npm manager to install the packages required. Go back to Terminal and enter the following command:

npm i

During installation, you may see warning messages in red starting with:

npm WARN

You should ignore them if the installation finishes successfully. After installation, the npm executes the `postinstall` script to run `typings` installation.

Creating and bootstrapping an Angular component

The Angular 2 application must always have a top-level component, where all other components and logic lie. Let's create it. Go to the Visual Studio code and create a sub-folder app of the root directory where we will keep the source code. Create the file `app.component.ts` under `app` folder, and copy/paste the following:

```
// Import the decorator class for Component
import { Component } from '@angular/core';

@Component({
  selector: 'my-app',
  template: '<h1> Hello, World</h1>'
})
export class AppComponent { }
```

As you can see, we have added metadata via @Component decorator to the class AppComponent. This decorator tells Angular how to process the class via configuration with the following options:

- The selector defines the name of an HTML tag which our component will link
- We pass in any service in the providers property. Any service registered here becomes available to this component and its children
- We give away any number of style files to styles a particular component
- The template property will hold the template of the component
- The template url is a URL to an external file containing a template for the view

We need to export the class AppComponent to make it visible from other modules and Angular can instantiate it.

The Angular application is a composition of multiple modules marked with NgModule decorator. Any application must have at least one root module, so let's create AppModule in the app.module.ts file:

```
import { NgModule } from '@angular/core';
import { BrowserModule } from '@angular/platform-browser';

@NgModule({
  imports: [ BrowserModule ]
})
export class AppModule { }
```

The WebBrowser is a collection of modules and providers specific for web browsers such as document DomRootRenderer, and so on. We import WebBrowser into the application module to make all of those providers and modules available in our application, thereby reducing the amount of boilerplate code-writing required. Angular contains the ServerModule: a similar module for the server side.

Now we need to start up our application. Let's create main.ts file under app folder, and copy/paste the following:

```
import { platformBrowserDynamic } from
    '@angular/platform-browser-dynamic';

import { AppModule } from './app.module';

const platform = platformBrowserDynamic();

platform.bootstrapModule(AppModule);
```

Last but not least, we rely on the bootstrap function to load top-level components. We import it from '@angular/platform-browser-dynamic'. Angular has a different kind of bootstrap function for:

- Web workers
- Development on mobile devices
- Rendering the first page of an application on a server

Angular does several tasks after instantiation of any component:

- It creates a shadow DOM for it
- It loads the selected template into the shadow DOM
- It creates all the injectable objects configured with 'providers' and 'viewProviders'

In the end, Angular 2 evaluates all template expressions and statements against the component instance.

Now, create index.html file in Microsoft Visual Studio code under the root folder with the following content:

```
<html>
  <head>
    <title>Angular 2 First Project</title>
    <meta charset="UTF-8">
    <meta name="viewport" content="width=device-width, initial-scale=1">
    <link rel="stylesheet" href="styles.css">

    <!-- 1. Load libraries -->
     <!-- Polyfill(s) for older browsers -->
    <script src="node_modules/core-js/client/shim.min.js">
    </script>
    <script src="node_modules/zone.js/dist/zone.js"></script>
    <script src="node_modules/reflect-metadata/Reflect.js">
    </script>
    <script src="node_modules/systemjs/dist/system.src.js">
</script>

    <!-- 2. Configure SystemJS -->
    <script src="systemjs.config.js"></script>
    <script>
      System.import('app')
      .catch(function(err){ console.error(err);  });
    </script>
  </head>
```

```
    <!-- 3. Display the application -->
    <body>
      <my-app>Loading...</my-app>
    </body>
</html>
```

Because we are referencing the `systemjs.config.js` file, let's create it in the root folder with the code:

```
(function (global) {
  System.config({
    paths: {
      // paths serve as alias
      'npm:': 'node_modules/'
    },
    // map tells the System loader where to look for things
    map: {
      // our app is within the app folder
      app: 'app',
      // angular bundles
      '@angular/core': 'npm:@angular/core/bundles/core.umd.js',
      '@angular/common': 'npm:@angular/common/bundles/common.umd.js',
      '@angular/compiler': 'npm:@angular/compiler/bundles/compiler.umd.js',
      '@angular/platform-browser': 'npm:@angular/platform-
browser/bundles/platform-browser.umd.js',
      '@angular/platform-browser-dynamic': 'npm:@angular/platform-browser-
dynamic/bundles/platform-browser-dynamic.umd.js',
      '@angular/http': 'npm:@angular/http/bundles/http.umd.js',
      '@angular/router': 'npm:@angular/router/bundles/router.umd.js',
      '@angular/forms': 'npm:@angular/forms/bundles/forms.umd.js',
      // other libraries
      'rxjs':                         'npm:rxjs',
      'angular-in-memory-web-api': 'npm:angular-in-memory-web-api',
    },
    // packages tells the System loader how to load when no filename and/or
no extension
    packages: {
      app: {
        main: './main.js',
        defaultExtension: 'js'
      },
      rxjs: {
        defaultExtension: 'js'
      },
      'angular-in-memory-web-api': {
        main: './index.js',
        defaultExtension: 'js'
      }
```

```
    }
  });
}) (this);
```

Compiling and running

We are ready to run our first application. Go back to Terminal and type:

```
npm start
```

This script runs two parallel Node.js processes:

- The TypeScript compiler in watch mode
- The static lite-server loads index.html and refreshes the browser when the application file changes

In your browser you should see the following:

You can find the source code in the chapter_1/1.hello-world folder.

Adding user input

We now need to include our text input and also, specify the model we want to use. When a user types in the text input, our application shows the changed value in the title. Also, we should import the `FormsModule` into the `AppModule`:

```
import { NgModule }      from '@angular/core';
import { BrowserModule } from '@angular/platform-browser';
import { FormsModule }   from '@angular/forms';

import { AppComponent }   from './app.component';

@NgModule({
  imports:      [ BrowserModule, FormsModule ],
  declarations: [ AppComponent ],
  bootstrap:    [ AppComponent ]

})
export class AppModule { }
```

Here is the updated version of `app.component.ts`:

```
import { Component } from '@angular/core';

@Component({
  selector: 'my-app',
  template: `
<h1>Hello, {{name || 'World'}}</h1>
<input type="text" [(ngModel)]="name" placeholder="name">
`})
export class AppComponent {
  name: string = 'World';
}
```

The `ngModel` attribute declares a model binding on that element, and anything we type into the input box will be automatically bound to it by Angular. Obviously, this isn't going to be displayed on our page by magic; we need to tell the framework where we want it echoed. To show our model on the page, we just need to wrap the name of it in double curly braces:

```
{{name}}
```

I popped this in place of World in our `<h1>` tag and refreshed the page in my browser. If you pop your name in the input field, you'll notice that it's automatically displayed in your heading in real time. Angular does all of this for us, and we haven't written a single line of code:

Now, while that's great, it would be nice if we could have a default in place so it doesn't look broken before a user has entered their name. What's awesome is that everything in between those curly braces is parsed as an Angular expression, so we can check and see if the model has a value, and if not, it can echo `'World'`. Angular calls this an expression and it's just a case of adding two pipe symbols as we would in TypeScript:

```
{{name || 'World'}}
```

It's good to remember that this is TypeScript, and that's why we need to include the quotation marks here, to let it know that this is a string and not the name of a model. Remove them and you'll notice that Angular displays nothing again. That's because both the name and `World` models are undefined.

You can find the source code into the `chapter_1/2.hello-input.` folder.

Integrating Bootstrap 4

Now that we've created our `Hello World` application, and everything is working as expected, it's time to get involved with Bootstrap and add a bit of style and structure to our app. At the time of writing this book Bootstrap 4 was in alpha version, so bear in mind that the code and markup of your application might be slightly different. We need to add the Bootstrap 4 style sheet into the `index.html` file:

```
<meta name="viewport" content="width=device-width, initial-scale=1">
<link rel="stylesheet"
href="node_modules/bootstrap/dist/css/bootstrap.css">
<link rel="stylesheet" href="styles.css">
```

The application is currently misaligned to the left, and everything is looking cramped, so let's sort that out first with a bit of scaffolding. Bootstrap comes with a great *mobile first* responsive grid system that we can utilize with the inclusion of a few `div` elements and classes. First, though, let's get a container around our content to clean it up immediately:

 Mobile first is a way of designing/developing for the smallest screens first and adding to the design rather than taking elements away.

```
<div class="container">
  <h1>Hello, {{name || 'World'}}</h1>
  <input type="text" [(ngModel)]="name">
</div>
```

If you resize your browser window, you should start to notice some of the responsiveness of the framework coming through and see it collapsing:

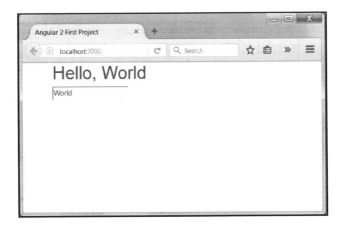

Now, I think it's a good idea to wrap this in what Bootstrap calls a Jumbotron (in previous versions of Bootstrap this was a hero unit). It'll make our headline stand out a lot more. We can do this by wrapping our H1 and input tags in a new div with the jumbotron class:

```
<div class="container">
  <div class="jumbotron">
    <h1>Hello, {{name || 'World'}}</h1>
    <input type="text" ng-model="name">
  </div>
</div>
```

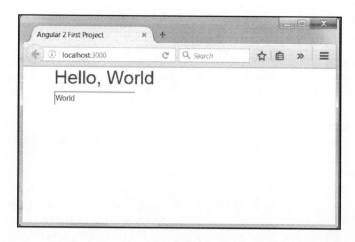

It's starting to look a lot better, but I'm not too happy about our content touching the top of the browser like that. We can make it look a lot nicer with a page header, but that input field still looks out of place to me.

First, let's sort out that page header:

```
<div class="container">
  <div class="page-header">
    <h2>Chapter 1 <small>Hello, World</small></h2>
  </div>
  <div class="jumbotron">
    <h1>Hello, {{name || 'World'}}</h1>
    <input type="text" [(ng-model)]="name">
  </div>
</div>
```

I've included the chapter number and title here. The `<small>` tag within our `<h2>` tag gives us a nice differentiation between the chapter number and the title. The page-header class itself just gives us some additional margin and padding as well as a subtle border along the bottom.

The utmost thing I think we could improve upon is that input box. Bootstrap comes with some cool input styles so let's include those. First, we need to add the class of form-control to the text input. This will set the width to 100% and also bring out some beautiful styling such as rounded corners and glowing when we focus on the element:

```
<input type="text" [(ngModel)]="name" class="form-control">
```

Much better, but to me it looks a little small when you compare it with the heading. Bootstrap provides two additional classes we can include that will either make the element smaller or larger: `form-control-lg` and `form-control-sm` respectively. In our case, the `form-control-lg` class is the one we want, so go ahead and add that to the input.

```
<input type="text" [(ngModel)]="name"
       class="form-control form-control-lg">
```

You can find the source code in the `chapter_1/3.hello-bootstrap`.

Summary

Our app's looking great and working exactly how it should, so let's recap what we've learnt in the first chapter.

To begin with, we saw just how to setup a working environment and finish the TypeScript crash course.

The `Hello World` app we've created, while being very basic, demonstrates some of Angular's core features:

- Component directives
- Application bootstrapping
- Two-way data binding

All of this was possible without writing a single line of TypeScript, as the component we created was just to demonstrate two-way data binding.

With Bootstrap, we utilized a few of the many available components such as the Jumbotron and the page-header classes to give our application some style and substance. We also saw the framework's new mobile first responsive design in action without cluttering up our markup with unnecessary classes or elements.

In Chapter 2, *Working with Bootstrap Components*, we're going to explore more Bootstrap fundamentals and introduce the project we're going to be building over the course of this book.

2

Working with Bootstrap Components

In the world of web designing and development, we have heard a lot about **Twitter Bootstrap 3**. The hero of our days is **Bootstrap 4**, a CSS framework that ultimately helps to design web applications easier and faster.

In this chapter, I will explain how you can start using Bootstrap 4 by showcasing a demo layout page, and how you can explore the framework and customize it to your requirements. At the end of the chapter, you will have a solid understanding of the following:

- How to use **Syntactically Awesome Style Sheets (Sass)**
- How to add Bootstrap 4 into your project
- How to design layouts with grids and containers
- How to add navigation elements
- How to customize selected components

Bootstrap 4

In the first chapter, we spoke briefly about Twitter Bootstrap 4, but it's time to look at this CSS framework more closely. However, before delving deeper into Bootstrap 4 let's talk about all of the newly introduced features:

- The source CSS files of Bootstrap 4 are based on Sass
- The `rem` is the primary CSS unit instead of `px`
- Global font size increased from `14px` to `16px`

- New grid tiers have been added for small devices (from ~480px and below)
- Bootstrap 4 optionally supports **Flex Box Grid**
- Adds improved **Media Queries**
- The new **Card** component replaces the **Panel**, **Well**, and **Thumbnail**
- There is the new reset component called Reboot.css
- Everything is customizable with Sass variables
- Dropped support for IE 8 and iOS 6
- It no longer supports non-responsive usage

Introduction to Sass

If you are not familiar with Sass, I think now is the right moment to introduce to you that fantastic CSS preprocessing framework. It is not a secret that the preprocessing of a CSS file allows you to write more concise and less verbose stylesheets. The syntax of the first version of Sass used indentations, didn't require semi-colons, had shorthand operators, and used .sass file extension. It was so different from CSS that Sass version 3 started to support new formats with brackets, semicolons, and .scss file extensions. Let's compare the various forms to each other.

Here is a vanilla CSS style:

```
#container {
        width:100px;
        padding:0;
}
#container p {
        color: red;
}
```

In files with the .sass extension, we should use only indentation, and it is heavily dependent on white spaces:

```
$red: #ff0000
#container
        width:100px
        padding: 0
                p
                        color:$red
```

In files with .scss extension, we use brackets and semicolons:

```scss
$red: #ff0000;
#container {
        width:100px;
        padding:0;
        p {
                color :$red;
        }
}
```

It is ultimately up to you which style you prefer, but I will use the newest one based on .scss files in this book.

Setting up of Ruby

Before you start using Sass, you will need to install Ruby, but first check if you already has it. Open the Terminal and type ruby -v.
If you don't get an error, skip install Ruby step. Otherwise, you'll install a fresh Ruby from the official Ruby website https://www.ruby-lang.org/en/documentation/installation.

Setting up of Sass

After finishing the installation of Ruby, open Terminal and type the following commands.

- For Windows:

    gem install sass

- For Linux and Mac:

    sudo gem install sass

This command will install Sass and necessary dependencies for you. Run the following command to check installation of Saas on your PC:

sass -v

The Sass must respond with a version number:

Sass 3.4.22 (Selective Steve)

Bear in mind that the version of Sass installed on my computer could be different from yours. If these commands gave you a version number, you are ready to go with Sass development.

Now, that we have installed Sass, we can explore its files and output them into CSS. You can use CLI or GUI to get you started with Sass. If you prefer a GUI style of development, please use one from the following list:

- CodeKit (Mac, Paid): `http://incident57.com/codekit`
- Compass.app (Windows, Mac, Linux, Paid, Open Source): `http://compass.hand lino.com`
- Ghostlab (Web-based, Paid): `http://www.vanamco.com/ghostlab`
- Hammer (Mac, Paid): `http://hammerformac.com`
- Koala (Windows, Mac, Linux, Open Source): `http://koala-app.com`
- LiveReload (Mac, Paid, Open Source): `http://livereload.com`
- Prepros (Windows, Mac, Linux, Paid): `https://prepros.io`
- Scout (Windows, Mac, Open Source): `http://mhs.github.io/scout-app`

Personally, I prefer the Scout GUI, which runs Sass and Compass in a self-contained Ruby environment; it does all of the heavy lifting, so we will never have to worry about technical issues such as setting up Ruby.

Another interesting option I would recommend is a web-based Sass playground **SassMeister** which you can find at `http://www.sassmeister.com`. We will use it a bit in our Sass crash course.

Sass crash course

The main idea behind Sass is that we create reusable, less verbose code which is easy to read, and understand. Let's see what features make that happens. Please open the SassMeister website and prepare for our exercises.

Variables

We can create variables in Sass, especially to reuse them throughout our document. Acceptable values for variables include:

- number
- string

- color
- null
- list
- map

We use the $ symbol to define a variable. Switch to SassMeister and create our first variables:

```
$my-pad: 2em;
$color-primary: red;
$color-secondary: #ff00ed;
```

The SassMeister compiles them but without output any CSS. We just define variables in the scope, and that is it. We need to use them in the CSS declaration to see the result of compilation:

```
body {
    background-color: $color-primary;
}

.container {
    padding: $my-pad;
    color: $color-secondary;
}
```

Here is the result of compilation from Sass to CSS:

```
body {
    background-color: red;
}

.container {
    padding: 2em;
    color: #ff00ed;
}
```

Mathematical expressions

Sass allows us to use the following mathematical operators in arithmetical expressions:

- Addition (+)
- Subtraction (-)
- Division (/)
- Multiplication (*)

- Modulo (%)
- Equality (==)
- Inequality (!=)

Jump to SassMeister and play with some introduced mathematical operations:

```
$container-width: 100%;
$font-size: 16px;

.container {
  width: $container-width;
}

.col-4 {
  width: $container-width / 4;
  font-size: $font-size - 2;
}
```

Here is some CSS compiler code:

```
.container {
  width: 100%;
}

.col-4 {
  width: 25%;
  font-size: 14px;
}
```

I would like to warn you against the use of incompatible units in mathematical operators. Try the following Sass code in your playground:

```
h2 {
  // Error: Incompatible units: 'em' and 'px'.
  width: 100px + 2em;
  // Result: 52px
  height: 50px + 2;
}
```

However, multiplying two numbers of the same unit produces an invalid CSS value:

```
h2 {
  // Error: 100px*px isn't a valid CSS value.
  width: 50px * 2px;
}
```

The forward slash symbol (/) is a part of CSS shorthand properties. For example, here are the font declarations:

```
font-style: italic;
font-weight: bold;
font-size: .8em;
line-height: 1.2;
font-family: Arial, sans-serif;
```

It can be shortened to the following:

```
font: italic bold .8em/1.2 Arial, sans-serif;
```

To avoid any possible issues, you should always wrap an expression that containing the division operator of non-variable values in parentheses such that:

```
h2 {
    // Result: Outputs as CSS
    font-size: 16px / 24px;
    // Result: Does division because uses parentheses
    width: (16px / 24px);
}
```

 You should avoid using different units in mathematical operators.

Functions

Sass has a reach set of built-in functions and here is the address where you can find all of them:

```
http://sass-lang.com/documentation/Sass/Script/Functions.html
```

Here is the simplest example of the use of the rgb($red, $green, $blue) function. It creates a color from red, green, and blue values:

```
$color-secondary: rgb(ff,00,ed);
```

Nesting

Sass allows us to have a declaration inside another declaration. In the following vanilla CSS code we define two statements:

```
.container {
    width: 100px;
}

.container h1 {
    color: green;
}
```

We have a container class and header within container style declarations. In Sass we can create the compact code:

```
.container {
  width: 100px;
  h1 {
    color: green;
  }
}
```

Nesting makes code more readable and less verbose.

Imports

Sass allows you to break styles into separate files and import them into another. We can use @import directive with or without the file extensions. There are two lines of code giving the same result:

```
@import "components.scss";
@import "components";
```

Extends

If you need to inherit style from an existing one, Sass has @extend directive to help you:

```
.input {
  color: #555;
  font-size: 17px;
}

.error-input {
  @extend .input;
```

```
    color: red;
  }
```

Here is the result of how the Sass compiler properly handled the compiled code:

```
.input, .error-input {
  color: #555;
  font-size: 17px;
}

.error-input {
  color: red;
}
```

Placeholders

In the case when you want to extend a declaration with a set of styles that don't exist, Sass helps with the placeholder selector:

```
%input-style {
  font-size: 14px;
}

.input {
  @extend %input-style;
  color: #555;
}
```

We use % sign to prefix a class name and with the help of @extend, magic happens. Sass doesn't render the placeholder. It renders only the result of its extending elements. Here is the compiled code:

```
.input {
  font-size: 14px;
}

.input {
  color: #555;
}
```

Mixins

We can create reusable chunks of CSS styles with mixins. Mixins always return markup code. We use the `@mixin` directive to define mixins and `@include` to use them in the document. You may have seen the following code quite often before:

```
a:link { color: white; }
a:visited { color: blue; }
a:hover { color: green; }
a:active { color: red; }
```

Indeed, changing the color of an element depends on states. Usually we write this code over and over again, but with Sass we can do it like this:

```
@mixin link ($link, $visit, $hover, $active) {
  a {
    color: $link;
    &:visited {
      color: $visit;
    }
    &:hover {
      color: $hover;
    }
    &:active {
      color: $active;
    }
  }
}
```

The `&` symbol here points to the parent element, that is, to the anchor element. Let's use this mixin in the following example:

```
.component {
  @include link(white, blue, green, red);
}
```

Here is the mixin compiled to CSS code:

```
.component a {
  color: white;
}
.component a:visited {
  color: blue;
}
.component a:hover {
  color: green;
}
.component a:active {
```

```
    color: red;
}
```

Function directives

The function directive is another feature of Sass that helps to create reusable chunks of CSS style return values via the @return directive. We use the @function directive to define it:

```
@function getTableWidth($columnWidth,$numColumns,$margin){
    @return $columnWidth * $numColumns + $margin * 2;
}
```

In this function we calculate that the width of the table depends on individual column widths, the number of columns, and margin values:

```
$column-width: 50px;
$column-count: 4;
$margin: 2px;

.column {
  width: $column-width;
}

.table {
  background: #1abc9c;
  height: 200px;
  width: getTableWidth($column-width,$column-count,$margin);
  margin: 0 $margin;
}
```

The resulting CSS code looks like this:

```
.column {
  width: 50px;
}

.table {
  background: #1abc9c;
  height: 200px;
  width: 204px;
  margin: 0 2px;
}
```

I think it's time to leave our Sass crash course, but please don't think that you know everything about it. Sass is big and incredibly powerful, so if you decide to continue the journey we started here, please get more information here: `http://sass-lang.com/docume ntation/file.SASS_REFERENCE.html`.

Example project

Let's talk about what web application we will develop while reading this book. I have decided that an e-commerce application is the best candidate to demonstrate the full flavor of different Bootstrap 4 components tightly in one place.

The term e-commerce, as we think of it today, refers to the buying and selling of goods or services over the Internet, so we design the web application based on a real-world scenario. After the introduction, we will consolidate a high-level list of customer requirements. We will then prepare a series of mockups which will help you get a clearer picture of how the final application will look to an end-user. Finally, we will break down the customer requirements into a set of implementation tasks and structure the application so that the responsibilities and interactions among functional components are clearly defined.

The scenario

The Dream Bean is a small grocery store which collaborates with several local farms to supply organic food and produce. The store has a long-standing customer base and is bringing increasing profits to the area. The store has decided to investigate the possibility of providing an online delivery service to customers because a recent survey has indicated that 9% of its regular clientele has continuous Internet access, and 83% would be interested in using this service.

The manager of the grocery store has asked you to create a website that will enable their customers to shop online from a broad range of devices includes cell phones, tablets, and desktop computers.

Gathering customer requirements

Before making any design or implementation decisions, you need to collect information from the client; thus, after direct communication with client, we have the following conditions:

- The customer can buy products available in the physical store. There are the following product categories:
  - Meat
  - Seafood
  - Bakery
  - Dairy
  - Fruit and vegetables
  - Take away

- The customer can browse all the goods or filter them by category
- The customer has a virtual shopping cart
- The customer can add, remove, or update item quantities in the shopping cart
- The customer can view a summary of everything
- The customer can place an order and make payment through a secure checkout process

Preparing use-cases

Now, when the requirements are in place, it is time to work with managers from the Dream Bean to gain an understanding of how the website should look and behave. We create a set of use-cases that describe how the customer will use the web application:

- The customer visits the welcome page and selects a product by category
- The customer browses products within the selected category page, then adds a product to shopping cart
- The customer clicks on the **Info** button to open a separate sheet which contains full information about the product and then adds a product to the shopping cart
- The customer continues shopping and selects a different category
- The customer adds several products from this class to the shopping cart
- The customer selects **View Cart** option and updates quantities for products in the cart
- The client verifies the shopping cart contents and proceeds to checkout
- On the checkout page, the customer views the cost of the order and other information, fills in personal data, then submits the details

We continue to work with staff of Dream Bean and need to create mockups in one of the following ways:

- Using storyboard software
- Creating a set of wireframes
- Using paper prototyping

I use **Balsamiq Mockups** to help me quickly create wireframes. The fully functional trial version of Balsamiq Mockups works for 30 days and is available from the official website: `https://balsamiq.com`.

Welcome page

The welcome page is an entry point for the application. It introduces the business and service to the customer and enables him or her to navigate to any of the product categories. We add a slideshow in the middle of the welcome page, as shown here:

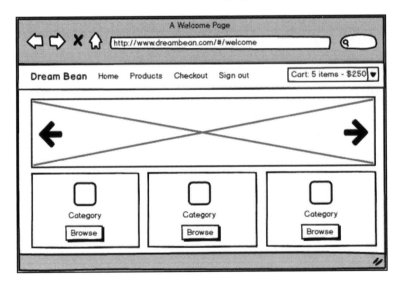

The wireframe of the welcome page

Products page

The products page provides a listing of all goods within the chosen category. From this page, a customer can view all product information, and add any of the listed products to his or her shopping cart. A user can also navigate to any of the provided categories or use the **Quick Shop** feature to search products by name, as shown here:

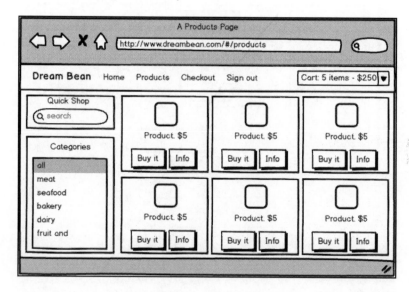

The wireframe of the products page

Products page

The products page displays information about the product. On this page the customer can do the following:

- Check the availability of the product
- Update the quantity of the product
- Add the product to the cart by clicking **Buy it**

- Return to the products list by clicking on **Continue Shopping**

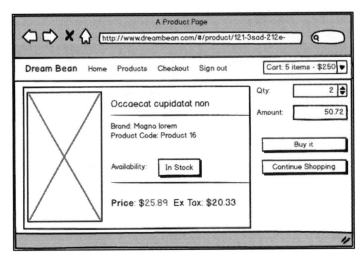

The wireframe of the product page

Cart page

The cart page lists all items held in the user's shopping cart. It displays product details for each item and from this page, a user can do the following:

- Remove all goodies from his or her cart by clicking **Clear Cart**
- Update the quantity for any listed item
- Return to the products list by clicking on **Continue Shopping**
- Proceed to checkout by clicking **Checkout**

The following is how the cart page might look:

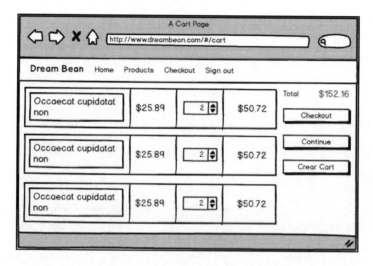

The wireframe of the cart page

Checkout page

The checkout page displays the customer details form, purchase conditions, and order information. The customer should fill in the form, confirm payment, and click on the **Submit** button to start the payment process, as shown here:

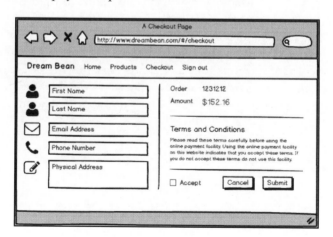

The wireframe of the checkout page

We have everything to initiate the journey with Angular 2 and Bootstrap 4. We projected the business requirements onto mockups, and now we need to do the following:

1. Open Terminal, create folder `ecommerce` and move in this folder
2. Copy the contents of the project from the `ecommerce-seed` folder into the new project
3. Run the following script to install npm modules:

```
npm install
```

4. Start the **TypeScript** watcher and lite server with the following command:

```
npm run start
```

This script opens the web browser and navigates to the welcome page of the project. We are ready to start development.

 You can find the source code in the `chapter_2/1.ecommerce-seed` folder.

Designing layouts with grids and containers

Bootstrap includes a powerful mobile-first grid system for building designs of all shapes and sizes, and that sounds very promising because we need to create several pages for our project. We will use the grid systems for creating the page layouts through a series of rows and columns. Since Bootstrap is developed to be mobile first, we use a handful of `media queries` to create sensible breakpoints for our layouts and interfaces. These breakpoints are mostly based on minimum viewport widths and allow us to scale up elements as the viewport changes. There are three main components of the grid system, they are:

- Container
- Row
- Column

The container is the core and requires layout element in Bootstrap. There are two classes to create the containers for all other items:

- You can create a responsive, fixed-width container with a `container` class. This one doesn't have extra space on both sides of the hosting element and it's `max-width` property changes at each breakpoint.
- You can use the full-width container with a `container-fluid` class. This one always has 100% width of a viewport.

To create a simple layout for our project open `app.component.html` file, and insert a `div` element with a `container` class inside:

```
<div class="container">
</div>
```

We can nest containers, but most layouts do not require that. The container is just a placeholder for rows, so let's add the row inside:

```
<div class="container">
  <div class="row">
  </div>
</div>
```

The row has a `row` class, and the container can contain as many rows as you need.

 I recommend using one or several containers with all of the rows inside to wrap the page content and center elements on the screen.

A row is a horizontal group of columns. It exists only for one purpose: to keep columns lined up correctly. We must put the substance of the page only inside columns and indicate the number of columns to use. Each row can contain up to 12 of them.

We can add the column to the row as a combination of a `col` class, and it prefixes size:

```
<div class="col-md-12">
```

Bootstrap 4 supports five different sizes of displays, and the columns classes names depend on them:

- `col-xs`: For an extra small display (screen width less than 34em or 544px)
- `col-sm`: For a smaller display (screen width 34em or 544ps and up)
- `col-md`: For a medium display (screen width 48em or 768px and up)

- `col-lg`: For a larger display (screen width 62em or 992px and up)
- `col-xl`: For an extra large display (screen width 75em or 1200px and up)

The column class names always apply to devices with screen widths greater than or equal to the breakpoint sizes.

The width of a column sets in percentage, so it is always fluid and sized about the parent element. Each column has a horizontal padding to create a space between individual columns. The first and last columns have negative margins, and this is why the content within the grid lines up with the substance outside. Here is an example of a grid for extra small devices:

col-xs-1	col-xs-1	col-xs-1	col-xs-1	col-xs-1	col-xs-1	col-xs-1	col-xs-1	col-xs-1	col-xs-1	col-xs-1	col-xs-1
col-xs-2		col-xs-3			col-xs-7						
col-xs-4			col-xs-4			col-xs-4					
col-xs-5				col-xs-7							
col-xs-6					col-xs-6						
col-xs-12											

Look at the welcome page mockup of our project and imagine splitting it into rows and columns:

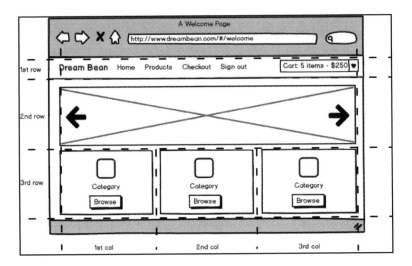

The wireframe of the welcome page

Our markup has a minimum of three rows. The first has a header with company logo and menu. It spans 12 mid-sized columns marked with `col-md-12`. I have used grid for now, but later I will change it to a more suitable component:

```
<div class="container">
  <div class="row">
    <div class="col-md-12 table-bordered">
      <div class="product-menu">Logo and Menu</div>
    </div>
  </div>
  <!-- /.row -->
</div>
```

The second one has a single column, contains an image 1110x480px, and spans all 12 mid-sized columns marked with `col-md-12` like the previous one:

```
<div class="container">
  <div class="row">
    <div class="col-md-12 table-bordered">
      <img class="img-fluid center-block product-item"
           src="http://placehold.it/1110x480" alt="">
    </div>
  </div>
  <!-- /.row -->
```

The last one includes the places with six product categories, and each of them occupies a different number of columns depending on the size of the layout:

- Four middle-sized columns marked with `col-md-4`
- Six small columns marked as `col-sm-6`
- Twelve extra small columns marked with `col-xs-12`

The size of each image is 270x171px. The markup of the bottom part of the screen is quite long, so I cut it off:

```
<div class="row">
    <div class="col-xs-12 col-sm-6 col-md-4 table-bordered">
      <a href="#">
        <img class="img-fluid center-block product-item"
             src="http://placehold.it/270x171" alt="">
      </a>
    </div>
    <!-- /.col -->
    <div class="col-xs-12 col-sm-6 col-md-4 table-bordered">
      <a href="#">
        <img class="img-fluid center-block product-item"
```

```
                     src="http://placehold.it/270x171" alt="">
        </a>
      </div>
      <!-- /.col -->
  ...
      <div class="col-xs-12 col-sm-6 col-md-4 table-bordered">
        <a href="#">
          <img class="img-fluid center-block product-item"
               src="http://placehold.it/270x171" alt="">
        </a>
      </div>
      <!-- /.col -->
    </div>
    <!-- /.row -->
  </div>
  <!-- /.container -->
```

I intentionally added the Bootstrap class `table-bordered` to display the boundaries of columns. I will remove it later. Here is the result of how the website looks like:

If I change the viewport to a smaller size, Bootstrap immediately transforms columns into rows, as you see on the preceding diagram. I didn't use real images on the page but pointed to `http://placehold.it`. This is a service on the web that generates placeholder images of specified sizes on the fly. The link like this `http://placehold.it/270×171` returns the placeholder image with 270x171px size.

Using images

In our markup I used images, so pay attention to the `img-fluid` class which opts the image into responsive behavior:

```
<img class="img-fluid center-block product-item"
     src="http://placehold.it/270x171" alt="">
```

The logic behind the class will never allow the image to become larger than the parent element. At the same time, it adds lightweight styles management via classes. You can easily design the shape of the picture as follow:

- Rounded it with `img-rounded` class. The border radius is 0.3rem
- Circle it with the help of `img-circle`, so the border radius became to 50%
- Transform it with `img-thumbnail`

In our example, the `center-block` centered the image, but you can align it with helper float or text alignment classes:

- The class `pull-sm-left` floats left on small or wider devices
- The class `pull-lg-right` floats right on large and bigger devices
- The class `pull-xs-none` prevents floating on all viewport sizes

 You can find the source code in the `chapter_2/2.ecommerce-grid` folder.

Now, I would like to create the plates and change them with images at the bottom of the page. The best one that we can use for this purposes is a **Card** component.

Using Cards

A Card component is a very flexible and extensible content container requiring a small amount of markup and classes to make fantastic things. The Cards replaces the following elements that exist in Bootstrap 3:

- Panels
- Wells
- Thumbnails

The simplest way to create it is to add the `card` and `card-block` classes to the element:

```
<div class="col-xs-12 col-sm-6 col-md-4">
  <div class="card">
    <img class="card-img-top center-block product-item"
         src="http://placehold.it/270x171" alt="Bakery">
    <div class="card-block">
      <h4 class="card-title">Bakery</h4>
      <p class="card-text">The best cupcakes, cookies, cakes,
                  pies, cheesecakes, fresh bread,
                  biscotti, muffins, bagels, fresh coffee
                  and more.</p>
      <a href="#" class="btn btn-primary">Browse</a>
    </div>
  </div>
</div>
```

The `card-block` class adds a padding space between the content and the card border. In my example, I moved it inside to allow the card header to line up flush with the card edge. If you need to, you can create a header with `card-header` and footer with `card-footer` classes. As your see, it includes a broad range of components in the Card like images, texts, list groups, and more. Here is how our Card component looks:

But this is not only a single place where we use Card components. We will use them a lot in the following chapters.

You can find the source code in the `chapter_2/3.ecommerce-cards` folder.

Using buttons

I have added a button to the Card component, and I want to talk about it. You can apply the button style to the following elements:

- The standard `button` works correctly across all browsers.
- The `input` element with `type="button"`.
- The anchor element, only behaves like a button with `role="button"`. Use it only to trigger in-page functionality rather than linking to new a page or section within the current one.
- The label when working with checkboxes and radio buttons.

General button styles

In Bootstrap 4, we can find seven styles for buttons and each of them for a different semantic purpose. The class `btn` adds style for contextual variations, sizes, states of buttons placed standalone, in forms, or dialogs:

The primary actions style provides an extra visual weight:

```
<button type="button" class="btn btn-primary">Primary</button>
```

The secondary, less important than primary actions style provides for reduced background color:

```
<button type="button" class="btn btn-secondary">Secondary</button>
```

The success indicates any success operations or position actions:

```
<button type="button" class="btn btn-success">Success</button>
```

The info is to guide users for informational actions or alerts:

```
<button type="button" class="btn btn-info">Info</button>
```

The warning one offers warning with cautions actions:

```
<button type="button" class="btn btn-warning">Warning</button>
```

The danger indicates dangerous or potentially negative actions:

```
<button type="button" class="btn btn-danger">Danger</button>
```

The link one presents a button as a link:

```
<button type="button" class="btn btn-link">Link</button>
```

Outline button styles

You can remove hefty background images and colors on any button of any predefined styles by replacing the default modified classes with the `.btn-outline-*` styles.

```
<button type="button"
        class="btn btn-outline-primary">Primary</button>
<button type="button"
        class="btn btn-outline-secondary">Secondary</button>
<button type="button"
        class="btn btn-outline-success">Success</button>
<button type="button"
        class="btn btn-outline-info">Info</button>
<button type="button"
        class="btn btn-outline-warning">Warning</button>
<button type="button"
        class="btn btn-outline-danger">Danger</button>
```

There is no outline for link buttons (that is, there is no `btn-outline-link` class).

Button sizes

Buttons may have small and big sizes:

Use `btn-sm` and `btn-lg` classes to make that happen:

```
<button type="button"
        class="btn btn-primary btn-lg">Large button</button>
<button type="button"
        class="btn btn-primary btn-sm">Small button</button>
```

Block level button styles

If you planning to create block level buttons that span the full width of parent element, just add `btn-block` class:

```
<button type="button"
        class="btn btn-primary btn-lg btn-block">Block</button>
```

The button with active style

The pseudo-classes in button styles update the visual state of elements according to user actions, but if you need to change the states manually use `active` class:

```
<a href="#" class="btn btn-primary btn-lg active"
   role="button">Primary link</a>
```

The button with inactive state

We can make button looks inactive with the `disabled` property:

```
<button type="button" disabled
        class="btn btn-lg btn-primary">Primary button</button>
```

Radio buttons and checkboxes

Bootstrap 4 provides button styles with toggle features to `input` elements similar to radio buttons and checkboxes. To achieve that you need to create the massive construction that includes a group element, a label, and the input element itself:

```
<div class="btn-group" data-toggle="buttons">
  <label class="btn btn-primary active">
    <input type="checkbox" checked autocomplete="off">
      Checkbox 1 (active)
  </label>
  <label class="btn btn-primary">
    <input type="checkbox" autocomplete="off"> Checkbox 2
  </label>
```

```
    <label class="btn btn-primary">
      <input type="checkbox" autocomplete="off"> Checkbox 3
    </label>
</div>
```

Checkbox 1 (active)   Checkbox 2   Checkbox 3

```
<div class="btn-group" data-toggle="buttons">
  <label class="btn btn-primary active">
    <input type="radio" name="options" id="option1"
           autocomplete="off" checked> Radio 1 (preselected)
  </label>
  <label class="btn btn-primary">
    <input type="radio" name="options" id="option2"
           autocomplete="off"> Radio 2
  </label>
  <label class="btn btn-primary">
    <input type="radio" name="options" id="option3"
           autocomplete="off"> Radio 3
  </label>
</div>
```

Radio 1 (preselected)   Radio 2   Radio 3

Navs

Bootstrap 4 provides a base style for navigation elements. It exposes the base nav class that shares general mark-up and styles by extending it. All navigation components are built on top of this by specifying additional styles. It doesn't have styles for the active state. By the way, you can use these methods for disabled buttons.

The base Nav

Any **Nav** component must have the outer navigation element based on ul or nav elements. Here is a list-based approach displaying navigation elements vertically:

```
<ul class="nav">
  <li class="nav-item">
    <a class="nav-link" href="#">Link</a>
  </li>
```

```
  <li class="nav-item">
    <a class="nav-link" href="#">Link</a>
  </li>
  <li class="nav-item">
    <a class="nav-link" href="#">Another link</a>
  </li>
  <li class="nav-item">
    <a class="nav-link disabled" href="#">Disabled</a>
  </li>
</ul>
```

Our mark-up can be very flexible because all components are based on classes. We can use nav with regular anchor elements to layout navigation horizontally:

```
<nav class="nav">
  <a class="nav-link active" href="#">Active</a>
  <a class="nav-link" href="#">Link</a>
  <a class="nav-link" href="#">Another link</a>
  <a class="nav-link disabled" href="#">Disabled</a>
</nav>
```

I like this approach because it is less verbose than the list-based one.

Inline navigation

You can easily add inline navigation elements with spacing horizontally as shown in the preceding example with the help of the nav-inline class:

```
<ul class="nav nav-inline">
  <li class="nav-item">
    <a class="nav-link" href="#">Link</a>
  </li>
  <li class="nav-item">
    <a class="nav-link" href="#">Link</a>
  </li>
  <li class="nav-item">
    <a class="nav-link" href="#">Another link</a>
  </li>
```

```
      <li class="nav-item">
        <a class="nav-link disabled" href="#">Disabled</a>
      </li>
    </ul>
```

Tabs

We can quickly transform Nav components from the preceding, to generate a tabbed interface with the nav-tabs class:

```
<ul class="nav nav-tabs">
  <li class="nav-item">
    <a class="nav-link active" href="#">Active</a>
  </li>
  <li class="nav-item">
    <a class="nav-link" href="#">Link</a>
  </li>
  <li class="nav-item">
    <a class="nav-link" href="#">Another link</a>
  </li>
  <li class="nav-item">
    <a class="nav-link disabled" href="#">Disabled</a>
  </li>
</ul>
```

Pills

Just change nav-tabs to nav-pills to display the **pills** instead:

```
<ul class="nav nav-pills">
  <li class="nav-item">
    <a class="nav-link active" href="#">Active</a>
  </li>
  <li class="nav-item">
    <a class="nav-link" href="#">Link</a>
  </li>
  <li class="nav-item">
    <a class="nav-link" href="#">Another link</a>
  </li>
  <li class="nav-item">
    <a class="nav-link disabled" href="#">Disabled</a>
```

```
      </li>
    </ul>
```

Stacked pills

If you need layout pills vertically, use the `nav-stacked` class:

```html
<ul class="nav nav-pills nav-stacked">
  <li class="nav-item">
    <a class="nav-link active" href="#">Active</a>
  </li>
  <li class="nav-item">
    <a class="nav-link" href="#">Link</a>
  </li>
  <li class="nav-item">
    <a class="nav-link" href="#">Another link</a>
  </li>
  <li class="nav-item">
    <a class="nav-link disabled" href="#">Disabled</a>
  </li>
</ul>
```

Navigation with dropdowns

You can add a drop-down menu to inline navigation, tabs, or pills by applying a `dropdown` class to the list item and with a little extra HTML and drop-down JavaScript plugins:

```html
<ul class="nav nav-tabs">
  <li class="nav-item">
    <a class="nav-link active" href="#">Active</a>
  </li>
  <li class="nav-item dropdown">
    <a class="nav-link dropdown-toggle" data-toggle="dropdown"
       href="#" role="button" aria-haspopup="true"
```

```
        aria-expanded="false">Dropdown</a>
    <div class="dropdown-menu">
      <a class="dropdown-item" href="#">Action</a>
      <a class="dropdown-item" href="#">Another action</a>
      <a class="dropdown-item" href="#">Something else here</a>
      <div class="dropdown-divider"></div>
      <a class="dropdown-item" href="#">Separated link</a>
    </div>
  </li>
  <li class="nav-item">
    <a class="nav-link" href="#">Another link</a>
  </li>
  <li class="nav-item">
    <a class="nav-link disabled" href="#">Disabled</a>
  </li>
</ul>
```

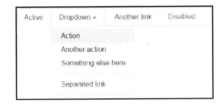

Navbars

I mentioned earlier the header with company logo and menu, temporarily implemented as a grid. Now we change this construction to the suitable component. Please welcome the **Navbars**.

The Navbar is just a simple wrapper helping to position containing elements. Usually, it displays as a horizontal bar, but you can configure it to collapse on smaller layouts.

Like many other components of Bootstrap the Navbar container requires a small amount of markup and classes to make it work:

- To create one, you must use a `navbar` class in conjunction with a color scheme
- The topmost must be a `nav` or `div` element with `role="navigation"`

Content

We can include built-in sub-components to add the placeholders when necessary:

- Use `navbar-brand` class for your company, product, or project name.
- Use `navbar-nav` class for full-height and lightweight navigation. It includes support for drop-downs as well.
- Use `navbar-toggler` class to organize collapsible behavior.

Let's use what we know about Navbar to build our header. First of all, I use `nav` to create the topmost element:

```
<nav class="navbar navbar-light bg-faded">
```

Then, I need `navbar-brand` class for the company name. We can apply this class to most elements, but an anchor works best:

```
<a class="navbar-brand" href="#">Dream Bean</a>
```

At the end, I add a set of navigation links with `active` first:

```
<ul class="nav navbar-nav">
  <lii class="nav-tem active">
    <a class="nav-link" href="#">
      Home <span class="sr-only">(current)</span>
    </a>
  </li>
  <li class="nav-item">
    <a class="nav-link" href="#">Products</a>
  </li>
  <li class="nav-item">
    <a class="nav-link" href="#">Checkout</a>
  </li>
  <li class="nav-item">
    <a class="nav-link" href="#">Sign out</a>
  </li>
</ul>
</nav>
<!-- /.navbar -->
```

Here is our header with branding and a set of links:

Dream Bean   Home   Products   Checkout   Sign out

With the help of `nav` classes we can make navigation simple by avoiding the list-based approach entirely:

```
<nav class="navbar navbar-light bg-faded">
  <a class="navbar-brand" href="#">Dream Bean</a>
  <div class="nav navbar-nav">
    <a class="nav-item nav-link active" href="#">
      Home <span class="sr-only">(current)</span>
    </a>
    <a class="nav-item nav-link" href="#">Products</a>
    <a class="nav-item nav-link" href="#">Checkout</a>
    <a class="nav-item nav-link" href="#">Sign out</a>
  </div>
</nav>
```

Colors

You can manage the colors of Navbar very elegantly:

- Specify the scheme with `navbar-light` or `navbar-dark` classes
- Add color values via one of the Bootstrap color classes or create your own color with CSS

In my example I used a light scheme and a Bootstrap faded background color. Let's change it to a dark scheme and a custom color:

```
<nav class="navbar navbar-dark" style="background-color: #666">
  <a class="navbar-brand" href="#">Dream Bean</a>
  <div class="nav navbar-nav">
    <a class="nav-item nav-link active" href="#">
      Home <span class="sr-only">(current)</span>
    </a>
    <a class="nav-item nav-link" href="#">Products</a>
    <a class="nav-item nav-link" href="#">Checkout</a>
    <a class="nav-item nav-link" href="#">Sign out</a>
  </div>
</nav>
```

It looks nice, but Navbar is spanning the full width of the viewport. This is not what managers from Dream Bean want. The header must be centered and have a specific size.

Containers

We will wrap our Navbar in a `container` class to center it on the page:

```
<div class="container">
  <nav class="navbar navbar-dark" style="background-color: #666">
    <a class="navbar-brand" href="#">Dream Bean</a>
    <div class="nav navbar-nav">
      <a class="nav-item nav-link active" href="#">
        Home <span class="sr-only">(current)</span>
      </a>
      <a class="nav-item nav-link" href="#">Products</a>
      <a class="nav-item nav-link" href="#">Checkout</a>
      <a class="nav-item nav-link" href="#">Sign out</a>
    </div>
  </nav>
</div>
```

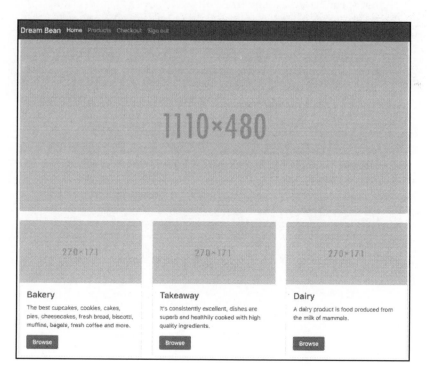

Another correction they would like to have is that the header must be statically placed at top of the page. I used the `navbar-fixed-top` class to place it at the top of the viewport:

```
<div class="container">
  <nav class="navbar navbar-fixed-top navbar-dark"
       style="background-color: #666">
    <a class="navbar-brand" href="#">Dream Bean</a>
    <div class="nav navbar-nav">
      <a class="nav-item nav-link active" href="#">
        Home <span class="sr-only">(current)</span>
      </a>
      <a class="nav-item nav-link" href="#">Products</a>
      <a class="nav-item nav-link" href="#">Checkout</a>
      <a class="nav-item nav-link" href="#">Sign out</a>
    </div>
  </nav>
</div>
```

You can use the `navbar-fixed-bottom` class to reach the same effect but at the bottom of the page.

With these last changes, the header spans the full width of the viewport again. To fix that issue, we need to move `container` inside `navbar` to wrap up its content:

```
<nav class="navbar navbar-fixed-top navbar-dark"
     style="background-color: #666">
  <div class="container">
    <a class="navbar-brand" href="#">Dream Bean</a>
    <div class="nav navbar-nav">
      <a class="nav-item nav-link active" href="#">
        Home <span class="sr-only">(current)</span>
      </a>
      <a class="nav-item nav-link" href="#">Products</a>
      <a class="nav-item nav-link" href="#">Checkout</a>
      <a class="nav-item nav-link" href="#">Sign out</a>
    </div>
  </div>
</nav>
```

Our Navbar hides the part of the viewport underneath, so we need to add a padding to compensate this issue:

```
body {
  padding-top: 51px;
}
```

If your Navbar was fixed at the bottom add padding for it as well:

```
body {
  padding-bottom: 51px;
}
```

Responsive Navbar

Another issue the staff of Dream Bean would like to fix is that the content must collapse at the given viewport width. Let's do it with `navbar-toggler` class along with `navbar-toggleable` classes, and their prefix sizes:

```
<nav class="navbar navbar-fixed-top navbar-dark bg-inverse">
  <div class="container">
    <button class="navbar-toggler hidden-sm-up"
            type="button" data-toggle="collapse"
            data-target="#exCollapsingNavbar">&#9776;
    </button>
    <div class="collapse navbar-toggleable-xs"
         id="exCollapsingNavbar">
      <a class="navbar-brand" href="#">Dream Bean</a>
      <div class="nav navbar-nav">
        <a class="nav-item nav-link active" href="#">
          Home <span class="sr-only">(current)</span>
        </a>
        <a class="nav-item nav-link" href="#">Products</a>
        <a class="nav-item nav-link" href="#">Checkout</a>
        <a class="nav-item nav-link" href="#">Sign out</a>
      </div>
    </div>
  </div>
</nav>
```

As I mentioned earlier, the `navbar-toggler` class helps to organize collapsible behavior. The collapsible plugin uses information from the `data-toggle` property to trigger the action and one element defined in `data-target`. The `data-target` keeps the ID of an element contained with `navbar-toggleable` classes, and it prefixes the size.

The collapsible header will only work responsively with a combination of all of them:

Responsive utilities

To make the life of developers easy, Bootstrap provides utility classes for faster mobile-friendly development. They could help in:

- Showing and hiding content by a device via a media query

- Toggling content when printed

I don't want to create entirely different versions of the same web application for different mobile devices. Instead, I will use the following utility classes to complement each device's presentation:

- The utility class `hidden-*-up` hides the element when the viewport is at the given breakpoint or wider

- The utility class `hidden-*-down` hides the element when the viewport is at the given breakpoint or smaller

- We can show an element only on a given interval of screen sizes by combining `hidden-*-up` and `hidden-*-down` utility classes

Bear in mind that there are no exit responsive utility classes to show an element explicitly. Indeed, we do not hide it at the particular breakpoint size.

In our project we show the UI element we like to call the hamburger button only for devices with a screen size less than 544px:

```
<button class="navbar-toggler hidden-sm-up"
        type="button" data-toggle="collapse"
        data-target="#exCollapsingNavbar">&#9776;
</button>
```

Here is a quick tip table that can help you to choose the right utility class to show elements on screen:

- The `hidden-xs-down` shows elements from small devices (landscape phones) and up (>= 544px)

- The `hidden-sm-down` shows elements from medium devices (tablets) and up (>= 768px)

- The `hidden-md-down` shows elements from large devices (desktops) and up (>= 992px)

- The `hidden-lg-down` shows elements from small devices (desktops) and up (>= 1200px)

- The `hidden-sm-up` shows elements for extra small devices (portrait phones) (< 544px)

- The `hidden-md-up` shows elements for small devices (portrait phones) and down (< 768px)

- The `hidden-lg-up` shows elements for medium devices (tablets) and down (< 992px)

- The `hidden-xl-up` shows elements for large devices (desktops) and down (< 1200px)

The Navbar content alignment

The last thing we need to fix is the placement of a menu in the Navbar. We can use any of `pull-*left` or `pull-*right` classes to align the menu and all other components in Navbar. The managers of Dream Bean want to add the cart item with a drop-down as the last item of the menu and align it to the right side:

```
<ul class="nav navbar-nav pull-xs-right">
  <li class="nav-item dropdown">
    <a class="nav-link dropdown-toggle"
       data-toggle="dropdown" href="#" role="button"
       aria-haspopup="true" aria-expanded="false">Cart</a>
    <div class="dropdown-menu">
      <span>The Cart Placeholder</span>
    </div>
  </li>
</ul>
```

I have created a separate menu group and aligned it to the right with `pull-xs-right` on all sizes of layout:

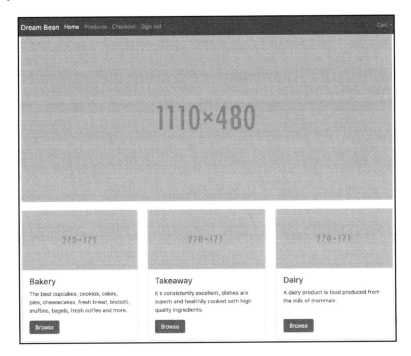

You can find the source code in the
`chapter_2/4.ecommerce-responsive` folder.

Summary

In this chapter, we discovered the world of Sass; the CSS preprocessing framework allows you to write more concise stylesheets. The Sass files are formatted nicely and require less repetitive techniques commonly found when writing CSS code. As a result, we had more dynamic styling and saved time developing quality websites and applications. We will use Sass in customizing our project in the following chapters.

We introduced the project we're going to be building over the course of this book. This information includes important aspects about how to start a project development from scratch.

We explored the most fundamental grid component helping us to layout all other elements across the page.

We introduced the flexible Card component and built the plates that contain categories of products from the building project.

We now know how to use Nav and Navbar components to organize responsively collapsible headers with a menu, and how to customize it.

In Chapter 3, *Advanced Bootstrap Components and Customization*, we're going to explore more Bootstrap fundamentals and continue to build the project we started to develop in this chapter.

3

Advanced Bootstrap Components and Customization

In this chapter, we continue to discover the world of Bootstrap 4. You will meet new components, and we will continue to demonstrate the use of Bootstrap 4 by showcasing a project we started to build in the preceding chapter. At the end of the chapter, you will have a solid understanding of:

- How to display content with Jumbotron
- How create a slideshow with Bootstrap
- How use typography in text
- How create input, button, and list groups
- Getting attention with images and labels
- Using drop-down menus and tables

How to capture a customer's attention

The Welcome page presents core marketing messages to website users, and it needs to get extra attention from them. We can use two different components to make that happen. Let's start with:

1. Open Terminal, create folder `ecommerce` and move in.
2. Copy the content of the project from the folder `chapter_3/1.ecommerce-seed` into the new project.
3. Run the following script to install npm modules:

```
npm install
```

4. Start the TypeScript watcher and lite server with the next command:

```
npm run start
```

This script opens a web browser and navigates to the Welcome page of the project. Now, we are ready to start development.

Displaying content with Jumbotron

We can use the **Jumbotron** component to draw significant attention to marketing messages. It is a lightweight component, styled with large text and dense padding. We need to show:

- The marketing message
- The slogan
- Essential information for customers

Open the `app.component.html` page, find the first container under Navbar and change its content to the Jumbotron component:

```html
<div class="jumbotron">
  <h1>FRESH ORGANIC MARKET</h1>
  <p>Nice chance to save a lot of money</p>
  <hr>
  <p>We are open 7 Days a Week 7:00am to 10:00pm</p>
</div>
```

You can force Jumbotron to use the full width of the page with the help of the `jumbotron-fluid` class and `container` or the `container-fluid` class within.

I used standard HTML markup elements inside Jumbotron, but it might look better with a different style.

Typography

In the preceding code, we used text elements without any classes, to see how Bootstrap renders them on the page. It uses the global default `font-size` of `16px` and `line-height` `1,5`. `Helvetica Neue`, `Helvetica`, `Arial`, `Sans Serf` are the default `font-family` in Bootstrap 4. Every element has a `box-sizing` to avoid exceeding the width due to padding or borders. The paragraph element has a bottom margin of `1rem`. The body has a declared white `background-color`. Any page linked to Bootstrap 4 style sheets renders with those page-wide defaults.

Headings

All heading elements, `<h1>` through `<h6>`, have a weight of `500` and a `line-height` of `1,1`. Bootstrap's developers have removed `margin-top` from them, but added the `margine-bottom` of `0,5rem` for easy spacing.

In cases when you need to display some inline text you can use the `h1` through `h6` classes to style elements that mimic headings:

```
<p class="h1">.h1 (Semibold 36px)</p>
<p class="h2">.h2 (Semibold 30px)</p>
<p class="h3">.h3 (Semibold 24px)</p>
<p class="h4">.h4 (Semibold 18px)</p>
<p class="h5">.h5 (Semibold 14px)</p>
<p class="h6">.h6 (Semibold 12px)</p>
```

.h1 (Semibold 36px)

.h2 (Semibold 30px)

.h3 (Semibold 24px)

.h4 (Semibold 18px)

.h5 (Semibold 14px)

h6 (Semibold 12px)

Sub-headings

If you require the inclusion of a sub-heading or secondary text smaller than the original, you may use the `<small>` tag:

```
<h1>Heading 1 <small>Sub-heading</small></h1>
<h2>Heading 2 <small>Sub-heading</small></h2>
<h3>Heading 3 <small>Sub-heading</small></h3>
<h4>Heading 4 <small>Sub-heading</small></h4>
<h5>Heading 5 <small>Sub-heading</small></h5>
<h6>Heading 6 <small>Sub-heading</small></h6>
```

Heading 1 Sub-heading

Heading 2 Sub-heading

Heading 3 Sub-heading

Heading 4 Sub-heading

Heading 5 Sub-heading

Heading 6 Sub-heading

We can show faded and smaller text with the help of the `text-muted` class:

```
<h3>
  The heading
  <small class="text-muted">with faded secondary text</small>
</h3>
```

The heading with faded secondary text

Display headings

When the standard heading is not enough and you need to draw the user's attention to something special, I recommend using the `display-*` classes. There are four different sizes, and that means you can render the `<h1>` element with four different styles:

```
<h1 class="display-1">Display 1</h1>
<h1 class="display-2">Display 2</h1>
<h1 class="display-3">Display 3</h1>
<h1 class="display-4">Display 4</h1>
```

```
Display 1
Display 2
Display 3
Display 4
```

Lead

We can add the `lead` class to any paragraph to make it stand out from other text:

```
<p class="lead">
This is the article lead text.
</p>
<p>
This is the normal size text.
</p>
```

This is the article lead text.

This is the normal size text.

Let's update the Jumbotron component to make it look better:

```
<div class="jumbotron">
  <h1 class="display-3">FRESH ORGANIC MARKET</h1>
  <p class="lead">Nice chance to save a lot of money</p>
  <hr class="m-y-2">
  <p>We are open 7 Days a Week 7:00am to 10:00pm</p>
</div>
```

FRESH ORGANIC MARKET

Nice chance to save a lot of money

We are open 7 Days a Week 7:00am to 10:00pm

The marketing message looks gorgeous, the slogan is in place, but we did not change the essential information for customers because there was no need.

Inline text elements

Here is a set of different styles we can use as inline text:

```
<p>The mark tag is <mark>highlight</mark> text.</p>
<p>The del tag marks <del>text as deleted.</del></p>
<p>The s tag marks <s> text as no longer accurate.</s></p>
<p>The ins tag marks <ins>text as an addition to the document.</ins></p>
<p>The u tag renders <u>text as underlined.</u></p>
<p>The small tag marks <small>text as fine print.</small></p>
<p>The strong tag renders <strong>text as bold.</strong></p>
<p>The em tag mark renders <em>text as italicized.</em></p>
```

The mark tag is highlight text.

The del tag marks ~~text as deleted.~~

The s tag marks ~~text as no longer accurate.~~

The ins tag marks <u>text as an addition to the document.</u>

The u tag renders <u>text as underlined.</u>

The small tag marks text as fine print

The strong tag renders **text as bold**.

The em tag mark renders *text as italicized.*

Abbreviations

To mark any text as an abbreviation or acronym, we can use the `<abbr>` tag. It shows the standing out of other text and provides the expanded version when you hover over it with the help of the `title` attribute:

```
<p>The Ubuntu is <abbr >OS</abbr>.</p>
```

The Ubuntu is OS

Operation System

The class `initialism` makes an abbreviation for a slightly smaller font size.

Blockquotes

We can quote the content from another source within our document with the help of the blockquote tag and class:

```
<blockquote class="blockquote">
  <p>Love all, trust a few, do wrong to none.</p>
</blockquote>
```

> Love all, trust a few, do wrong to none.

Also, we can add the author at the bottom of the blockquote with nested footer and cite tags.

```
<blockquote class="blockquote">
  <p>Love all, trust a few, do wrong to none.</p>
  <footer class="blockquote-footer">William Shakespeare in
    <cite>All's Well That Ends Well</cite>
  </footer>
</blockquote>
```

> Love all, trust a few, do wrong to none.
>
> — William Shakespeare in *All's Well That Ends Well*

Do you prefer blockquotes aligned to the right side? Let's use the blockquote-reverse class:

```
<blockquote class="blockquote blockquote-reverse">
  <p>Love all, trust a few, do wrong to none.</p>
  <footer class="blockquote-footer">William Shakespeare in
    <cite>All's Well That Ends Well</cite>
  </footer>
</blockquote>
```

> Love all, trust a few, do wrong to none.
>
> William Shakespeare in *All's Well That Ends Well* —

Address

We use the `address` element to display customer contact information at the bottom of the page:

```
<footer class="footer">
  <div class="container">
    <address>
      <strong>Contact Info</strong><br>
      0000 Market St, Suite 000, San Francisco, CA 00000,
      (123) 456-7890, <a href="mailto:#">support@dream-bean.com</a>
    </address>
  </div>
</footer>
```

 You can find the source code in the `chapter_3/2.ecommerce-jumbotron` folder

Displaying content with a carousel

Another component we can use to get customers' extra attention is the carousel. It helps us create elegant and interactive images or text slideshows. The carousel is a combination of different components, each of them playing a very specific role.

Carousel container

The container wraps all other content so the plugin JavaScript code can find it by the `carousel` and `slide` classes. It must have an `id` for the carousel controls and inner components to function properly. If you want the carousel to start an animation when the page loads, use the `data-ride="carousel"` property:

```
<div id="welcome-products"
     class="carousel slide" data-ride="carousel">
```

Carousel inner

This container holds carousel items as scrollable content and marks them with the `carousel-inner` class:

```
<div class="carousel-inner" role="listbox">
```

Carousel item

The `carousel-item` class keeps the content of slides such as images, text, or a combination of them. You need to wrap text-based content with a `carousel-caption` container. The `active` class marks the item as initialized and without it the carousel won't be visible.

```
<div class="carousel-item active">
  <img src="http://placehold.it/1110x480" alt="Bread & Pastry">
  <div class="carousel-caption">
    <h3>Bread & Pastry</h3>
  </div>
</div>
```

Carousel indicators

The carousel may have indicators to display and control the slideshow via a click or a tap to select a particular slide. Usually, it is an ordered list marked with a `carousel-indicators` class. Every item on the list must have the `data-target` property keeping the carousel container id. Because it's an ordered list, you don't need to sort it. If you need to alter the slide position around the current location use the `data-slide` property to accept the keywords `prev` and `next`. Another option is to use the `data-slide-to` property to pass the index of the slide. Use the `active` class to mark the initial indicator:

```
<ol class="carousel-indicators">
  <li data-target="#welcome-products" data-slide-to="0"
```

```
                    class="active"></li>
    <li data-target="#welcome-products" data-slide-to="1"></li>
    <li data-target="#welcome-products" data-slide-to="2"></li>
</ol>
```

Carousel controls

You can use an alternative way to display slides via carousel control buttons. In this case, the two anchor elements play the role of the buttons. Add the `left` or the `right` classes to a particular button together with `carousel-control`. Use the carousel container `id` as a link in the `href` property. Set `prev` or `next` to the `data-slide` property:

```
<a class="left carousel-control" href="#welcome-products"
    role="button" data-slide="prev">
    <span class="icon-prev" aria-hidden="true"></span>
    <span class="sr-only">Previous</span>
</a>
<a class="right carousel-control" href="#welcome-products"
    role="button" data-slide="next">
    <span class="icon-next" aria-hidden="true"></span>
    <span class="sr-only">Next</span>
</a>
```

Let's compare the final result and wireframe of the Welcome page:

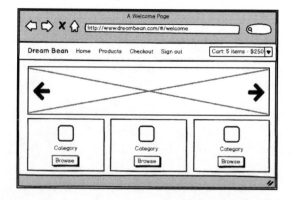

The wireframe of the Welcome page

As you can see, they look absolutely the same. Actually, we have finished with the Welcome page, and now it's time to move on to the Products page development.

 You can find the source code in the `chapter_3/3.ecommerce-carousel` folder

Products page layout

Let's have a look at a wireframe of the Products page and imagine splitting it into rows and columns as we did for the Welcome page:

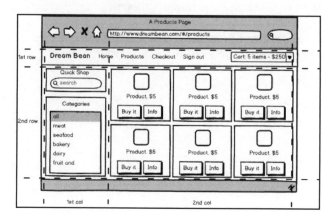

The first row still contains our navigation header, but I put the other content into another single row. There are two columns with **Quick Shop** and **Categories** in one, and the grid includes a set of products in another one. Why have I split the Products page like that? The answer is pretty straightforward. Bootstrap always renders content by rows and then by columns inside them. On devices with a small layout, the header in the first row usually collapses into a hamburger menu. At the bottom, it displays the second row with **Quick Shop**, **Categories** and, below, the set of products aligned vertically.

I cloned the last project and cleaned the code but saved the navigation header and footer, because I don't want to mix the development of the Products page with the original one. Let's talk about the components in the first column.

Quick Shop component

This component is just a search input with a button. I don't implement business logic, but just design the page. This one is based on the Card element we explored in Chapter 2, *Working with Bootstrap Components*. I would like to use the input group component, so let's see what it can do.

Input group

This is a group of form controls and text combined in one line. It was designed to extend form controls by adding text, buttons, or groups of buttons on either side of the input field and aligning them against each other. Creating an input group component is very easy. Just wrap the input with an element marked with the input-group class and append or prepend another one with an input-group-addon class. You can use the input group out of any form, but we need to mark the input element with the form-control class to have it width 100%.

 Use the input group for textual input elements only.

Text addons

Here is an example of a text field with an appended addon:

```
<div class="input-group">
  <input type="text" class="form-control"
```

```
            placeholder="Pricein USD">
    <span class="input-group-addon">.00</span>
</div>
```

Another example with a prepended addon is:

```
<div class="input-group">
    <span class="input-group-addon">https://</span>
    <input type="text" class="form-control"
           placeholder="Your address">
</div>
```

And finally we can combine all of them together:

```
<div class="input-group">
    <span class="input-group-addon">$</span>
    <input type="text" class="form-control"
           placeholder="Price per unit">
    <span class="input-group-addon">.00</span>
</div>
```

Sizing

There are two form sizing classes, `input-group-lg` and `input-group-sm`, which make an input group bigger or smaller than the standard one. You need to apply one to the element marked with `input-group` class, and the content within will automatically resize:

```
<div class="input-group input-group-lg">
    <input type="text" class="form-control"
           placeholder="Large">
    <span class="input-group-addon">.00</span>
</div>
<div class="input-group">
    <input type="text" class="form-control"
           placeholder="Standard">
```

```
      <span class="input-group-addon">.00</span>
</div>
<div class="input-group input-group-sm">
   <input type="text" class="form-control"
          placeholder="Small">
   <span class="input-group-addon">.00</span>
</div>
```

Checkboxes and radio option addons

We can use a checkbox or radio option instead of text addons:

```
<div class="input-group">
   <span class="input-group-addon">
     <input type="checkbox">
   </span>
   <input type="text" class="form-control"
          placeholder="Select">
</div>

<div class="input-group">
   <span class="input-group-addon">
     <input type="radio">
   </span>
   <input type="text" class="form-control"
          placeholder="Choose">
</div>
```

Button addons

The most familiar elements are buttons, and you can use them within the input group. Just add one extra level of complexity:

```html
<div class="input-group">
  <input type="text" class="form-control"
         placeholder="Search for...">
  <span class="input-group-btn">
    <button class="btn btn-secondary" type="button">Go!</button>
  </span>
</div>
```

Drop-down menu addons

We can use buttons to show drop-down menus. We will speak about drop-down menus a bit later in this chapter. The following code demonstrates the use of drop-down menus:

```html
<div class="input-group">
  <input type="text" class="form-control">
  <div class="input-group-btn">
    <button type="button"
            class="btn btn-secondary dropdown-toggle"
            data-toggle="dropdown">
      Action
    </button>
    <div class="dropdown-menu dropdown-menu-right">
      <a class="dropdown-item" href="#">Action</a>
      <a class="dropdown-item" href="#">Another action</a>
      <a class="dropdown-item" href="#">Something else here</a>
      <div role="separator" class="dropdown-divider"></div>
      <a class="dropdown-item" href="#">Separated link</a>
    </div>
  </div>
</div>
```

Segmented buttons

Sometimes it can be useful to split button and drop-down menus, so that the layout is available as well:

```html
<div class="input-group">
  <input type="text" class="form-control">
  <div class="input-group-btn">
    <button type="button" class="btn btn-secondary">Action</button>
    <button type="button" class="btn btn-secondary dropdown-toggle"
            data-toggle="dropdown">
      <span class="sr-only">Toggle Dropdown</span> 
    </button>
    <div class="dropdown-menu dropdown-menu-right">
      <a class="dropdown-item" href="#">Action</a>
      <a class="dropdown-item" href="#">Another action</a>
      <a class="dropdown-item" href="#">Something else here</a>
      <div role="separator" class="dropdown-divider"></div>
      <a class="dropdown-item" href="#">Separated link</a>
    </div>
  </div>
</div>
```

Now that we know how to use input groups, let's create a **Quick Shop** component:

```html
<div class="container">
  <div class="row">
    <div class="col-md-3">
      <div class="card">
        <div class="card-header">
          Quick Shop
        </div>
        <div class="card-block">
          <div class="input-group">
            <input type="text" class="form-control"
                   placeholder="Search for...">
            <span class="input-group-btn">
              <button class="btn btn-secondary"
                      type="button">Go!</button>
```

```
        </span>
      </div>
    </div>
  </div>
  <!-- /.card -->
  </div>
  <!-- /.col -->
  </div>
  <!-- /.row -->
</div>
<!-- /.container -->
```

 You can find the source code in the `chapter_3/4.ecommerce-input-group` folder.

Categories component

The Categories component lies under the **Quick Shop**. I would like to use the list group component to hold categories from which the customer can choose.

List group

This one is a flexible component for displaying an unordered list of elements, such as simple items or custom content, with ease. Just mark any unordered list element with the `list-group` class and every item with `list-group-item` to quickly create the **list group** component:

```html
<ul class="list-group">
  <li class="list-group-item">Apple</li>
  <li class="list-group-item">Banana</li>
  <li class="list-group-item">Grapefruit</li>
  <li class="list-group-item">Carrot</li>
</ul>
```

Listing with tags

Sometimes we need to display a bit more information about every item such as counts, activities, and others. For that purpose we can add **tag** to each item and list group automatically to position it to the right:

```
<ul class="list-group">
  <li class="list-group-item">
    <span class="tag tag-default tag-pill
              pull-xs-right">15</span>
    Apple
  </li>
  <li class="list-group-item">
    <span class="tag tag-default tag-pill
              pull-xs-right">5</span>
    Banana
  </li>
  <li class="list-group-item">
    <span class="tag tag-default tag-pill
              pull-xs-right">0</span>
    Grapefruit
  </li>
  <li class="list-group-item">
    <span class="tag tag-default tag-pill
              pull-xs-right">3</span>
    Carrot
  </li>
</ul>
```

Linked list groups

We can quickly create a vertical menu with a linked list group component. This kind of list is based on the `div` tag instead of `ul`. The whole item of this list is an anchor element, and it can be:

- Clickable
- Hoverable
- Highlighted with the help of an `active` class
- Disabled with the aid of a class with the same name

```
<div class="list-group">
  <a href="#" class="list-group-item">Apple</a>
  <a href="#" class="list-group-item active">Banana</a>
  <a href="#" class="list-group-item disabled">Grapefruit</a>
  <a href="#" class="list-group-item">Carrot</a>
</div>
```

Button list groups

If you prefer, use buttons instead of anchor elements, then you need to change the tag name of each item and add the `list-group-item-action` class into it. We can use `active` or `disabled` to make the item appear different:

```
<div class="list-group">
  <button type="button" class="list-group-item list-group-item-action
active ">Apple</button>
  <button type="button" class="list-group-item item list-group-item-action
">Banana</button>
  <button type="button" class="list-group-item item list-group-item-action
disabled">Grapefruit</button>
  <button type="button" class="list-group-item item list-group-item-action
">Carrot</button>
</div>
```

Using the standard `btn` class in list groups is prohibited.

Contextual classes

You can also style individual list items with contextual classes. Just add a contextual class suffix to the `list-group-item` class. The item with the `active` class displays as a darkened version:

```
<div class="list-group">
  <a href="#" class="list-group-item
          list-group-item-success">Apple</a>
  <a href="#" class="list-group-item
          list-group-item-success active">Watermelon</a>
  <a href="#" class="list-group-item
          list-group-item-info">Banana</a>
  <a href="#" class="list-group-item
          list-group-item-warning">Grapefruit</a>
  <a href="#" class="list-group-item
          list-group-item-danger">Carrot</a>
</div>
```

Custom content

Finally, you can add HTML within every item of a list group component, and make it clickable with an anchor element. Bootstrap 4 provides the `list-group-item-heading` and `list-group-item-text` classes for heading and text content. Any item with the `active` class displays custom content as a darkened version:

```
<div class="list-group">
  <a href="#" class="list-group-item list-group-item-success">
```

```
    <h4 class="list-group-item-heading">Apple</h4>
    <p class="list-group-item-text">It is sweet.</p>
  </a>
  <a href="#" class="list-group-item list-group-item-success active">
    <h4 class="list-group-item-heading">Watermelon</h4>
    <p class="list-group-item-text">
      It is a fruit and a vegetable.
    </p>
  </a>
</div>
```

Now, it's time to create our **Categories** component:

```
<div class="card">
  <div class="card-header">
    Categories
  </div>
  <div class="card-block">
    <div class="list-group">
      <a href="#" class="list-group-item">All</a>
      <a href="#" class="list-group-item">Meat</a>
      <a href="#" class="list-group-item">Seafood</a>
      <a href="#" class="list-group-item">Bakery</a>
      <a href="#" class="list-group-item">Dairy</a>
      <a href="#" class="list-group-item">Fruit & Vegetables</a>
    </div>
  </div>
</div>
```

We are finished with the first column, so let's go on to develop the second one, which contains the grid with a set of products.

You can find the source code in the `chapter_3/5.ecommerce-list-group` folder.

Creating a product grid

We need to display a set of products in a grid of rows and columns inside the second column.

Nested rows

We can nest additional rows inside any column to create a more complex layout similar to the one we have:

```
<div class="col-md-9">
  <div class="row">
    <div class="col-xs-12 col-sm-6 col-lg-4">
      <!-- The Product 1 -->
    </div>
    <!-- /.col -->
    <div class="col-xs-12 col-sm-6 col-lg-4">
      <!-- The Product 2 -->
    </div>
    <!-- /.col -->
    <div class="col-xs-12 col-sm-6 col-lg-4">
      <!-- The Product N -->
    </div>
    <!-- /.col -->
  </div>
</div>
```

We create as many columns as we need within one row and Bootstrap will display them properly, based on the viewport size:

- One column takes the whole size on an extra small viewport
- Two columns on a small viewport
- Three columns on large and bigger viewports

Product component

In a similar way, we use the Card to display information and controls in the product component:

```html
<div class="card">
  <img class="card-img-top img-fluid center-block product-item"
      src="http://placehold.it/270x171" alt="Product 1">
  <div class="card-block text-xs-center">
    <h4 class="card-title">Product 1</h4>
    <h4 class="card-subtitle">
      <span class="tag tag-success">$10</span>
    </h4>
    <hr>
    <div class="btn-group" role="group">
      <button class="btn btn-primary">Buy</button>
      <button class="btn btn-info">Info</button>
    </div>
  </div>
</div>
<!-- /.card -->
```

Let's talk a bit about the elements we have used here.

You can find the source code in the `chapter_3/6.ecommerce-grid-in-grid` folder.

Images

To the extent that we use images in the Card element, I think it's a good idea to talk about images with responsive behavior and image shapes.

Responsive images

You can make any image responsive with the `img-fluid` class. It applies the following to the picture and scales it with the parent element:

- Sets the `max-width` property to `100%`
- Sets the `height` property to `auto`

```
<div class="container">
  <div class="row">
    <div class="col-md-3">
      <img class="img-fluid" src="http://placehold.it/270x171">
    </div>
  </div>
</div>
```

Image shapes

In cases when you need to render images:

- With rounded corners, use the `img-rounded` class
- Within a circle, use the `img-circle` class
- As a thumbnail, use the `img-thumbnail` class

Image alignment

To align images horizontally, we can use either text alignment or helper float classes:

- Use `text-*-center` classes on the parent of the picture to center it
- Use the `center-block` class on an image to center it

- Use the `pull-*-left` or `pull-*-right` classes to float the image to the left or right respectively

```
<div class="container">
  <div class="row">
    <div class="col-md-6 table-bordered">
      This is text around pull image to left
      <img class="img-rounded pull-xs-left"
          src="http://placehold.it/270x171">
    </div>
    <div class="col-md-6 table-bordered">
      This is text around pull image to right
      <img class="img-circle pull-xs-right"
          src="http://placehold.it/270x171">
    </div>
    <div class="col-md-6 table-bordered">
      This is text around center block image
      <img class="img-thumbnail center-block"
          src="http://placehold.it/270x171">
    </div>
    <div class="col-md-6 text-xs-center table-bordered">
      This is centered<br>
      <img class="img-thumbnail"
          src="http://placehold.it/270x171">
    </div>
  </div>
</div>
```

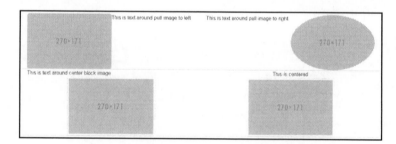

I used the `table-border` class in the preceding code only to display borders.

Tags

If I need to highlight some information in a text string, I will use a tag. To create a tag I need to apply the `tag` class together with a contextual `tag-*` to `span` the element:

```html
<div class="container">
  <div class="row">
    <div class="col-md-12">
      <h1>Example heading
        <span class="tag tag-default">Default</span>
      </h1>
      <h2>Example heading
        <span class="tag tag-primary">Primary</span>
      </h2>
      <h3>Example heading
        <span class="tag tag-success">Success</span>
      </h3>
      <h4>Example heading
        <span class="tag tag-info">Info</span>
      </h4>
      <h5>Example heading
        <span class="tag tag-warning">Warning</span>
      </h5>
      <h6>Example heading
        <span class="tag tag-danger">Danger</span>
      </h6>
    </div>
  </div>
</div>
```

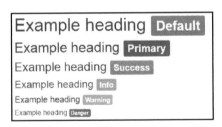

The tag uses the relative font size of the parent element so it always scales to match its size. If you need tag to looks like a badge use the `tag-pill` class to achieve this:

```html
<div class="container">
  <div class="row">
    <div class="col-md-12">
      <span class="label label-pill label-default">Default</span>
      <span class="label label-pill label-primary">Primary</span>
```

```
      <span class="label label-pill label-success">Success</span>
      <span class="label label-pill label-info">Info</span>
      <span class="label label-pill label-warning">Warning</span>
      <span class="label label-pill label-danger">Danger</span>
    </div>
  </div>
</div>
```

Button groups

We can group buttons together either horizontally or vertically with the **button group** component. Buttons are oriented horizontally by default. To create a button group use buttons with the btn class in a container with the btn-group class:

```
<div class="container">
  <div class="row">
    <div class="col-md-12">
      <div class="btn-group" role="group">
        <button type="button" class="btn btn-default">Left</button>
        <button type="button" class="btn btn-secondary">Middle</button>
        <button type="button" class="btn btn-danger">Right</button>
      </div>
    </div>
  </div>
</div>
```

Sizing

There are two sizes to make the button group bigger or smaller than the standard size. Add either the btn-group-lg or btn-group-sm class to the button group to resize all buttons in the group at once:

```
<div class="btn-group btn-group-lg" role="group">
  <button type="button" class="btn btn-default">Left</button>
  <button type="button" class="btn btn-secondary">Middle</button>
  <button type="button" class="btn btn-danger">Right</button>
</div><br><br>
<div class="btn-group" role="group">
```

```
      <button type="button" class="btn btn-default">Left</button>
      <button type="button" class="btn btn-secondary">Middle</button>
      <button type="button" class="btn btn-danger">Right</button>
</div><br><br>
<div class="btn-group btn-group-sm" role="group">
      <button type="button" class="btn btn-default">Left</button>
      <button type="button" class="btn btn-secondary">Middle</button>
      <button type="button" class="btn btn-danger">Right</button>
</div>
```

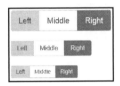

Button toolbars

We can combine button groups into a **button toolbar** for more complex components:

```
<div class="btn-toolbar" role="toolbar">
  <div class="btn-group" role="group">
    <button type="button" class="btn btn-primary">Create</button>
    <button type="button" class="btn btn-secondary">Edit</button>
    <button type="button" class="btn btn-danger">Delete</button>
  </div>
  <div class="btn-group" role="group">
    <button type="button" class="btn btn-default">Fetch</button>
  </div><br><br>
</div>
```

Nesting drop-downs

We can make a drop-down as a part of a button group by nesting it into another button group:

```
<div class="btn-group" role="group">
  <button type="button" class="btn btn-secondary">Create</button>
  <button type="button" class="btn btn-secondary">Delete</button>

  <div class="btn-group" role="group">
```

```
<button id="btnGroupDrop1" type="button"
        class="btn btn-secondary dropdown-toggle"
        data-toggle="dropdown" aria-haspopup="true"
        aria-expanded="false">
  Actions
</button>
<div class="dropdown-menu" aria-labelledby="btnGroupDrop1">
  <a class="dropdown-item" href="#">Get One</a>
  <a class="dropdown-item" href="#">Get Many</a>
</div>
</div>
</div>
```

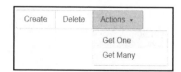

Also, you can create a split drop-down menu component with a button group:

```
<div class="btn-group" role="group">
  <button type="button" class="btn btn-secondary">Actions</button>
  <button id="btnGroupDrop1" type="button"
          class="btn btn-secondary dropdown-toggle"
          data-toggle="dropdown" aria-haspopup="true"
          aria-expanded="false">
    <span class="sr-only">Toggle Dropdown</span> 
  </button>
  <div class="dropdown-menu" aria-labelledby="btnGroupDrop1">
    <a class="dropdown-item" href="#">Get One</a>
    <a class="dropdown-item" href="#">Get Many</a>
  </div>
</div>
```

Vertical button groups

If you need to orient a button group vertically, replace btn-group with the btn-group-vertical class:

```
<div class="btn-group-vertical" role="group">
```

```
    <button type="button"
           class="btn btn-default">Left</button>
    <button type="button"
           class="btn btn-secondary">Middle</button>
    <button type="button"
           class="btn btn-danger">Right</button>
</div>
```

The vertical button group doesn't support split drop-down menus.

Drop-down menus

We talk a lot about drop-down menus, so let's have a closer look at them. A drop-down menu is a toggle overlay for displaying a list of links. It is a combination of several components.

Drop-down containers

This one wraps all other elements. Usually, it is a `div` element with a `dropdown` class, or another one uses `position: relative`.

Drop-down triggers

This is any item that the user can click or tap to expand the drop-down. We need to mark it with a `dropdown-toggle` class and set the `data-toggle="dropdown"` property.

Drop-down menus with items

A drop-down menu itself is a combination of elements with `dropdown-item` classes, and the wrapper contains all of them marked with the `dropdown-menu` class. It is a list-less component. For menu items, you can use anchor or button elements:

```
<div class="dropdown">
  <button class="btn btn-secondary dropdown-toggle" type="button"
      id="dropdownMenu1" data-toggle="dropdown" aria-haspopup="true"
```

```
        aria-expanded="false">
    Action
  </button>
  <div class="dropdown-menu" aria-labelledby="dropdownMenu1">
    <a class="dropdown-item" href="#">Create</a>
    <a class="dropdown-item" href="#">Edit</a>
    <a class="dropdown-item" href="#">Delete</a>
  </div>
</div>
```

Menu alignment

Drop-down menus are aligned to the left by default. If you need align one to the right, then you need to apply the `dropdown-menu-right` class to it. I have added the `text-xs-right` class to the parent element to align the whole component to the right:

```
<div class="col-md-3 text-xs-right">
  <div class="dropdown">
    <button class="btn btn-secondary dropdown-toggle"
            type="button" id="dropdownMenu1"
            data-toggle="dropdown" aria-haspopup="true"
            aria-expanded="false">
      Action
    </button>
    <div class="dropdown-menu dropdown-menu-right"
         aria-labelledby="dropdownMenu1">
      <a class="dropdown-item" href="#">Create</a>
      <a class="dropdown-item" href="#">Edit</a>
      <a class="dropdown-item" href="#">Delete</a>
    </div>
  </div>
</div>
```

Menu headers and dividers

A drop-down menu may have several header elements. You can add them with the help of heading elements and the `dropdown-header` classes:

```
<div class="dropdown">
  <button class="btn btn-secondary dropdown-toggle" type="button"
          id="dropdownMenu1" data-toggle="dropdown"
          aria-haspopup="true" aria-expanded="false">
    Action
  </button>
  <div class="dropdown-menu" aria-labelledby="dropdownMenu1">
    <h6 class="dropdown-header">Document</h6>
    <a class="dropdown-item" href="#">Create</a>
    <a class="dropdown-item" href="#">Edit</a>
    <a class="dropdown-item" href="#">Delete</a>
    <h6 class="dropdown-header">Print</h6>
    <a class="dropdown-item" href="#">Print Now</a>
    <a class="dropdown-item" href="#">Configuration</a>
  </div>
</div>
```

Menu dividers

We can segregate groups of menu items not only with headers but also with dividers. Use the `dropdown-divider` class to mark menu items as dividers:

```
<div class="dropdown">
  <button class="btn btn-secondary dropdown-toggle" type="button"
          id="dropdownMenu1" data-toggle="dropdown"
          aria-haspopup="true" aria-expanded="false">
    Action
  </button>
  <div class="dropdown-menu" aria-labelledby="dropdownMenu1">
```

```
      <a class="dropdown-item" href="#">Create</a>
      <a class="dropdown-item" href="#">Edit</a>
      <a class="dropdown-item" href="#">Delete</a>
      <div class="dropdown-divider"></div>
      <a class="dropdown-item" href="#">Print Now</a>
      <a class="dropdown-item" href="#">Configuration</a>
   </div>
</div>
```

Disabling menu items

If necessary we can disable menu items via the disabled class:

```
<div class="dropdown">
   <button class="btn btn-secondary dropdown-toggle" type="button"
            id="dropdownMenu1" data-toggle="dropdown"
            aria-haspopup="true" aria-expanded="false">
      Action
   </button>
   <div class="dropdown-menu" aria-labelledby="dropdownMenu1">
      <a class="dropdown-item" href="#">Create</a>
      <a class="dropdown-item" href="#">Edit</a>
      <a class="dropdown-item disabled" href="#">Delete</a>
   </div>
</div>
```

Tables

There are new classes to build consistently styled and responsive tables. Because we need **table** to design the shopping cart component I would like to look at it now. It is an opt-in, so it's very easy to transform any table to a Bootstrap table by adding a `table` class. As a result we have a basic table with horizontal dividers:

```
<table class="table">
  <thead>
    <tr>
      <th>#</th>
      <th>First Name</th>
      <th>Last Name</th>
      <th>Username</th>
    </tr>
  </thead>
  <tfoot>
    <tr>
      <th colspan="4">Number <strong>2</strong></th>
    </tr>
  </tfoot>
  <tbody>
    <tr>
      <th scope="row">1</th>
      <td>Mark</td>
      <td>Otto</td>
      <td>@mdo</td>
    </tr>
    <tr>
      <th scope="row">2</th>
      <td>Jacob</td>
      <td>Thornton</td>
      <td>@fat</td>
    </tr>
  </tbody>
</table>
```

#	First Name	Last Name	Username
1	Mark	Otto	@mdo
2	Jacob	Thornton	@fat
Number 2			

table-inverse

The `table-inverse` class inverts the colors of a table:

```
<table class="table table-inverse">
```

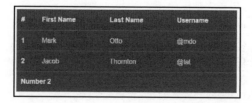

Striped rows

We can alter the background colors of rows with the `table-striped` class:

```
<table class="table table-striped">
```

Bordering tables

If you need a table with borders all around, use the `table-bordered` class:

```
<table class="table table-bordered">
```

Making rows hoverable

To achieve a *hover* effect while hovering the mouse over table rows, use the `table-hover` class:

```
<table class="table table-hover">
```

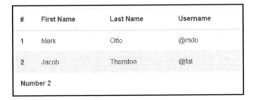

Table head options

There are two classes to change the `thead` element of `table`. Add the `thead-default` class to apply a slightly gray background color:

```
<table class="table">
  <thead class="thead-default">
```

The `thead-inverse` class inverts the text and background colors of `thead`:

```
<table class="table">
  <thead class="thead-inverse">
```

Making table smaller

We can halve the padding of a table to make it smaller with the `table-sm` class:

```
<table class="table table-sm">
```

#	First Name	Last Name	Username
1	Mark	Otto	@mdo
2	Jacob	Thornton	@fat
Number 2			

Contextual classes

There are five contextual classes to apply to individual rows or cells: `table-active`, `table-success`, `table-info`, `table-warning`, and `table-danger`.

Responsive tables

Responsive tables support horizontal scrolling on small and extra small devices (under 768px). On devices bigger than small you won't see any difference. Wrap a table with the `div` element with the `table-responsive` class to achieve this effect:

```
<div class="table-responsive">
  <table class="table">
    ...
  </table>
</div>
```

Reflowing tables

There is a `table-reflow` class to help make the contents of a table reflow:

```
<table class="table table-reflow">
  <thead>
    <tr>
      <th>#</th>
      <th>First Name</th>
      <th>Last Name</th>
      <th>Username</th>
    </tr>
  </thead>
  <tbody>
```

```
    <tr>
      <th scope="row">1</th>
      <td>Mark</td>
      <td>Otto</td>
      <td>@mdo</td>
    </tr>
    <tr>
      <th scope="row">2</th>
      <td>Jacob</td>
      <td>Thornton</td>
      <td>@fat</td>
    </tr>
  </tbody>
</table>
```

Shopping cart component

We haven't yet touched on the last component on the wireframe of the Products page: the shopping cart. This is the union of the cart information and the dropdown contains a table of items the customer has added to the cart:

We display the cart information as button text:

```
<button class="btn btn-primary dropdown-toggle" type="button"
        id="cartDropdownMenu" data-toggle="dropdown"
        aria-haspopup="true" aria-expanded="false">
    Cart: 2 item(s) - $20.00
</button>
```

I used an inversed, bordered table to print out a set of products the cusomer added to the cart:

```
<div class="dropdown-menu dropdown-menu-right"
     aria-labelledby="cartDropdownMenu">
  <table class="table table-bordered table-inverse">
   <thead>
    <tr>
      <th>Name</th><th>Amount</th><th>Qty</th><th>Sum</th>
```

```
        </tr>
      </thead>
      <tfoot>
        <tr>
          <td colspan="4" style="text-align:center">
            Total:<strong>$20.00</strong><br>
            <div class="btn-group">
              <button class="btn btn-primary">View Cart</button>
              <button class="btn btn-success">Checkout</button>
            </div>
          </td>
        </tr>
      </tfoot>
      <tbody>
        <tr>
          <td >Product 1</td><td >$10</td><td >x1<br>
            <span class="delete-cart">Del</span>
          </td>
          <td >$10.00</td>
        </tr>
        <tr>
          <td >Product 2</td><td >$5.00</td><td >x2<br>
            <span class="delete-cart">Del</span>
          </td>
          <td >$10.00</td>
        </tr>
      </tbody>
    </table>
  </div>
```

I combined everything we have learned and here is what the Products page looks like for now:

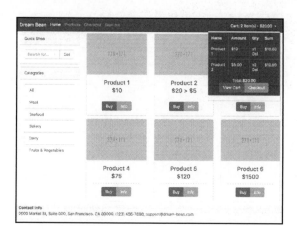

You can find the source code in the `chapter_3/7.ecommerce-dropdown` folder.

Summary

We've covered a lot in this chapter, and it's time to interrupt our journey, take a break, and recap it all.

Bootstrap allowed us to capture our customer's attention with Jumbotron and carousel slideshow quite easily.

We also looked at the powerful responsive grid system included with Bootstrap and created a simple two-column layout. While we were doing this, we learned about the five different column class prefixes and also nested our grid. To adapt our design, we discovered some of the helper classes included with the framework to allow us to float, center, and hide elements.

In this chapter, we saw in detail how to use input, button, and list groups in our project. A simple but powerful component such as dropdowns and tables helped us to create our components quickly and more efficiently.

In Chapter 4, *Creating the Template,* we're going to explore more Bootstrap fundamentals and continue to build the project we started to develop in this and the previous chapter.

In the next chapter, the readers will learn how to create a UI template using some built-in Angular 2 directives. Readers will become familiar with the template syntax. We will show you how to bind properties and events in an HTML page and transform displays using pipes.

4

Creating the Template

In this chapter, we'll learn how to build a UI template using built-in Angular 2 directives. You'll become familiar with the template syntax, and how to bind properties and events in an HTML page, and transform displays using pipes. Of course, we need to discuss the design principles behind Angular 2.

At the end of the chapter, you will have a solid understanding of:

- Template expressions
- Various binding types
- Input and output properties
- Using built-in directives
- Local template variables
- Pipe and Elvis operators
- Custom pipes
- Design components of our application

Diving deeper into Angular 2

We've read three chapters and haven't touched Angular 2 yet. I think it's time to invite Angular 2 on stage to demonstrate how this framework can help us in creating components for our project. As I mentioned in `Chapter 1`, *Saying Hello!*, the architecture of Angular 2 builds on top of standard web components so we can define custom HTML selectors and program them. That means we can create a set of Angular 2 elements to use in the project. In previous chapters, we designed and developed two pages, and you can find many repetitive markups so that we can reuse our Angular 2 components there as well.

Let's, start:

- Open the Terminal, create the folder `ecommerce` and move in
- Copy the contents of the project from the folder `chapter_4/1.ecommerce-seed` into the new project
- Run the following script to install `npm` modules:

```
npm install
```

- Start the TypeScript watcher and lite server with the following command:

```
npm run start
```

This script opens the web browser and navigates to the welcome page of the project. Now open Microsoft Visual Studio code and open `app.component.html` from the `app` folder. We are ready to analyze the welcome page.

Welcome page analysis

The welcome page has quite a simple structure, so I would like to create the following Angular 2 components to encapsulate inside the current markup and future business logic:

- `Navbar` with menus
- Slideshow based on the carousel Bootstrap component
- Grid of Products based on the card Bootstrap component

I will follow the Angular 2 *Style Guide* (`https://angular.io/docs/ts/latest/guide/styl e-guide.html`) while developing our project to keep our application code cleaner, and easy to read and maintain. I recommend following my example on your plans, otherwise, the development results could be unpredictable and extremely costly.

Single responsibility principle

We will apply the **single responsibility principle** to all aspects of the project, so whenever we need to create a component or service, we will create the new file for it and try to keep inside maximum 400 lines of code. The benefits of keeping one component per file are evident:

- Makes code more reusable and less error prone
- Easy to read, test and maintain

- Prevents collisions with team in source control
- Avoids unwanted code coupling
- The component router can lazily load it at runtime

Naming conventions

It is no secret that **naming conventions** are crucial to readability and maintainability. The ability to find files and understand what they contain may have a significant impact on future development, so we should be consistent and descriptive in naming and organizing files to find content at a glance. The conventions comprise the following rules:

- The recommended pattern for all features describes the name then its type: `feature.type.ts`
- The words in descriptive name should be separated by dashes: `feature-list.type.ts`
- There are well-known types of names including `service`, `component`, `directive`, and `pipe`: `feature-list.service.ts`

Barrels

There are barrel modules—TypeScript files that import, aggregate, and re-export other modules. They have one purpose—to reduce the number of `import` statements in code. They provide a consistent pattern introducing everything that is exported in the barrel from a folder. The conventional name for this file is `index.ts`.

Application structure

We keep application code in the `app` folder. For easy and quick access to files, it is recommended to maintain a flat folder structure for as long as possible until there is clear value in creating a new folder.

Folders-by-feature structure

For small projects, you can save all files in the `app` folder. Our project has many features, so we put each of them in their folders, including TypeScript, HTML, Style Sheet, and Spec files. The name of each folder represents the feature it has.

Shared folder

There are some features we can use in multiple places. Better move them into the `shared` folder and separate them into folders if necessary. If features exist in your project, define the overall layout to save them here as well.

Navigation component

There is a navigation component needed for the entire application, so we need to create files `navbar.component.ts` and `navbar.component.html` into the `navbar` folder. Here is the folder structure of our project as it stands now:

Open the `navbar.component.ts` file and paste the following content:

```
import { Component } from '@angular/core';

@Component({
  selector: 'db-navbar',
  templateUrl: 'app/navbar/navbar.component.html'
})
export class NavbarComponent {}
```

In the code, we just defined the `NavbarComponent` class with a `@Component` decorator to tell Angular that the class, which it attached to, is a component. We use an `import` statement here to specify the module, where the TypeScript compiler can find the `@Component` decorator.

Decorators

The decorators are a proposed standard for ECMAScript 2016 and available as a crucial part of TypeScript defining a reusable structural pattern. Each decorator follows the form of `@expression`. The `expression` is a function that evaluates at runtime with information about the decorated statement to change the behavior and state of it. We can use a **decorator function**, which returns as a result of evaluation of the `expression`, to customize how decorator applies to a declaration. It is possible to attach one or multiple decorators to any class, method, accessor, property, or parameter declarations.

The `@Component` is a class decorator applied at compile time to the constructor of `NavbarComponent` class for the following purposes:

- To modify the class definition with a set of parameters passing through
- To add proposed methods organizing the component lifecycle

We must define the `selector` parameter for every `@Component` decorator and use `kebab-case` for naming it. The *style guide* recommends identifying components as elements via the `selector` because it provides consistency for components that represent the content with a template. I use the `db-navbar` selector name for `NavigationComponent` as a combination of:

- The `db` prefix displays the Dream Bean company name abbreviations
- The `navbar` as the name of the feature

 Always use the prefix for selector names to prevent name collision with components from other libraries.

The template is a required part of the @Component decorator because we associate it with putting content on the page. You can supply the template as an inline string in the code or templateUrl as an external resource. It is better to keep the content of the template as an external resource:

- When it has more than three lines
- Because some editors do not support the syntax hints for inline templates
- As it is easier to read the logic of a component when not mixed with inline templates

Now, open the app.component.html and find the nav element on the top. Cut it with content and paste into navbar.component.html and replace it with:

```
<db-navbar></db-navbar>
```

Now we need to add the NavbarComponent into AppModule. Open app.module.ts to add a reference on NavbarComponent there:

```
import { NgModule } from '@angular/core';
import { BrowserModule } from '@angular/platform-browser';

/*
 * Components
 */
import { AppComponent }  from './app.component';
import { NavbarComponent } from './navbar/navbar.component';

@NgModule({
  imports: [BrowserModule],
  declarations: [AppComponent, NavbarComponent],
  bootstrap: [AppComponent]
})
export class AppModule { }
```

Tree of components

Every Angular application has a top level element to display the content. In our application, it is an AppComponent. In Chapter 3, *Advanced Bootstrap Components and Customization*, we split the welcome page into Bootstrap components, now we move them into separate modules, and compose them back with the help of an Angular framework. The Angular framework renders an application as a tree of components, from a top level element, its children, and further down. When we need to add a child to any component, we register it via the declarations property of Angular module. The NavigatorComponent does not belong to any Angular feature module, so I register it in the top most module which is the AppModule.

Let's come back to the navbar.component.html to find other repetitive elements. In the place where we display the navigation bar we have navigation items:

```
<div class="nav navbar-nav">
  <a class="nav-item nav-link active" href="#">
    Home <span class="sr-only">(current)</span>
  </a>
  <a class="nav-item nav-link" href="#">Checkout</a>
  <a class="nav-item nav-link" href="#">Create Account</a>
  <a class="nav-item nav-link" href="#">Login</a>
</div>
```

Because we have duplicates in the markup, I propose creating an array of links and keeping them inside the NavbarComponent as a property, so Angular can display them here.

NavItem object

I suggest you create a separate NavItem interface to keep information about navigation, because each item should have href, label, and active properties:

```
export interface NavItem {
  // Navigation link
  href: string;
  // Navigation Label
  label: string;
  // Status of Navigation Item
  active: boolean;
}
```

Copy and paste the code in between the top of NavbarComponent class and the last import statement. Now we can add the navItems property into NavbarComponent which exposes the navigation items:

```
@Component({
    selector: 'db-navbar',
    templateUrl: 'app/navbar/navbar.component.html'
})
export class NavbarComponent {
    // App name
    appName: string = 'Dream Bean';
    // Navgation items
    navItems: NavItem[] = [
        {href: '#', label: 'Home', active: true},
        {href: '#', label: 'Products', active: false},
        {href: '#', label: 'Checkout', active: false},
        {href: '#', label: 'Sign out', active: false}
    ];
}
```

I add the appName property to keep the application name out of the template as well. We are ready to use the data binding, but before we do, let's take a closer look at template expressions and statements.

Template expressions

The **template expression** is the central part of data binding. Its primary purpose is to execute expressions to produce a value so that Angular can assign it to a binding property of an HTML element, directive, or component. We can put expressions into the template in two forms:

- Within the interpolation curly braces. Angular first evaluates the content inside the braces and then converts to a string: {{a + 1 - getVal()}}.

- Within the quotes when setting a property of view element to the value of template expression: <button [disabled]="isUnchanged">Disabled</button>.

The template expression is based on a JavaScript-like language. We can use any JavaScript expressions with the following restrictions:

- It is prohibited to use assignments like =, +=, -=
- Do not use the `new` keyword
- Do not create chaining expressions with ; or ,
- Avoid the use of increment ++ and decrement -- operators
- Bitwise operators | and & and new template expression operators | and ? are not supported

Expression context

The content of template expressions only belongs to the component instance and cannot refer to variables or functions in the global context. The component instance provides everything the template expression can use. It is usually the context of the expression but can include objects other than components, like a template reference variable.

Template reference variable

The **template reference variable** is a reference to a DOM element or directive within a template. You can use it as a variable with any native DOM element and Angular 2 component. We can reference it on someone, on a sibling or any child elements. There are two forms in which we can define it:

- Within prefix hash (#) and variable name:

```
<input #product placeholder="Product ID">
<button (click)="findProduct(product.value)">Find</button>
```

- The canonical alternative with `ref-` prefix and variable name:

```
<input ref-product placeholder="Product ID">
<button (click)="findProduct(product.value)">Find</button>
```

In both places, the variable `product` passes its `value` to the `findProduct` method. The `(click)` is the form of data binding, which we will talk about shortly.

Expression guidelines

Authors of the Angular framework recommend following these guidelines in your template expressions:

- They should change only the value of the target property. Changes to other application states are prohibited.
- They must be as quick as possible because they execute more often than other code. Consider caching values of computation for better performance when the computation is expensive.
- Please avoid creating complex template expressions. Usually, you can get value from the property or call the method. Move complex logic into the method of the component.
- Please create idempotent expressions that always return the same thing until one of its dependent values changes. It is not allowed to change dependent values in the period of the event loop.

Expression operators

Template expression language includes a few operators for specific scenarios.

The Elvis operator

There are very common situations where the data we want to bind to the view is undefined temporarily. Say we render a template and simultaneously fetch data from the server. There is a period where the data is unclear since the fetch call is asynchronous. As Angular doesn't know this by default, it throws an error. In the following markup we see that the product can be equals null:

```
<div>Product: {{product.name | uppercase}}</div>
```

The render view may fail with a null reference error, or worse yet, entirely disappear:

```
TypeError: Cannot read property 'name' of null in [null]
```

Every time you write markup, you need to analyze it. If you decide that the `product` variable must never be `null`, but it is `null`, you find the programming error that should be caught and fixed, so this is the reason to throw an exception. Contrariwise, a `null` value can be on the property from time to time, since the fetch call is asynchronous. In the last case, the view must render without exceptions, and the `null` property path must display as blank. We can solve this problem in a few ways:

- Include undefined checks
- Make sure that data always has an initial value

Both of them are useful and have merit but look cumbersome. As an example, we can wrap code in `ngIf` and check the existence of `product` variable and its properties:

```
<div *ngIf="product && product.name">
  Product: {{product.name | uppercase}}
</div>
```

This code is noteworthy, but it becomes cumbersome and looks ugly especially if the path is long. No solution is as elegant as the *Elvis* operator. The Elvis or **safe navigation operator** is a convenient way to protect template expression evaluation out of `null` or `undefined` exceptions in the property path.

```
<div>Product: {{product?.name | uppercase}}</div>
```

Angular stops expression evaluation when it hits the first null value, displays blank, and the application doesn't crash.

The pipe operator

One of the primary purposes of the template is displaying data. We can show the raw data with string values directly to the view. But most of the time we need to transform the raw dates into a simple format, add currency symbols to raw floats, and so on, so we understand that some values need a bit of message before display. I feel like we desire lot of the same transformations in many applications. The Angular framework gives us pipes, a way to write display-value transformations that we can declare in templates.

Pipes are simple functions that accept an input value and return a transformed value. We can use them within template expressions, using the pipe operator (`|`):

```
<div>Product: {{product.name | uppercase}}</div>
```

The `uppercase` is a pipe function we placed after the pipe operator. It is possible to chain expressions through multiple pipes:

```
<div>Product: {{product.name | uppercase | lowercase}}</div>
```

Pipe chains always start the transformation from when the first pipe converts the product name into `uppercase`, then to `lowercase`. It is possible to pass the parameters to a pipe:

```
<div>Expiry Date: {{product.expDate | date:'longDate'}}</div>
```

Here we have a pipe with configuration argument dictates to transform the expiry date into the long date format: `August 2, 1969`. There is a list of common pipes available in Angular 2:

- The `async` pipe subscribes to an observable or promise and returns the latest value it has emitted.
- The `date` formats a value to a string based on the requested format.
- The `i18nSelect` is a generic selector that displays the string that matches the current value.
- `percent` formats a number as a local percent.
- `uppercase` implements uppercase transforms to text.
- The `number` formats a number as local text. i.e. group sizing and the separator and other locale-specific configurations base on the active locale.
- The `json` transforms any input value using `JSON.stringify`. Useful for debugging.
- `replace` creates a new string with some or all of the matches of a pattern replaced by a replacement.
- `currency` formats a number as local currency.
- `i18nPlural` maps a value to a string that pluralizes the value correctly.
- `lowercase` transforms text to lowercase.
- `slice` creates a new list or string containing only a subset (slice) of the elements.

The custom pipes

We can create a custom pipe similar to `json` for our needs as follows:

- Import `Pipe` and `PipeTransform` from the Angular core module
- Create a `JsonPipe` class which implements `PipeTransform`

- Apply the `@Pipe` decorator to the `JsonPipe` class and give it a name `db-json`
- Write the `transform` function with input values of `string` type

Here is the final version of our pipe:

```
import {Pipe, PipeTransform} from '@angular/core';

@Pipe({name: 'db-json'})
export class JsonPipe implements PipeTransform {
  transform(value: any): string {
    return JSON.stringify(value);
  }
}
```

Now we need a component to demonstrate our pipe:

```
import {Component} from '@angular/core';
import {JsonPipe} from './shared/json.pipe';

@Component({
selector: 'receiver',
template: `
<h2>Receiver</h2>
<p>Received: {{data | db-json}}</p>
`
})
export class PowerBoosterComponent {
  data: any = {x: 5, y: 6};
}
```

Template statements

The **template statement** is another important part of data binding. We use template statements to respond to an event raised by binding targets like element, directive or component. It is based on a JavaScript-like language like the template expression, but Angular parses it differently because:

- It supports the basic assignment =
- It supports chaining expressions with ; or ,

Statement context

The statement expression, like the template expression, can refer only to the component instance to which it is a binding event or to a template reference variable. You may use reserved `$event` in an event binding statement that represents the payload of the raised event.

Statement guidelines

Authors of the Angular framework recommend avoiding creating the complex statement expressions. Usually, you can assign a value to the property or call the method. Move complex logic into the method of the component.

Data binding

I mentioned **data binding** in `Chapter 1`, *Saying Hello!*, in passing, but now we dive deeper into this crucial tool of the Angular framework. The data binding is the mechanism for updating parts of the template with binding markup via properties or methods of a component.

The data binding flow supports three directions between data sources and targets HTML elements:

- One-way binding from the data source to target HTML. This group includes interpolation, property, attribute, class, and style binding types:

  ```
  {{expression}}
  [target] = "expression"
  bind-target = "expression"
  ```

- One-way binding from the target HTML to the data source. This one is event data binding:

  ```
  (target) = "statement"
  on-target = "statement"
  ```

- Two-way data binding:

  ```
  [(target)] = "expression"
  bindon-target = "expression"
  ```

The `target` is the directive or component input property that receives data from outside. We must explicitly declare any input property before starting to use it. There are two ways to do that:

Mark the property with `@Input` decorator:

```
@Input() product: Product;
```

Identify the property as an element of `inputs` array of directive or component metadata:

```
@Component({
  inputs: ['product']
})
```

The hosting parent element can use `product` property name:

```
<div>
  <db-product [product]="product"></db-product>
</div>
```

It is possible to use *alias* for the property to get it a different public name from the internal one to meet conventional expectations:

```
@Input('bestProduct') product: Product;
```

Now any hosting parent element can use the `bestProduct` property name instead of `product`:

```
<div>
  <db-product [bestProduct]="product"></db-product>
</div>
```

HTML attributes versus DOM properties

HTML attributes and DOM properties are not the same thing. We are using HTML attributes only to initialize DOM properties, and we cannot change their values later.

> Template binding works with DOM properties and events, not HTML attributes.

Interpolation

When we need to show the property value of a component on the page we use double curly brackets markup to tell Angular how to display it. Let's update our code inside the `navbar.component.html` in such a way:

```
<a class="navbar-brand" href="#">{{appName}}</a>
```

Angular automatically pulls the value of the property `appName` from the `NavbarComponent` class and inserts it into the page. When the property changes, the framework updates the page. Interpolation is just syntactic sugar to make our life easy. In reality, it is one of the forms of property binding.

Property binding

Property binding is a technique to set the property of an element, component, or directive. We can change the preceding markup in this way:

```
<a class="navbar-brand" href="#" [innerHTML]="appName"></a>
```

We can change the classes via the `ngClass` property:

```
<div [ngClass]="classes">Binding to the classes property</div>
```

Here is how can we change the property of the component or directive:

```
<product-detail [product]="currentProduct"></product-detail>
```

For the reason that template expressions may contain malicious content, Angular sanitizes the values before displaying them. Neither interpolation nor property binding allows the HTML with script tags to leak into the web browser.

Attribute binding

There are several attributes of an HTML element that do not have corresponding DOM properties like `ARIA`, `SVG`, and table span. If you try to write code like this:

```
<tr><td colspan="{{1 + 1}}">Table</td></tr>
```

You will immediately get the following exception because the table data tag has a `colspan` attribute, but does not have a `colspan` property:

```
browser_adapter.js:77 EXCEPTION: Error: Uncaught (in promise): Template
```

```
parse errors:
Can't bind to 'colspan' since it isn't a known native property ("
<tr><td [ERROR ->]colspan="{{1 + 1}}">Three-Four</td></tr>
")
```

In this particular case, we can use **attribute binding** as part of property binding. It uses the prefix `attr` followed by the dot (`.`) and the name of the attribute. Everything else is the same:

```
<tr><td [attr.colspan]="1 + 1">Three-Four</td></tr>
```

Class binding

Angular provides support for **class binding**. By analogy to attribute binding, we use the prefix `class`, optionally followed by a dot (`.`) and the name of a CSS class.

```
<div class="meat special">Meat special</div>
```

We can replace it with binding to a string of the desired class name `meatSpecial`:

```
<div [class]="meatSpecial">Meat special</div>
```

Or add the template expression `isSpecial` to evaluate true or false to tell Angular to add or remove the `special` class from the target elements:

```
<div [class.special]="isSpecial">Show special</div>
```

 Use the **NgClass** directive for managing multiple class names at the same time.

Style binding

It is possible to manage the styles of the target element via **style binding**. We use the prefix `style`, optionally followed by a dot (`.`) and the name of a CSS style property:

```
<button [style.color]="isSpecial?'red':'green'">Special</button>
```

 Use the **NgStyle** directive when setting several inline styles at the same time.

The data always flows in one direction in property binding, from the data property of the component to the target element. We cannot use property binding to get the value from the target element or call a method on the target element. If the element raises the events, we can listen to them via an event binding.

Event binding

Any user action on the page generates events, so the authors of Angular framework introduced **event binding**. The syntax of this binding is quite simple and it consists of a **target event** within the parentheses, equal sign, and a quoted template statement. The target event is the name of the event:

```
<button (click)="onSave()">Save</button>
```

You can use the canonical format of event binding if you prefer. It supports the prefix on- in front of the name without parentheses in such a way:

```
<button on-click="onSave()">Save</button>
```

In cases where the name of an event does not exist on the element or the output property is unknown, Angular reports this as an `unknown directive` error.

We can use the information event binding transfers about the event via an **event object name** `$event`. Angular uses the target event to determine the shape of the `$event` whereby if the DOM element generates an event, the `$event` is a DOM event object, and it contains `target` and `target.value` properties. Check this code:

```
<div #product>
  <input [value]="product.name"
         (input)="product.name=$event.target.value"><br>
  {{product.name}}
</div>
```

We define the local variable product and bind the value of the input element to its name, and we attach the input event to listen to changes. When the user starts to type, the component generates the DOM input event, and the binding executes the statement.

Custom events

JavaScript provides a dozen events for a whole bunch of scenarios out of the box, but sometimes we want to fire our own custom events for particular needs. It would be good to use them because custom events provide an excellent level of decoupling in the application. JavaScript provides `CustomEvent` that does all sorts of awesome things, but Angular exposes an `EventEmitter` class we can use in *directives* and *components* to emit custom events. What we need to do is to create a property of type `EventEmitter` and call the `emit` method to fire the event. It is possible to pass in a message payload that can be anything. This property regarding Angular works as output because it fires events from the directive or component to outside. We must explicitly declare any output property before we start to use it. There are two ways to do that:

Mark the property with the `@Output` decorator:

```
@Output() select:EventEmitter<Product>
```

Identify the property as an element of `outputs` array of directive or component metadata:

```
@Component({
  outputs: ['select']
})
```

If necessary, we can use *alias* for the property to give it a different public name from the internal one to meet conventional expectations:

```
@Output('selected') select:EventEmitter<Product>
```

Assume the customer selects the product in the grid of products. We can listen to mouse `click` events in markup and handle them in the `browse` method of the component:

```
<a class="btn btn-primary" (click)="browse(product)">Browse</a>
```

When the method handles the mouse event, we can fire the custom event with the selected product:

```
import {Component, Input, Output, EventEmitter} from
      '@angular/core';

export class Product {
  name: string;
  price: number;
}

@Component({
  selector: 'db-product',
```

```
    templateUrl: 'app/product/product.component.html'
})
export class ProductComponent {
  @Input product: Product;

  @Output() select:EventEmitter<Product> =
            new EventEmitter<Product>();

  browse($event) {
    this.select.emit(<Product>$event);
  }
}
```

From now on, any hosting parent component can bind to the `select` event firing by the `ProductComponent`:

```
<db-product [product]="product"
            (select)="productSelected($event)"></db-product>
```

When the `select` event fires, Angular calls the `productSelected` method in the parent component and passes the `Product` in the `$event` variable.

Two-way data binding

Most of the time we need only one-way binding, where data follows from component to view or vice verse. Usually, we do not capture input that needs to be applied back to the DOM, but in some scenarios, it might be very useful. This is why Angular supports **two-way data binding**. As shown previously, we can use the property binding to input the data into directive or component properties with the help of square brackets:

```
<input [value]="product.selected"></input>
```

The opposite direction is denoted by surrounding an event name with parentheses:

```
<input (input)="product.selected=$event.target.value">Browse</a>
```

We can combine those techniques to have the best of both worlds with the help of the `ngModel` directive. There are two forms of two-way data binding:

- Where the parentheses go inside the brackets. It is easy to remember as it shapes like "banana in a box":

  ```
  <input [(ngModel)]="product.selected"></input>
  ```

- Using the canonical prefix `bindon-`:

```
<input bindon-ngModel="product.selected"></input>
```

When Angular parses the markup and meets one of these forms, it uses the `ngModel` input and `ngModelChange` output to create two-way data binding and hide the details behind the scene.

> The `ngModel` directive only works for HTML elements supported by a `ControlValueAccessor`.

We cannot use `ngModel` in a custom component until we implement a suitable value accessor.

Built-in directives

Angular has a small number of powerful built-in directives to cover many routine operations we need to do in templates.

NgClass

We use a class binding to add and remove a single class:

```
<div [class.special]="isSpecial">Show special</div>
```

In scenarios when we need to manage many classes at once it's better to use the `NgClass` directive. Before use, we need to create a `key:value` control object, where the key is a CSS class name and the value is a boolean. If the value is `true`, Angular adds the class from the key to the element and if it is `false` then it removes it. Here is the method that returns the `key:value` control object:

```
getClasses() {
  let classes =  {
    modified: false,
    special: true
  };
  return classes;
}
```

So, it's time to add the `NgClass` property and bind it to the `getClasses` method:

```
<div [ngClass]="getClasses()">This is special</div>
```

NgStyle

The style binding helps set inline styles, based on the state of the component.

```
<button [style.color]="isSpecial?'red':'green'">Special</button>
```

If we need to set many inline styles it's better to use the `NgStyle` directive, but before using it we need to create the `key:value` control object. The key of the object is the style name, the value is anything appropriated for the particular style. Here is the `key:value` control object:

```
getStyles() {
  let styles = {
    'font-style':  'normal',
    'font-size':   '24px'
  };
  return styles;
}
```

Let's add the `NgStyle` property and bind it to the `getStyles` method:

```
<div [ngStyle]="getStyles()">
  This div has a normal font with 8 px size.
</div>
```

NgIf

We can use different techniques to manage the appearance of elements in DOM. One of them uses `hidden` property to hide any unwanted part of the page:

```
<h3 [hidden]="!specialName">
  Your special is: {{specialName}}
</h3>
```

In the preceding code, we bind the `specialName` variable to the HTML `hidden` property. Another one uses a built-in directive like `NgIf` to add or remove the element from the page entirely:

```
<h3 *ngIf="specialName">
  Your special is: {{specialName}}
```

```
</h3>
```

The difference between hiding and deleting is material. The benefits of invisible elements are evident:

- It shows very quickly
- It preserves the previous state and is ready to display
- It is not necessary to reinitialize

The side effects of a hidden element are that:

- It still exists on the page and its behavior continues
- It ties up resources, utilizes connections to the backend, etc.
- Angular keeps listening to events and checking for changes that could affect data bindings and so on

The NgIf directive works differently:

- It removes the component and all children entirely
- Removed elements do not utilize resources
- Angular stops change detection, detaches the element from DOM and destroys it.

 I recommend you use ngIf to remove unwanted components rather than hide them.

NgSwitch

If we want to display only one element tree from many element trees based on some condition, we can use the NgSwitch directive. To make it work we need:

- To define a container element which contains the NgSwitch directive with a switch expression
- Define inner elements with a NgSwitchCase directive per element
- Establish no more than an item with the NgSwitchDefault directive

The NgSwitch inserts nested elements based on which match expressions in NgSwitchCase and which match the value evaluated from the switch expression:

```
<div [ngSwitch]="condition">
```

```
    <p *ngSwitchWhen="true">The true value</p>
    <p *ngSwitchWhen="false">The false value</p>
    <p *ngSwitchDefault>Unknown value</p>
</div>
```

If a matching expression is not found, then an element with a `NgSwitchDefault` directive is displayed.

NgFor

The `NgFor` directive, in contrast to `NgSwitch`, renders each item in the collection. We can apply it to simple HTML elements or components with the following syntax:

```
<div *ngFor="let product of products">{{product.name}}</div>
```

The text assigned to the `NgFor` directive is not a template expression. It is **microsyntax**—the language that Angular interprets how to iterate over the collection. Further, Angular translates an instruction into a new set of elements and bindings. The `NgFor` directive iterates over the `products` array to return the instance of the `Product` and stamps out instances of the DIV element to which it is applied. The `let` keyword in an expression creates a *template input variable* called the `product`, available in the scope of host and its children elements, so we can use its properties like we are doing in interpolation `{{product.name}}`.

 A template input variable is neither the template nor the state reference variables.

Sometimes it can be useful to know a bit more about the currently iterated element. The `NgFor` directive provides several exported index-like values:

- The `index` value sets to the current loop iteration from 0 to the length of collection
- The `first` is the boolean value indicating whether the item is the first in the iteration
- The `last` is the boolean value indicating whether the item is the last one in the collection
- The `even` is the boolean value indicating whether the item has an even index
- The `odd` is the boolean value indicating whether the item has an odd index

So we can use any of those values to capture one in a local variable and use it inside an iteration context:

```
<div *ngFor="let product of products; let i=index">
    {{i + 1}} - {{product.name}}
</div>
```

Now, let's imagine an array of products we query from the backend. Each refresh operation returns the list containing some, if not all, of the number of changed items. Because Angular doesn't know about changes, it discards the old DOM elements and rebuilds a new list with new DOM elements. With a huge number of items in the list, the NgFor directive can perform poorly, freeze the UI, and make a web application entirely unresponsive. We can fix the problem if we give Angular a function to track items inside the collection, and so avoid this DOM rebuild nightmare. The tracking relies on object identity so that we can use any one or many properties to compare new and old items inside the collection. The term *object identity* refers to object equality based on the === identity operator. Here is an example of track by the ID property of product:

```
<div *ngFor="let product of products; trackBy: product.id; let i=index">
    {{i + 1}} - {{product.name}}
</div>
```

Hence, we can use the tracking function such that:

```
trackByProductId(index: number, product: Product): any {
    return product.id;
}
```

It's time to add the tracking function to the NgFor directive expression:

```
<div *ngFor="let product of products; trackBy:trackByProductId;
             let i=index">
  {{i + 1}} - {{product.name}}
</div>
```

The tracking function cannot remove the DOM changes but it can reduce the number of them and make the UI smoother and more responsive.

Structural directives

We quite often see the asterisk prefix in built-in directives, but I haven't explain the purpose. It's time to unveil the *secret* Angular developers keep from us.

We are developing single page applications and at some time, we end up with the necessity to manipulate DOM efficiently. The Angular framework helps with appearing and disappearing portions of the page according to the application state with several built-in directives. In general, Angular has three kinds of directives:

- **Component**: This is a directive with a template, and we will create a lot of them in our project.
- **Attribute directive:** This kind of directive changes the appearance or behavior of an element.
- **Structural directive**: This changes the DOM layout by adding or removing DOM elements.

Structural directives use the HTML 5 `template` tag to manage the appearance of components on the page. Templates allow the declaration of fragments of HTML markup as prototypes. We can insert them into the page anywhere—the head, body, or frameset, but without display:

```
<template id="special_template">
  <h3>Your are special</h3>
</template>
```

To use the template we must clone and insert it into the DOM:

```
// Get the template
var template: HTMLTemplateElement =
    <HTMLTemplateElement>document.
    querySelector("#special_template");
// Find place where
var placeholder: HTMLElement =
    <HTMLElement>document.
    querySelector("place");
// Clone and insert template into the DOM
placeholder.appendChild(template.content.cloneNode(true));
```

Angular keeps the content of structural directives in the `template` tag, replaces it with a `script` tag, and uses it when it is necessary. Because the template form is verbose, the Angular developers introduced the **syntactic sugar**—asterisk (*) prefix for directives to hide verbosity:

```
<h3 *ngIf="condition">Your are special</h3>
```

When Angular reads and parses the above HTML markup, it replaces the asterisk back to template form:

```
<template [ngIf]="condition">
```

```
    <h3>Your are special</h3>
</template>
```

Custom structural directive

Let's create the structural directive similar to `NgIf` that we can use to display the content on the page dependent on the condition. Open the project in Microsoft Studio Code and create `if.directive.ts` file with the following content:

```
import {Directive, Input} from '@angular/core';

@Directive({ selector: '[dbIf]' })
export class IfDirective {
}
```

We import `Directive` to apply it to the `IfDirective` class. We can use our directive in any HTML element or component as a property. Because we manipulate it with the content of the template, we need `TemplateRef`. Moreover, Angular uses a special renderer `ViewContainerRef` to render the content of template, so we need to import both of them and inject them into constructor as private variables:

```
import {Directive, Input} from '@angular/core';
import {TemplateRef, ViewContainerRef} from '@angular/core';

@Directive({ selector: '[dbIf]' })
export class IfDirective {
    constructor(
        private templateRef: TemplateRef<any>,
        private viewContainer: ViewContainerRef
    ) { }
}
```

And lastly, the property to keep the boolean condition so that the directive adds or removes the template based on that value: it must have the same name as the directive, plus we can make it read-only:

```
@Input() set dbIf(condition: boolean) {
    if (condition) {
        this.viewContainer.createEmbeddedView(this.templateRef);
    } else {
        this.viewContainer.clear();
    }
}
```

If the `condition` is `true`, the preceding code calls the view container to create an embedded view that references the template content, or otherwise, removes it. Here is the final version of our directive:

```
import {Directive, Input} from '@angular/core';
import {TemplateRef, ViewContainerRef} from '@angular/core';

@Directive({ selector: '[dbIf]' })
export class IfDirective {
    constructor(
        private templateRef: TemplateRef<any>,
        private viewContainer: ViewContainerRef
    ) { }

    @Input() set dbIf(condition: boolean) {
        if (condition) {
            this.viewContainer.
                createEmbeddedView(this.templateRef);
        } else {
            this.viewContainer.clear();
        }
    }
}
```

Now we can add our directive into the `directives` array of the host component to use it instead of `NgIf`.

You can find the source code at `chapter_4/2.ecommerce-navbar`.

Category product component

We will continue to create Angular components for our application. Now, we know everything about templates, it's time to create the `Category` product. Let's create the `category` directory and the file `category.ts`. Copy and paste the following code:

```
export class Category {
    // Unique Id
    id: string;
    // The title
    title: string;
    // Description
```

```
    desc: string;
    // Path to image
    image: string;
}
```

So, each category of product has a unique identifier, title, description, and image. Now create the file `category-card.component.ts`, copy and paste the following code:

```
import {Component, Input, Output, EventEmitter}
from '@angular/core';

import {Category} from './category';

@Component({
    selector: 'db-category-card',
    templateUrl:
        'app/category/category-card.component.html'
})
export class CategoryCardComponent {
    @Input() category: Category;
    @Output() select: EventEmitter<Category> =
                new EventEmitter<Category>();

    browse() {
        this.select.emit(this.category);
    }
}
```

This is a Category component that we use in a grid of categories. It has the input property category and output event `select`. Let's have a look at what the markup looks like:

```
<div class="col-xs-12 col-sm-6 col-md-4">
    <div class="card">
    <img class="card-img-top img-fluid center-block product-item"
        src="{{category.image}}" alt="{{category.title}}">
    <div class="card-block">
        <h4 class="card-title">{{category.title}}</h4>
        <p class="card-text">{{category.desc}}</p>
        <a class="btn btn-primary" (click)="browse()">Browse</a>
    </div>
    </div>
</div>
<!-- /.col -->
```

It is an exact copy of the markup from `app.component.html`. We use interpolation data binding everywhere. Now create `category-slide.component.ts`, copy and paste the following code:

```
import {Component, Input, Output, EventEmitter} from '@angular/core';

import {Category} from './category';

@Component({
    selector: 'db-category-slide',
    templateUrl:
      'app/category/category-slide.component.html'
})
export class CategorySlideComponent {
    @Input() category: Category;
    @Output() select: EventEmitter<Category> =
                  new EventEmitter<Category>();

    browse() {
        this.select.emit(this.category);
    }
}
```

The source code of this file looks very similar to the card category, but the markup is not:

```
<img src="{{category.image}}" alt="{{category.title}}">
<div class="carousel-caption">
    <h2>{{category.title}}</h2>
</div>
```

This one is a copy of HTML from the carousel component. It's time to create our first Angular feature module. Create the file `category.module.ts` with the following content:

```
import { NgModule } from '@angular/core';
import { CommonModule } from '@angular/common';
import { RouterModule } from '@angular/router';

import { CategoryCardComponent } from './category-card.component';
import { CategorySlideComponent } from './category-slide.component';

@NgModule({
    imports: [CommonModule, RouterModule],
    declarations: [CategoryCardComponent, CategorySlideComponent],
    exports: [CategoryCardComponent, CategorySlideComponent]
})
export class CategoryModule { }
```

As we know, an Angular module is a class decorated with an `NgModule` decorator. Let's see what we are defining with it:

- There are the `CategoryCardComponent` and `CategorySlideComponent` components which belong to the module, so we must declare them as well as other components, directives, and pipes inside the `declarations` property
- We make the `CategoryCardComponent` and `CategorySlideComponent` components available publicly via the `exports` property so that other component templates can use them
- And lastly, we import the `CommonModule` and `RouterModule` inside the `imports` property because we use their components and services in this module

Now we can include this module file in other modules or in the application module, to make the export available there. Open the `app.module.ts` file and update it accordingly:

```
import { NgModule } from '@angular/core';
import { BrowserModule } from '@angular/platform-browser';

/**
 * Modules
 */
import { CategoryModule } from './category/category.module';

/*
 * Components
 */
import { AppComponent }  from './app.component';
import { NavbarComponent } from './navbar/navbar.component';

@NgModule({
  imports: [BrowserModule, CategoryModule],
  declarations: [AppComponent, NavbarComponent],
  bootstrap: [AppComponent]
})
export class AppModule { }
```

This change makes the `CategoryCardComponent` and `CategorySlideComponent` components available immediately for the application component. I defined two variables `slideCategories` and `cardCategories` to keep data for cards in grid and slides.

Here are the changes in `app.component.html`:

```html
<!-- Indicators -->
<ol class="carousel-indicators">
  <li data-target="#welcome-products"
*ngFor="let category of slideCategories; let first=first; let i=index"
      attr.data-slide-to="{{i}}" [ngClass]="{active: first}"></li>
</ol>
```

We use the NgFor directive here with `first` and `index` values to initialize the `data-slide-to` attribute and `active` class of the first component:

```html
<!-- Content -->
<div class="carousel-inner" role="listbox">
  <div *ngFor="let category of slideCategories; let first=first"
        class="carousel-item" [ngClass]="{active: first}">
    <db-category-slide
      [category]="category" (select)="selectCategory($event)">
    </db-category-slide>
  </div>
</div>
```

In this markup, we form the content of carousel images, so we use the NgFor directive in the `carousel-inner` component. We use the first value to manage the active class of the first component:

```html
<div class="row">
    <db-category-card *ngFor="let category of cardCategories"
      [category]="category" (select)="selectCategory($event)">
    </db-category-card>
  </div>
```

Here are the last changes where we create the cards grid with help of the NgFor directive.

 You can find the source code at `chapter_4/3.ecommerce-category`.

Summary

We have been speaking about the structure of the Angular application and how important it is to maintain a flat folder structure. Because we are following the single responsibility principles, we create only one component per file and keep it as small as possible. It is best practice for every angular application to have a shared folder.

We have spoken a lot about decorators, tree of components, and templates. We know that template expressions and template statements are the crucial part of data binding. Both of them are based on a restricted version of the JavaScript-like language.

Template expression includes the Elvis and pipe operators for specific scenarios. Data binding supports three flow directions and includes interpolation, property binding, attribute binding, class binding, style binding, event binding, and two-way binding.

Angular has several very powerful directives that help us to manipulate DOM elements like NgFor, NgIf, NgClass, NgStyle, and NgSwitch. We learned why we use the asterisk prefix and what Structural Directives are.

In Chapter 5, *Routing*, we will set up the top navigation with Bootstrap. You will become familiar with Angular's component router and how to configure it. Plus we will continue to build the project that we started to develop in previous chapters.

5
Routing

Many web applications require more than one page or view, and Angular is well equipped to handle this with its router. The router uses JavaScript code and manages the navigation between views as users perform application tasks. In this chapter, we will take a look at how we can create static routes, as well as routes containing parameters, and how to configure them. We will also discover some of the pitfalls we might face. In this chapter, we will set up the top navigation with Angular.

At the end of the chapter, you will have a solid understanding of the following:

- Component router
- Router configuration
- Router link and router outlet
- Creating components and navigation for our application

Modern web applications

You've heard about **Single-Page Applications (SPA)** many times, but why develop web applications like that? What are the benefits?

The main idea for using SPAs is quite simple—users would like to use web applications which look like and behave like native applications. An SPA is a web application that loads a single HTML page and dynamically updates it as the user interacts with multiple components on it. Some of the components support many states, such as open, collapsed, and so on. Implementing all of these features with server-side rendering is hard to do, therefore much of the work happens on the client side, in JavaScript. This is achieved by separating data from the presentation of data by having a model layer that handles data and a view layer that reads from the models.

This idea brings some level of complexity to the code and often results in changing people's minds about the development process. Now we start thinking about the conceptual parts of the application, file and module structures, performance issues over bootstrapping, and so on.

Routing

Since we are making an SPA and we don't want any page refreshes, we'll use the routing capabilities of Angular. The routing module is a crucial part of Angular. From one side it helps to update the URL of the browser as the user navigates through the application. From another side, it allows changes to the URL of the browser to drive navigation through the web application, thus allowing the user to create bookmarks to locations deep within the SPA. As a bonus, we can split the application into multiple bundles and load them on demand.

With the introduction of HTML 5, browsers acquired the ability to create programmatically new browser history entries that change the displayed URL without the need for a new request. This is achieved using the `pushState` method of history that exposes the browser's navigational history to JavaScript. So now, instead of relying on the anchor hack to navigate routes, modern frameworks can count on `pushState` to perform history manipulation without reloads.

The Angular router uses this model to interpret a browser URL as an instruction to navigate to a client-generated view. We can pass optional parameters along to the view component to help it decide what specific content to present.

Let's start with the following:

1. Open Terminal, create the folder `ecommerce` and move in.
2. Copy the content of the project from the folder `chapter_5/1.ecommerce-seed` into the new project.
3. Run the following script to install NPM modules:

   `npm install`

4. Start the TypeScript watcher and lite server with following command:

   `npm run start`

This script opens the web browser and navigates to the welcome page of the project.

Routing path

Before we begin, let's plan out exactly what routes we're going to need for the Dream Bean grocery store website:

- The welcome view uses the `/#/welcome` path. It is going to be our entry point for the application, which will list all categories in a grid and slideshow.
- The products view utilizes the `/#/products` path. We'll be able to see the goodies within the chosen category there.
- We show the products view on `/#/product/:id`. Here, we will display information about the product. The `:id` here and in the next example is a token for a route parameter. We will talk about it later in this chapter.
- The `/#/cart` path is where we will see the cart view list all items in the user's shopping cart.
- In the checkout view with the `/#/checkout/:id` path, we will include a form that will allow a user to add contact information; it also provides the order information and purchase conditions.

These are all of our essential routes; now let's take a look at how we can create them.

Installing the router

The router is packaged as a module inside Angular, but it is not a part of the Angular core, so we need to manually include it inside the bootstrapping configuration in the `systemjs.config.js` file:

```
// angular bundles
'@angular/core': 'npm:@angular/core/bundles/core.umd.js',
'@angular/common': 'npm:@angular/common/bundles/common.umd.js',
'@angular/compiler': 'npm:@angular/compiler/bundles/compiler.umd.js',
'@angular/platform-browser': 'npm:@angular/platform-
browser/bundles/platform-browser.umd.js',
'@angular/platform-browser-dynamic': 'npm:@angular/platform-browser-
dynamic/bundles/platform-browser-dynamic.umd.js',
'@angular/http': 'npm:@angular/http/bundles/http.umd.js',
'@angular/router': 'npm:@angular/router/bundles/router.umd.js',
'@angular/forms': 'npm:@angular/forms/bundles/forms.umd.js',
```

The base URL

If we have decided to use routing, then we should add the base element as the first child in the head tag. The reference in this tag resolves relative URLs and hyperlinks, and tells the router how to compose navigation URLs. For our project, I assigned the "/" to the href of the base element, because the app folder is the application root:

```
<base href="/">
```

If we deploy the application to the server within a particular context, such as portal, then we must change this value accordingly:

```
<base href="/portal">
```

The Angular router

The actual routing from one view to another happens with the help of the **Angular router**. It is an optional service, and represents the component view for a specific URL. It has its own library package, and we must import from it before use:

```
import { RouterModule } from '@angular/router';
```

The router configuration

The application must have only one router. We should configure it so that it knows how to map the browser's URL to the corresponding Route and determine the component to display. The primary way to do that uses the RouterModule.forRoot function with an array of routes which bootstraps the application with it.

Creating basic routes

Create the file app.routes.ts and import necessary elements from the router package:

```
import { Routes, RouterModule } from '@angular/router';
```

Now create the constants to keep the application routes:

```
const routes: Routes = [
  { path: 'welcome', component: WelcomeComponent },
  { path: 'products', component: ProductListComponent },
  // { path: 'products/:id', component: ProductComponent }
```

```
];
```

We define the array of route objects that describe how to navigate. Each route maps a URL `path` to a `component` to display. The router parses and constructs the URL, helping us to use the following:

- Path references to the base element, eliminating the necessity of using leading splashes
- Absolute path

Query parameters

The second item in the router configuration points only to `products`, but as I mentioned earlier, we'll be able to see the goodies within the chosen category there. It sounds like the information we would like to include in our URL is optional:

- We can leave the request without extra information to get all the products
- We can use the particular category to fetch the products belonging to it

These kinds of parameters do not fit easily into a URL path, so, usually, it is complicated or impossible to create the pattern matching required to translate an incoming URL to a named route. Fortunately, the Angular router supports the **URL query string** for conveying any arbitrary information during navigation.

Router parameters

The third element in the `routes` array has an `id` in its path. It is a token for a **route parameter**; the value corresponding with the view component will use it to find and present the product information. In our example, the URL `'product/20'` keeps the value `20` of the `id` parameter. The `ProductComponent` can use this value to find and display the product with an ID equaling `20`. This route is commented out because we don't have the `ProductComponent` implemented yet.

Route versus query parameters

Here are the general rules to help you choose what parameters to use. Use the route parameters when the following conditions are met:

- The value is required

- The value is necessary for navigation to another route

Use the query parameters when the following conditions are met:

- The value is optional
- The value is complex or contains multivariance

Register routing in bootstrap

In the end, we should use the `RouterModule.forRoot` method to return a new instance of `RouterModule` containing the configured and ready-to-use router service provider and required routing libraries:

```
export const routing = RouterModule.forRoot(routes);
```

After that, we need to register the returned module in `AppModule`:

```
/*
 * Routing
 */
import {routing}  from './app.routes';

@NgModule({
  imports: [BrowserModule, FormsModule,
            routing, CategoryModule],
  declarations: [AppComponent, NavbarComponent],
  bootstrap: [AppComponent]
})
export class AppModule { }
```

Redirecting routes

Usually, when a user types the address of the Dream Bean website, he/she provides the website domain name: `http://www.dreambean.com`.

This URL does not match any configured routes, and Angular cannot show any component at that moment. The user must click on some link to navigate to the view, or we can teach the configuration to display the particular route with the help of the `redirectTo` property:

```
const routes: Routes = [
  { path: '', redirectTo: 'welcome', pathMatch: 'full' },
  { path: 'welcome', component: WelcomeComponent },
  { path: 'products', component: ProductListComponent },
```

```
    //{ path: 'products/:id', component: ProductComponent }
];
```

After those changes, if the user navigates to the original URL, the router translates from the initial URL (`''`) to the default URL (`'welcome'`) and displays the Welcome View.

The redirected route has a required property, `pathMatch`, to tell the router how to match the URL to the path. We have two options for this value:

- The `full` shows that the selected route must match the entire URL
- The `prefix` dictates to the router to match the redirect route to any URL that begins with the prefixed value in the `path`.

Router outlet

Now, once we have settled the router configuration, it's time to present some components on the screen. But wait—we need a place for them, and this is why the router outlet is coming to the stage.

The `RouterOutlet` is a placeholder that Angular dynamically fills based on the application's route. The `RouterOutlet` is the part of the `RouterModule` imported before, so we don't need to import it elsewhere. Here is a wireframe that splits the SPA into three rows:

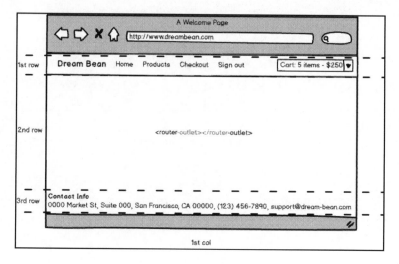

The wireframe of the SPA

In the first row, we keep the `NavigationComponent`; in the last row, the footer container. All space in between is the place where the `RouterOutlet` will display the corresponding view.

Welcome View

We configured the application routes and added them to the `AppModule`, so now we need to create the Welcome View because it is a crucial part of the routing. Create a `welcome` folder and two files inside `welcome.component.html` and `welcome.component.ts`. Now move the content of `app.component.html` between the `navbar` and the footer into `welcome.component.html` and replace it. Markup represents the `RouterOutlet` as a component:

```html
<db-navbar></db-navbar>
<router-outlet></router-outlet>
<footer class="footer">
  <div class="container">
    <address>
      <strong>Contact Info</strong><br>
      0000 Market St, Suite 000, San Francisco, CA 00000, (123) 456-7890,
      <a href="mailto:#">support@dream-bean.com</a>
    </address>
  </div>
</footer>
```

Copy and paste the following content into the `welcome.component.ts`:

```typescript
/*
 * Angular Imports
 */
import {Component} from '@angular/core';

@Component({
  selector: 'db-welcome',
  templateUrl: 'app/welcome/welcome.component.html'
})
export class WelcomeComponent { }
```

I moved almost all code from the `AppComponent` into `WelcomeComponent`, and it dramatically reduced its size:

```typescript
/*
 * Angular Imports
 */
import {Component} from '@angular/core';
```

```
@Component({
    selector: 'my-app',
    templateUrl: 'app/app.component.html',
})
export class AppComponent { }
```

I used the link to navigate from Welcome View to the products view with a selected category instead of making a call to the `selectCategory` method, so I deleted the last one as well.

The footer component

Now, when you have an idea how to create a component, you can do it yourself. Create the `footer` folder, `footer.component.ts`, and `footer.component.html`. Here, the source code of the `footer.component.ts` is the following :

```
/*
 * Components
 */
import {Component} from '@angular/core';

@Component({
    selector: 'db-footer',
    templateUrl: 'app/footer/footer.component.html'
})
export class FooterComponent {}
```

As you can see, it looks the same as other components that we created before. Move the content of the footer container from the `application.component.html` into the `footer.component.html` and replace it with the `FooterComponent` tag, so now the HTML of our application looks pretty neat:

```
<db-navbar></db-navbar>
<router-outlet></router-outlet>
<db-footer></db-footer>
```

The category data

I kept the category data as part of the AppComponent because it was a quick and obvious way at the moment when we started development. Now, as application grows, it's time to move all category data into the category file. Open the category.ts file and copy the following source code there:

```
export interface Category {
    // Unique Id
    id: string;
    // The title
    title: string;
    // Description
    desc: string;
    // Path to small image
    imageS: string;
    // Path to large image
    imageL: string;
}

var categories: Category[] = [
    { id: '1', title: 'Bread & Bakery', imageL:
'http://placehold.it/1110x480', imageS: 'http://placehold.it/270x171',
desc: 'The best cupcakes, cookies, cakes, pies, cheesecakes, fresh bread,
biscotti, muffins, bagels, fresh coffee and more.' },
    { id: '2', title: 'Takeaway', imageL: 'http://placehold.it/1110x480',
imageS: 'http://placehold.it/270x171', desc: 'It's consistently excellent,
dishes are superb and healthily cooked with high quality ingredients.' },
    { id: '3', title: 'Dairy', imageL: 'http://placehold.it/1110x480',
imageS: 'http://placehold.it/270x171', desc: 'A dairy product is food
produced from the milk of mammals, primarily cows, water buffaloes, goats,
sheep, yaks.' },
    { id: '4', title: 'Meat', imageL: 'http://placehold.it/1110x480',
imageS: 'http://placehold.it/270x171', desc: 'Only superior quality beef,
lamb, pork.' },
    { id: '5', title: 'Seafood', imageL: 'http://placehold.it/1110x480',
imageS: 'http://placehold.it/270x171', desc: 'Great place to buy fresh
seafood.' },
    { id: '6', title: 'Fruit & Veg', imageL:
'http://placehold.it/1110x480', imageS: 'http://placehold.it/270x171',
desc: 'A variety of fresh fruits and vegetables.' }
];

export function getCategories() {
    return categories;
}
```

```
export function getCategory(id: string): Category {
    for (let i = 0; i < categories.length; i++) {
        if (categories[i].id === id) {
            return categories[i];
        }
    }
    throw new CategoryNotFoundException(`Category ${id} not found`);
}

export class CategoryNotFoundException extends Error {
    constructor(message?: string) {
        super(message);
    }
}
```

The `getCategories` function returns the list of categories. The `getCategory` returns the category found by the ID or throws a `CategoryNotFoundException`.

Category card view

Let's open the `category-card.component.html` file and change the markup as follows:

```
<div class="col-xs-12 col-sm-6 col-md-4">
    <div class="card">
    <img class="card-img-top center-block product-item"
        src="{{category.image}}" alt="{{category.title}}">
    <div class="card-block">
        <h4 class="card-title">{{category.title}}</h4>
        <p class="card-text">{{category.desc}}</p>
        <a class="btn btn-primary"
            (click)="filterProducts(category)">Browse</a>
    </div>
    </div>
</div>
```

When a user clicks on the **Browse** button, Angular calls the `filterProducts` method with a category specified as a parameter.

Open the `category-card.component.ts` file, import the `Router` from the library, and add the reference in the constructor of the component:

```
import {Component, Input} from '@angular/core';
import {Router} from '@angular/router';

import {Category} from './category';
```

```
@Component({
    selector: 'db-category-card',
    templateUrl:
      'app/shared/category/category-card.component.html'
})
export class CategoryCardComponent {
    @Input() category: Category;

    constructor(private router: Router) {}

    filterProducts(category: Category) {
        this.router.navigate(['/products'],
            {queryParams: { category: category.id} });
    }
}
```

Pay attention to the `filterProducts` method. We use a router configured in the bootstrapping of the application and available in this component. Because we decided to use query parameters, I invoked a navigation method and passed the same name as the second parameter object. We can convey any information and Angular will convert it into the query string of URL like so:

```
/products?category=1
```

We are done with the Welcome View and are now moving to the Products View.

The product data

We don't use the back end server to return the products data yet, so let's create the `product.ts` file with the following content:

```
export interface Product {
    // Unique Id
    id: string;
    // Ref on category belongs to
    categoryId: string;
    // The title
    title: string;
    // Price
    price: number;
    // Mark product with specialproce
    isSpecial: boolean;
    // Description
    desc: string;
    // Path to small image
    imageS: string;
```

```
    // Path to large image
    imageL: string;
}

var products: Product[] = [
    // Bakery
    { id: '1', categoryId: '1', title: 'Baguette/French Bread', price: 1.5,
isSpecial: false, imageL: 'http://placehold.it/1110x480', imageS:
'http://placehold.it/270x171', desc: 'Great eaten fresh from oven. Used to
make sub sandwiches, etc.' },
    { id: '2', categoryId: '1', title: 'Croissants', price: 0.5, isSpecial:
true, imageL: 'http://placehold.it/1110x480', imageS:
'http://placehold.it/270x171', desc: 'A croissant is a buttery, flaky,
viennoiserie-pastry named for its well-known crescent shape.' },
    // Takeaway
    { id: '3', categoryId: '2', title: 'Pizza', price: 1.2, isSpecial:
false, imageL: 'http://placehold.it/1110x480', imageS:
'http://placehold.it/270x171', desc: 'Pizza is a flatbread generally topped
with tomato sauce and cheese and baked in an oven.' },
    // Dairy
    { id: '4', categoryId: '3', title: 'Milk', price: 1.7, isSpecial:
false, imageL: 'http://placehold.it/1110x480', imageS:
'http://placehold.it/270x171', desc: 'Milk is a pale liquid produced by the
mammary glands of mammals' },
    { id: '5', categoryId: '3', title: 'Cream Cheese', price: 2.35,
isSpecial: false, imageL: 'http://placehold.it/1110x480', imageS:
'http://placehold.it/270x171', desc: 'Cream cheese is a soft, mild-tasting
fresh cheese with a high fat content.' },
    // Meat
    { id: '6', categoryId: '4', title: 'Pork Tenderloin', price: 5.60,
isSpecial: false, imageL: 'http://placehold.it/1110x480', imageS:
'http://placehold.it/270x171', desc: 'The pork tenderloin, in some
countries called pork fillet, is a cut of pork. ' },
    { id: '7', categoryId: '4', title: 'Ribs, Baby Back', price: 4.85,
isSpecial: false, imageL: 'http://placehold.it/1110x480', imageS:
'http://placehold.it/270x171', desc: 'Pork ribs are a cut of pork popular
in North American and Asian cuisines. ' },
    { id: '8', categoryId: '4', title: 'Ground Beef', price: 9.20,
isSpecial: false, imageL: 'http://placehold.it/1110x480', imageS:
'http://placehold.it/270x171', desc: 'Ground beef, beef mince, minced beef,
minced meat is a ground meat made of beef that has been finely chopped with
a large knife or a meat grinder.' },
    // Seafood
    { id: '9', categoryId: '5', title: 'Tuna', price: 3.45, isSpecial:
false, imageL: 'http://placehold.it/1110x480', imageS:
'http://placehold.it/270x171', desc: 'A tuna is a saltwater finfish that
belongs to the tribe Thunnini, a sub-grouping of the mackerel family -
which together with the tunas, also includes the bonitos, ackerels, and
```

```
Spanish mackerels.' },
    { id: '10', categoryId: '5', title: 'Salmon', price: 4.55, isSpecial:
false, imageL: 'http://placehold.it/1110x480', imageS:
'http://placehold.it/270x171', desc: 'Salmon is the common name for several
species of ray-finned fish in the family Salmonidae.' },
    { id: '11', categoryId: '5', title: 'Oysters', price: 7.80, isSpecial:
false, imageL: 'http://placehold.it/1110x480', imageS:
'http://placehold.it/270x171', desc: 'The word oyster is used as a common
name for a number of different families of saltwater clams, bivalve
molluscs that live in marine or brackish habitats.' },
    { id: '12', categoryId: '5', title: 'Scalops', price: 2.70, isSpecial:
false, imageL: 'http://placehold.it/1110x480', imageS:
'http://placehold.it/270x171', desc: 'Scallop is a common name that is
primarily applied to any one of numerous species of saltwater clams or
marine bivalve mollusks in the taxonomic family Pectinidae, the scallops.'
},
    // Fruit & Veg
    { id: '13', categoryId: '6', title: 'Banana', price: 1.55, isSpecial:
false, imageL: 'http://placehold.it/1110x480', imageS:
'http://placehold.it/270x171', desc: 'The banana is an edible fruit,
botanically a berry, produced by several kinds of large herbaceous
flowering plants in the genus Musa.' },
    { id: '14', categoryId: '6', title: 'Cucumber', price: 1.05, isSpecial:
false, imageL: 'http://placehold.it/1110x480', imageS:
'http://placehold.it/270x171', desc: 'Cucumber is a widely cultivated plant
in the gourd family, Cucurbitaceae. ' },
    { id: '15', categoryId: '6', title: 'Apple', price: 0.80, isSpecial:
false, imageL: 'http://placehold.it/1110x480', imageS:
'http://placehold.it/270x171', desc: 'The apple tree is a deciduous tree in
the rose family best known for its sweet, pomaceous fruit, the apple.' },
    { id: '16', categoryId: '6', title: 'Lemon', price: 3.20, isSpecial:
false, imageL: 'http://placehold.it/1110x480', imageS:
'http://placehold.it/270x171', desc: 'The lemon is a species of small
evergreen tree native to Asia.' },
    { id: '17', categoryId: '6', title: 'Pear', price: 4.25, isSpecial:
false, imageL: 'http://placehold.it/1110x480', imageS:
'http://placehold.it/270x171', desc: 'The pear is any of several tree and
shrub species of genus Pyrus, in the family Rosaceae.' }
];

export function getProducts() {
    return products;
}

export function getProduct(id: string): Product {
    for (let I = 0; I < products.length; i++) {
        if (products[i].id === id) {
            return products[i];
```

```
        }
    }
    throw new ProductNotFoundException(`Product ${id} not found`);
}

export class ProductNotFoundException extends Error {
    constructor(message?: string) {
        super(message);
    }
}
```

If you look closely, you will find a similarity to the `category.ts` file. I'm just following the naming conventions.

Products View

The Products View provides a listing of all goodies within the chosen category. From it, a customer can see all product information, and add any of the listed products to his or her shopping cart. A user can also navigate to any of the provided categories or use the **Quick Shop** feature to search products by name.

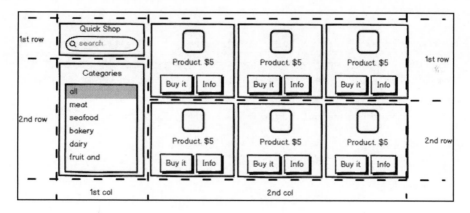

The wireframe of the products view

The layout of this component is a composition of two columns:

- The first column contains the **Quick Shop** and list of **Categories**
- The second column is a nested column combined into rows

Quick shop component

This one is an `input-group` field for searching and using `Quick Shop` to see the products available in the grocery. We use the URL query string for conveying the search information as we did for the category because we don't know what the user will type into the search field. Create the `product` folder where we will add all components and services belonging to `product`.

Let's create `product-search.component.html` in the `product` folder with the following markup:

```html
<div class="card">
    <div class="card-header">Quick Shop</div>
    <div class="input-group">
        <input #search type="text" class="form-control"
               placeholder="Search for...">
        <span class="input-group-btn">
            <button class="btn btn-secondary" type="button"
                    (click)="searchProduct(search.value)">Go!
            </button>
        </span>
    </div>
</div>
```

I use the Bootstrap 4 `input-groups` with a button inside the `Card` component. The template reference variable `search` grants us direct access to an input element so that we can use the text value in the `searchProduct` method when a user types the product name and clicks on the **Go!** button. Create the `product-search.component.ts` file and create the `ProductSearch` component similar to a `CategoryCard` one:

```typescript
import {Component} from '@angular/core';
import {Router} from '@angular/router';

import {Product} from './product';

@Component({
    selector: 'db-product-search',
    templateUrl: 'app/product/product-search.component.html'
})
export class ProductSearchComponent {

    constructor(private router: Router) {}

    searchProduct(value: string) {
        this.router.navigate(['/products'],
            { queryParams: { search: value} });
```

```
        }
    }
```

I use the navigation method of `Router` to search for a product by name with the following URL:

```
/products?search=Apple
```

Now, we are ready to create the `CategoryList` component so that the user can use it to select the category.

List of categories component

In Chapter 3, *Advanced Bootstrap Components and Customization*, we introduced the flexible Bootstrap 4 `list-group` component. `Categories` is a list of unordered items, so we can use this particular one to render categories quickly. I use the same mechanism to update the URL with the specific category that we used in `CategoryCard` component. Create `category-list.component.html` in the `category` folder with the following markup:

```html
<div class="card">
    <div class="card-header">Categories</div>
    <div class="card-block">
        <div class="list-group list-group-flush">
            <a class="list-group-item"
                *ngFor="let category of categories"
                (click)="filterProducts(category)">
            {{category.title}}</a>
        </div>
    </div>
</div>
```

The `Card` component wraps the `list-group`. The built-in `NgFor` directive helps to organize iteration through categories to display the items. Create the `category-list.component.ts`, and copy and paste the following code:

```
/*
 * Angular Imports
 */
import {Component} from '@angular/core';
import {Router} from '@angular/router';
```

```
/*
 * Components
 */
import {Category, getCategories} from './category';

@Component({
    selector: 'db-category-list',
    templateUrl: 'app/category/category-list.component.html'
})
export class CategoryListComponent {

    categories: Category[] = getCategories();

    constructor(private router: Router) {}

    filterProducts(category: Category) {
        this.router.navigate(['/products'], {
          queryParams: { category: category.id}
        });
    }
}
```

We use the getCategories function from the category file to assign all of them to the categories variable.

Update the CategoryModule

You should update the CategoryModule with the new component as follows:

```
import {NgModule} from '@angular/core';
import {CommonModule} from '@angular/common';
import {FormsModule} from '@angular/forms';
import {RouterModule} from '@angular/router';

import {CategoryListComponent} from './category-list.component';
import {CategoryCardComponent} from './category-card.component';
import {CategorySlideComponent} from './category-slide.component';

@NgModule({
    imports: [CommonModule, FormsModule, RouterModule],
    declarations: [CategoryListComponent, CategoryCardComponent,
CategorySlideComponent],
    exports: [CategoryListComponent, CategoryCardComponent,
CategorySlideComponent]
})
export class CategoryModule {}
```

I have exported the `CategoryListComponent` because we will use it in other modules.

Router links

Most of the time, the users navigate between views as a result of an action that they have performed on a link, such as a click happening on an anchor tag. We can bind the router to the links on a page, so that when the user clicks on the link, it will navigate to the appropriate application view.

 The router logs activity in the history journal of the browser so that the back and forward buttons work as expected.

The Angular team introduced a `RouterLink` directive to the anchor tag to bind it to the template expression containing the array of route link parameters. Let's create the `Product Card` component with the help of `RouterLink`.

Product card

I suppose it is a good idea to present the product as a card. I create the `product-card.component.html` in the `product` folder with the following markup:

```
<div class="col-xs-12 col-sm-6 col-md-4">
    <div class="card">
        <img class="card-img-top center-block product-item"
            src="{{product.imageS}}" alt="{{product.title}}">
        <div class="card-block">
            <h4 class="card-title">{{product.title}}</h4>
            <p class="card-text">{{product.desc}}</p>
            <a class="btn btn-primary"
                [routerLink]="['/product', product.id]">Browse</a>
        </div>
    </div>
</div>
```

In our code, the RouterLink binds in the anchor tag. Pay attention to the template expression we bind to the routerLink. Obviously, it is an array, which means that we can add more than one item, and Angular will combine them to build the URL. We can specify all the pieces of the route exclusively, like "product/1", but I intentionally leave them as separated items of an array as it's easy to maintain. Let's parse it:

- The first item identifies the parent root "/product" path
- There are no parameters for this parent element, such as "product/groups/1", so we are done with it
- The second item identifies the child route for the product and requires the ID

The navigation with RouterLink is very flexible, so we can write an application with multiple levels of routing with a link parameters array.

Create a product-card.component.ts in the product folder. The RouterLink belongs to RouterModule, so it's available on markup now. Copy and paste the following code into the product-card.component.ts:

```
import {Component, Input} from '@angular/core';

import {Product} from './product';

@Component({
    selector: 'db-product-card',
    templateUrl: 'app/product/product-card.component.html'
})
export class ProductCardComponent {
    @Input() product: Product;
}
```

We will bind the data from ProductGreedComponent into the instance of ProductCardComponent via the product property.

Products grid component

We need to show the products as a grid with three columns and multiple rows. The card component is the most suitable one to display the product information and navigate to the product view. All of the cards in the row must have the same width and height. How can we display them in a particular place inside the parent grid layout? Let's create `product-grid.component.html` and `product-grid.component.ts` files in the `product` folder. Copy and paste the following code into the `product-grid.component.ts` file:

```
/*
 * Angular Imports
 */
import {Component} from '@angular/core';

/*
 * Components
 */
import {Product, getProducts} from './product';

@Component({
    selector: 'db-product-grid',
    templateUrl: 'app/product/product-grid.component.html'
})
export class ProductGridComponent {
    products: Product[] = getProducts();
}
```

Card groups

We can use the **Bootstrap 4 Card** groups to present multiple cards as a single attached element with equal width and height. We need only include all cards within a parent element marked with the `card-group` class. Copy and paste the following code into the `product-grid.component.html` file:

```
<div class="card-group">
    <db-product-card *ngFor="let product of products"
        [product]="product"></db-product-card>
</div>
```

The result is not what I want because some cards are attached to each other:

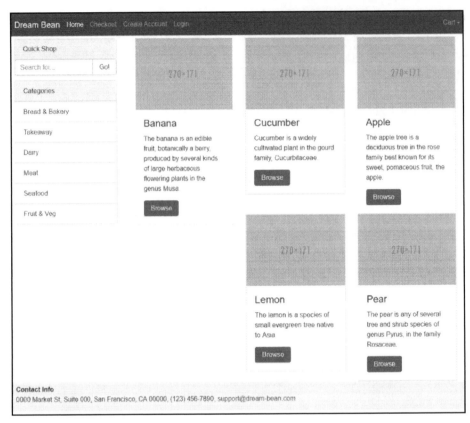

Card columns

Another layout is `card-columns` from Bootstrap 4. It allows you to display multiple cards in each column. Each card inside a column is stacked on top of another. Include all cards within a `card-columns` class. Copy and paste the following code into the `product-grid.component.html` file:

```
<div class="card-columns">
    <db-product-card *ngFor="let product of products"
        [product]="product"></db-product-card>
</div>
```

The result looks quite funny:

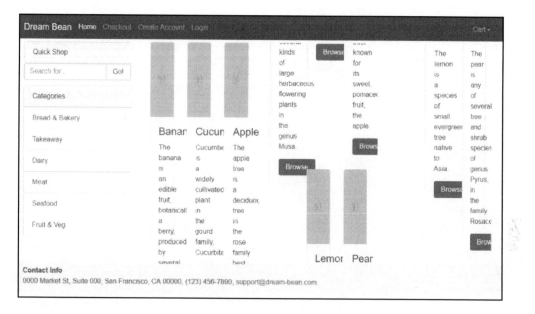

Card desks

The last layout is a card desk from Bootstrap 4. It is similar to the Card group, except the cards aren't attached to each other. This one requires two wrapping elements: `card-deck-wrapper` and a `card-deck`. It uses table styles for the sizing and the gutters on `card-deck`. The `card-deck-wrapper` is used to negative margin out the border-spacing on the `card-deck`.

Let's move back to the `product-card.component.html` file and update it with the following content:

```
<div class="card-deck-wrapper">
    <div class="card-deck">
        <div class="card" *ngFor="let product of products">
            <div class="card-header text-xs-center">
                {{product.title}}
            </div>
            <img class="card-img-top center-block product-item"
                src="{{product.imageS}}" alt="{{product.title}}">
            <div class="card-block text-xs-center"
                [ngClass]="setClasses(product)">
                <h4 class="card-text">
```

```
            Price: ${{product.price}}
        </h4>
    </div>
    <div class="card-footer text-xs-center">
        <a class="btn btn-primary"
            (click)="buy(product)">Buy Now</a>
        <a class="btn btn-secondary"
            [routerLink]="['/product', product.id]">
            More Info
        </a>
    </div>
    <div class="card-block">
        <p class="card-text">{{product.desc}}</p>
    </div>
        </div>
    </div>
</div>
```

The Card Desk works perfectly enough with one row, so we expose the `products` input in `ProductCardComponent`:

```
import {Component, Input} from '@angular/core';

import {Product} from './product';

@Component({
    selector: 'db-product-card',
    templateUrl: 'app/product/product-card.component.html',
    directives: [ROUTER_DIRECTIVES]
})
export class ProductCardComponent {
    @Input() products: Product[];

    setClasses(product: Product) {
        return {
            'card-danger': product.isSpecial,
            'card-inverse': product.isSpecial
        };
    }

    buy(product: Product) {
        console.log('We bought', product.title);
    }
}
```

The `setClasses` method helps change the card's background if the product has a `special` price. We call the `buy` method when the user clicks on the **Buy Now** button.

With all of that in place, we can update the markup of the `ProductGridComponent`:

```
<db-product-card *ngFor="let row of products"
                 [products]="row"></db-product-card>
```

Quite neat, isn't it?

But before we use our pretty component, we need to transform an array of products into an array of rows with three products per line. Please pay attention to the code in the constructor of the `ProductGridComponent`:

```typescript
import {Component} from '@angular/core';

import {Product, getProducts} from './product';

@Component({
    selector: 'db-product-grid',
    templateUrl: 'app/product/product-grid.component.html'
})
export class ProductGridComponent {
    products: any = [];

    constructor() {
        let index = 0;
        let products: Product[] = getProducts();
        let length = products.length;

        this.products = [];

        while (length) {
            let row: Product[] = [];
            if (length >= 3) {
                for (let i = 0; i < 3; i++) {
                    row.push(products[index++]);
                }
                this.products.push(row);
                length -= 3;
            } else {
                for (; length > 0; length--) {
                    row.push(products[index++]);
                }
                this.products.push(row);
            }
        }
    }
}
```

We split the products into multiple rows containing a maximum of three columns.

Combine them all together

Now we create the component that will combine all of our other product components to display them in a place provided by the router outlet tag. Will you please welcome the `ProductListComponent`!

Create a `product-list.component.ts` file with the following content:

```
/*
 * Angular Imports
 */
import {Component} from '@angular/core';

/*
 * Components
 */

@Component({
  selector: 'db-products',
  templateUrl: 'app/product/product-list.component.html'
})
export class ProductListComponent {}
```

Now, create the `product-list.component.html`, and copy and paste the next markup:

```
<div class="container">
    <div class="row">
        <div class="col-md-3">
            <db-product-search></db-product-search>
            <db-category-list></db-category-list>
        </div>
        <div class="col-md-9">
            <db-product-grid></db-product-grid>
        </div>
    </div>
</div>
```

As you can see, it draws the `ProductSearchComponent` and `CategoryListComponent` in the first column and the `ProductGridComponent` in the second one, which corresponds to our wireframe.

The product module

The last two cents in the `product` folder are the `ProductModule`. Create the `product.module.ts` file as follows:

```
import {NgModule} from '@angular/core';
import {CommonModule} from '@angular/common';
import {FormsModule} from '@angular/forms';
import {RouterModule} from '@angular/router';

import {ProductListComponent} from './product-list.component';
import {ProductCardComponent} from './product-card.component';
import {ProductSearchComponent} from './product-search.component';
import {ProductGridComponent} from './product-grid.component';

import {CategoryModule} from '../category/category.module';

@NgModule({
    imports: [CommonModule, FormsModule, RouterModule, CategoryModule],
    declarations: [ProductListComponent, ProductCardComponent,
ProductSearchComponent, ProductGridComponent],
    exports: [ProductListComponent, ProductCardComponent,
ProductSearchComponent, ProductGridComponent]
})
export class ProductModule {}
```

It imports the `CategoryModule` as well as system modules. We declare and export all of the four components that we created before.

Update the AllModule

Now, with `CategoryModule` and `ProductModule` in place, we need make all of their components available to the application so that we can import them into the `AppModule`:

```
import {NgModule} from '@angular/core';
import {BrowserModule} from '@angular/platform-browser';
import {FormsModule} from '@angular/forms';

/**
 * Modules
 */
import {CategoryModule} from './category/category.module';
import {ProductModule} from './product/product.module';

/*
```

```
 * Components
 */
import {AppComponent}  from './app.component';
import {NavbarComponent} from './navbar/navbar.component';
import {FooterComponent} from './footer/footer.component';
import {WelcomeComponent} from './welcome/welcome.component';

/*
 * Routing
 */
import {routing}  from './app.routes';

@NgModule({
  imports: [BrowserModule, FormsModule, routing,
           CategoryModule, ProductModule],
  declarations: [AppComponent, NavbarComponent, FooterComponent,
    WelcomeComponent],
  bootstrap: [AppComponent]
})
export class AppModule { }
```

The `NavbarComponent`, `FooterComponent`, and `WelcomeComponent` belong to the `AppModule` directly.

> You can find the source code at `chapter_5/2.ecommerce-router`.

Router change events

As we mentioned when looking at router configuration, the `ProductListComponent` can represent the Product View when a user navigates to the URL like the following:

```
/products?category=1
```

Or

```
/products?search=apple
```

The `ActivatedRouter` class contains the information about a route associated with a component loaded in an outlet. We can subscribe to route change events to inform the `ProductGridComponent` about the changes happening in the query parameters of the URL. Open the `product-grid.component.ts` file, import `ActivatedRouter` from the library, and inject it into the `router` property of the constructor. Now we can subscribe to the route changes:

```
constructor(private router: ActivatedRouter) {
        this.router
            .queryParams
            .subscribe(params => {
                let category: string = params['category'];
                let search: string = params['search'];
                // Return filtered data from getProducts function
                let products: Product[] =
                    getProducts(category, search);
                // Transform products to appropriate data
                // to display
                this.products = this.transform(products);
            });
    }
```

In the preceding code, we are listening to the changes that happen only in `queryParams` and using them to filter data in the `getProducts` function. Later, with the help of the `transform` method, we will translate the filtered products in the data appropriate to the display.

```
transform(source: Product[]) {
    let index = 0;
    let length = source.length;

    let products = [];

    while (length) {
        let row: Product[] = [];
        if (length >= 3) {
            for (let i = 0; i < 3; i++) {
                row.push(source[index++]);
            }
            products.push(row);
            length -= 3;
        } else {
            for (; length > 0; length--) {
                row.push(source[index++]);
            }
            products.push(row);
```

```
        }
    }

    return products;
}
```

Lastly, we must change the signature of the `getProducts` function because now we may pass two parameters:

```
export function getProducts(category?: string, search?: string) {
    if (category) {
        return products.filter(
          (product: Product, index: number, array: Product[]) => {
            return product.categoryId === category;
        });
    } else if (search) {
        let lowSearch = search.toLowerCase();
        return products.filter(
          (product: Product, index: number, array: Product[]) => {
            return product.title.toLowerCase().
              indexOf(lowSearch) != -1;
        });
    } else {
        return products;
    }
}
```

This function filters data by category, searches text, or leaves it as is, depending on the parameters that we send to the function. Save the code, and try to play with the filtered data:

Routing strategies

All of our essential routes have been configured, and we now have access to a separate view for all of them. That's great, but maybe you are not happy with the path following the # symbol in the URL. As I mentioned, modern web browsers support the pushState technique to help change a location and history in the browser without a request to the server. The Router uses this method to build the URL. The Angular router uses a different LocationStrategy to provide support for both old and new ways:

- The PathLocationStrategy provides the default, HTML 5 style based on pushState
- The HashLocationStrategy utilizes the hash in the URL style

Choosing the strategy is crucial for future development because it won't be easy to change it later, so it is better do it at the right time. You can use the HashLocationStrategy if your server doesn't support the ability to redirect to a fallback page when a route is not found. Likely, the lite-server we use in our development supports this feature.

Open the app.module.ts file and import the strategy from the common module:

```
import {LocationStrategy, HashLocationStrategy ,
        PathLocationStrategy} from '@angular/common';
```

We are registering the PathLocationStrategy or HashLocationStrategy as a provider to the LocationStrategy:

```
@NgModule({
  imports: [BrowserModule, FormsModule,
            routing, CategoryModule, ProductModule],
  declarations: [AppComponent, NavbarComponent, FooterComponent,
                 WelcomeComponent],
  providers: [{provide: LocationStrategy, useClass: HashLocationStrategy}],
  bootstrap: [AppComponent]
})
export class AppModule { }
```

Save it and check how the application works within and without hash in the browser's URL.

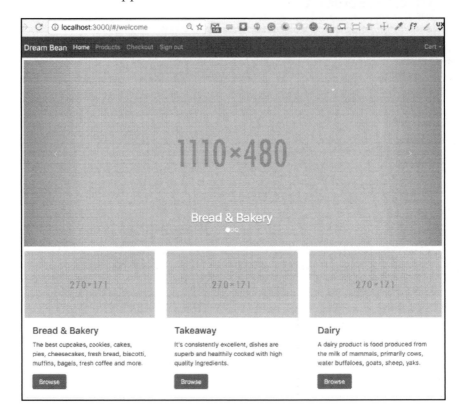

You can find the source code at `chapter_5/3.ecommerce-router-search`.

Summary

In this chapter, we transformed our application from a single page into a multipage view and multiroute app that we can build on the Dream Bean grocery store. We started by planning out the essential routes in our application before writing any lines of code.

We then built static and dynamic routes containing parameters.

Finally, we looked at how we can remove the # symbol from the URL using HTML 5's pushState and how we can link both types of routes.

In Chapter 6, *Dependency Injection*, we will talk about dependency injection, which teaches the readers how to decouple the requirements of an application and how to create a consistent source of data as a service. Plus, we will continue to build the project we started to develop in previous chapters.

6
Dependency Injection

This chapter is about dependency injection that teaches you how to decouple the requirements of an application and how to create a consistent source of data as a service. You will learn about Injector and Provider classes. We will also discuss Injectable decorator that is required for the creation of an object.

At the end of the chapter, you will have a solid understanding of:

- What is dependency injection?
- Separation of concerns
- Creating a service
- The injector and provider classes
- Injectable and inject decorators
- Creating data services for our application

What is dependency injection?

Here, I will talk about the concept of **dependency injection** with some concrete examples that will hopefully demonstrate the problems it tries to solve and the benefits it gives to the developer. Angular is mostly based on dependency injection, which you may or may not be familiar with. If you already know the concept of dependency injection, you can safely skip this chapter and just read the next one.

Dependency injection is probably one of the most famous design patterns I know, and you have probably already used it. I think it is one of the most difficult ones to explain well, partly due to the nonsense examples used in most introductions to dependency injection. I have tried to come up with examples that fit the Angular world better.

A real-life example

Imagine, you start your own business, and tend to travel a lot by air, so you need to arrange flights. You are always booking the flight yourself using the phone number of the airline agency.

Thus your typical travel planning routine might look like the following:

- Decide the destination, and desired arrival date and time
- Call up the airline agency and convey the necessary information to obtain a flight booking
- Pick up the tickets and be on your way

Now, if you suddenly change the preferred agency, and its contact mechanisms, you would be subject to the following relearning scenarios:

- The new agency, and its new contact mechanisms (say the new agency offers Internet based services and the way to make the bookings is over the Internet instead of over the phone)
- The typical conversational sequence through which the necessary bookings get done (data instead of voice)

You need to adjust yourself to the new scenario. It could lead to a substantial amount of time spent on the readjustment process.

Assume your business is growing and you get a secretary in the company, so whenever you needed to travel, you send an email to him or her to just state the destination, desired arrival date and time. The flight reservations are made for you and the tickets get delivered to you.

Now if the preferred agency gets changed, the secretary would become aware of the change, and would perhaps readjust his or her workflow to be able to communicate with the agency. However, you would have no relearning required. You still continue to follow the same protocol as before, since the secretary makes all the necessary adaptation in a manner that means you do not need to do anything differently.

In both the scenarios, you are the client and are dependent upon the services provided by the agency. However, the second scenario has a few differences:

- You don't need to know the contact point of the agency—the secretary does it for you

- You don't need to know the exact conversational sequence by which the agency conducts its activities via voice, email, website, and so on, as you are aware of a particular standardized conversational series with the secretary
- The services you are dependent upon are provided to you in a manner that you do not need to readjust should the service provider change

That is dependency injection in *real life*.

Dependency injection

Both, the Angular and custom components we used in our project are a part of a set of collaborating components. They depend upon each other to complete their intended purpose, and they need to know:

- Which components to communicate with?
- Where to locate them?
- How to communicate with them?

When the way to access is changed, such changes can potentially require the source of a lot of components to be modified. Here are the plausible solutions we can use to prevent dramatic changes of components:

- We can embed the logic of location and instantiation as part of our usual logic of components
- We can create the *external* piece of code to assume the responsibility of location and instantiation and supply the references when necessary

We can look at the last solution as the *secretary* from our *real life* example. We don't need to change the code of components when the way to locate any external dependency changes. This solution is the implementation of dependency injection, where an *external* piece of code is part of Angular Framework.

The use of dependency injection requires the declaration of the components and lets the framework work out of the complexities of instantiation, initialization, sequencing, and supplying the references as needed.

Passing of a dependency into a dependent object that would use it is a dependency injection. A component can accept a dependency in at least three common ways:

- **Constructor injection**: In this, the dependencies are provided through a class constructor.

- **Setter injection**: In this, the injector utilizes the component exposed setter methods to inject the dependency.
- **Interface injection**: In this, the dependency provides a method that will inject the dependency into any component passed to it.

Constructor injection

This method requires the component to provide a parameter in a constructor for the dependency. We injected the `Router` instance in the code of the `ProductGridService` component:

```
constructor(private router: ActivatedRoute) {
    this.router
        .queryParams
        .subscribe(params => {
            let category: string = params['category'];
            let search: string = params['search'];
            // Return filtered data
            let products: Product[] =
              getProducts(category, search);
            // Transform products to appropriate data
            // to display
            this.products = this.transform(products);
        });
}
```

Constructor injection is the most preferable method and can be used to ensure the component is always in a valid state, but its lacks the flexibility of being able to change its dependencies later.

Other injection methods

Setter and interface methods are not implemented in the Angular framework.

Components versus services

Angular 2 distinguishes the code of a web application on:

- The components that represent the visual part
- The reusable data services

The data service is a simple class that provides methods for returning or updating some data.

ReflectiveInjector

A `ReflectiveInjector` is an injection container that we use as a replacement for a `new` operator we are using to resolve the constructor dependencies automatically. When code in an application asks about dependencies in the constructor, the `ReflectiveInjector` resolves them.

```
import {Injectable, ReflectiveInjector} from '@angular/core';

@Injectable()
export ProductGridService {
  constructor(private router: ActivatedRoute) {...}
}

const injector = ReflectiveInjector.resolveAndCreate
      ([ActivatedRoute, ProductGridService]);
const service = injector.get(ProductGridService);
```

With a `resolveAndCreate` method, the `ReflectiveInjector` creates an instance of `Injector`. We are passing the array of service providers into the injector to configure it, or it won't know how to create them.

With an `Injector`, creating a `ProductGridService` is very easy, because it takes full responsibility of providing and injecting the `ActivatedRoute` into the `ProductGridService`.

Let's talk about why we imported and applied the `Injectable` decorator to the class?

Injectable decorator

We create multiple types in the application for particular needs. Some of them may have dependencies to others. We must mark any type available for an injector with an `Injectable` decorator. Injector uses class constructor metadata to get the parameter types and determine dependent types for instantiation and injection. Any dependent type must be marked with `Injectable` decorator or injector will report an error when trying to instantiate it.

Add `@Injectable()` to every service class to prevent dependency injection errors.

We must import and apply the `Injectable` decorator to all class of our services explicitly to make them available to an injector for instantiation. Without this decorator, the Angular doesn't know about the existence of those types.

Inject decorator

As I mentioned, the Injector uses a class constructor metadata to determine dependent types:

```
constructor(private router: ActivatedRoute) {...}
```

Injector uses the TypeScript generated metadata to inject the instance of `ActivatedRoute` type into the constructor. For injecting the TypeScript primitives such as `string`, `boolean`, or array we should define and use the Opaque Token:

```
import { OpaqueToken } from '@angular/core';

export let APP_TITLE = new OpaqueToken('appTitle');
```

Now, with the `APP_TITLE` token defined we can use it in the registration of dependency provider:

```
providers: [{ provide: APP_TITLE, useValue: 'Dream Bean' }]
```

We use the `@Inject` decorator when we inject the application title into any constructor of our application:

```
import {Inject} from '@angular/core';

constructor(@Inject('APP_TITLE') private appTitle) {...}
```

We will talk about tokens shortly.

Optional decorator

In cases when class has optional dependencies, we can use the @Optional decorator to mark the constructor parameters:

```
import {Optional} from '@angular/core';

constructor(@Optional('config') private config) {
  if (config) {
    // Use the config
    ...
  }
}
```

I added the conditional statement into the code above because I expected that config property will equal null.

Configuring the injector

In the preceding example, I used the resolveAndCreate method of the ReflectiveInjector to create Injector, but in real life, it's not necessary:

```
const injector = ReflectiveInjector.resolveAndCreate
        ([ActivatedRoute, ProductGridService]);
```

The Angular framework creates an application-wide injector for us during the Bootstrap of the application:

```
platformBrowserDynamic().bootstrapModule(AppModule);
```

We must configure the injector via registering the providers that create the services our application requires. We can do that in two ways:

- Register a provider within an NgModule
- Register a provider in an AppComponent

Which one is best? The services injected into the AppModule are widely available in the entire application and can be injected into lazy-loading modules and their components. The services injected into the AppComponent are available only to this component and its children and are not available to lazy-loading modules.

Register application-wide providers in the root `AppModule`, not in the `AppComponent`.

We can configure injector with alternative providers under the right circumstances:

- Provided an object behaves or looks like the original one
- Provides a substitute class
- Provides a factory function

For example for `AppModule` class:

```
@NgModule({
   imports: [BrowserModule, FormsModule,
            routing, CategoryModule, ProductModule],
   declarations: [AppComponent, NavbarComponent, FooterComponent,
               WelcomeComponent],
   providers: [ProductService],
   bootstrap: [AppComponent]
})
export class AppModule { }
```

We used a short-hand expression when registering the provider in the injector. Angular transforms it into the following verbose format:

```
[{provide: Router, useClass: Router]
```

The `provide` property in the first place is the *token* that serves as the key for:

- Locating a dependency value
- Registering the provider

The second property, `useClass`, is a definition object similar to many other *use* things such `useValue`, `useExisting`, and others. and tells the framework how to create the dependency. With the help of the *use* definitions, we can quickly switch implementations, define constants and factory functions. Let's look at all of them.

Class providers

Most of the time we will utilize the `useClass` definition to ask the different class to provide the service. We can create our own `BetterRouter` class as an extension of the original one and register it such that:

```
[{ provide: Router, useClass: BetterRouter }]
```

The injector knows how to build `BetterRouter` and will sort it out.

Aliased class providers

In scenarios when we need to use many providers of the same singleton, we can use the `useExisting` definition:

```
class BetterRouter extends Router {}

var injectorClass = ReflectiveInjector.resolveAndCreate([
  BetterRouter, {provide: Router, useClass: BetterRouter}
]);
var injectorAlias = ReflectiveInjector.resolveAndCreate([
  BetterRouter, {provide: Router, useExisting: BetterRouter}
]);
```

Look at the following example where `useExisting` helps organize mock requests:

```
var injector = Injector.resolveAndCreate([
    HTTP_PROVIDERS,
    MockBackend,
    { provide: XHRBackend, useExisting: MockBackend }
]);
var http = injector.get(Http);
var backend = injector.get(MockBackend);
```

The code below demonstrates how to use the `MockBackend` instead of the real one, making AJAX requests:

```
var people = [{name: 'Jeff'}, {name: 'Tobias'}];

// Listen for any new requests
backend.connections.observer({
  next: connection => {
    var response = new Response({body: people});
    setTimeout(() => {
      // Send a response to the request
      connection.mockRespond(response);
```

```
      });
    }
  });

  http.get('people.json').observer({
    next: res => {
      // Response came from mock backend
      console.log('first person', res.json()[0].name);
    }
  });
```

Another useful place for useExisting is in providing multiple values of custom pipes, custom directives, or custom validators:

```
@Directive({
    selector: '[custom-validator]',
    providers: [{ provide: NG_VALIDATORS,
                  useExisting: CustomValidatorDirective, multi: true }]
})
class CustomValidatorDirective implements Validator {
    validate(c: Control): { [key: string]: any } {
        return { "custom": true };
    }
}
```

With the help of the multi option, it is possible to add the CustomValidatorDirective to the default collections to have it available globally in the application.

Value providers

Sometimes we need to use a configuration object, string or function in our application is not always an instance of a class. Here the interface defines the structure of configuration:

```
export interface Config {
  url: string;
  title: string;
}

export const CUSTOM_CONFIG: Config = {
  url: 'www.dreambean.com',
  title: 'Dream Bean Co.'
};
```

We can register the ready-made objects with the `useValue` definition. There is no `Config` class, so we cannot use it for the token. Instead, we can use a string literal to register and resolve dependencies:

```
providers: [{ provide: 'app.config', useValue: CUSTOM_CONFIG }]
```

And now we can inject it into any constructor with the help of `@Inject` decorator:

```
constructor(@Inject('app.config') config: Config) {
  this.title = config.title + ':' + config.url;
}
```

Unfortunately, using string tokens opens up a potential for naming collisions. Angular comes to the rescue and provides an elegant solution with `Opaque Token` for non-class dependencies:

```
import { OpaqueToken } from '@angular/core';

export let CONFIG = new OpaqueToken('app.config');
```

We are registering the `CUSTOM_CONFIG` in the injector with the value provider:

```
providers: [{ provide: CONFIG, useValue: CUSTOM_CONFIG }]
```

Inject it into any constructor:

```
constructor(@Inject(CONFIG) config: Config) {
  this.title = config.title + ':' + config.url;
}
```

Multiple values

With the help of the `multi` option it is possible to add other values to the same binding later:

```
bootstrap(AppComponent, [
    provide('languages', {useValue: 'en', multi:true }),
    provide('languages', {useValue: 'fr', multi:true })
);
```

Somewhere in the code we can get multiple values of the `languages`:

```
constructor(@Inject('languages') languages) {
  console.log(languages);
  // Logs: "['en','fr']"
}
```

Factory providers

In cases when we need to create the dependent value dynamically based on information changed at any moment after the Bootstrap has happened, we can apply the `useFactory` definition.

Let's imagine we use `SecurityService` to authorize the user. `CategoryService` must know facts about the user. The authorization can change during the user session because he or she can log in and log out at any moment many times. The direct injection `SecurityService` into `CategoryService` creates a precedent to inject it into all services of the application.

The solution is quite neat, use the primitive Boolean `authorization` property instead of `SecurityService` to control `CategoryService`:

```
categories: Category[] = [...];

constructor(private authorized: boolean) { }

getCategories() {
        return this.authorized ? this.categories : [];
}
```

The authorized property will update dynamically, so we cannot use a value provider, but we have to take over the creation of a new instance of the `CategoryService` with a factory function:

```
let categoryServiceFactory = (securityService: SecurityService) => {
    return new CategoryService(securityService.authorized);
}
```

In the factory provider we inject the `SecurityService` along with the factory function:

```
export let categoryServiceProvider = {
    provide: CategoryService,
    useFactory: categoryServiceFactory,
    deps: [SecurityService]
};
```

The hierarchy of injectors

Angular 1 has only one injector across the application, and it manages the creation and resolving of all dependencies quite nicely. Every registered dependency becomes a singleton, so only one instance of it is available across the application. That solution has a side effect where you need to have more than one instance of the same dependency injecting into different parts of the application. Because the Angular 2 application is a tree of components, the framework has a **hierarchical dependency injection** system—the tree of injectors exists in parallel to the component tree of the application. Every component has an injector of its own or shared with other components at the same level in the tree. When the component at the bottom of the tree requests a dependency, Angular tries to find it with a provider registered in that component's injector. If the provider doesn't exist on this level, the injector passes the request to its parent injector and so on until finding the injector that can handle the request. Angular throws an exception if it runs out of ancestors. This solution helps us to create different instances of the same dependency on various levels and components. The particular service instance is still a singleton, but only in the scope of the host component instance and its children.

Let's start:

- Open Terminal, create folder `ecommerce` and move in
- Copy the contents of the project from the folder `chapter_6/1.ecommerce-seed` into the new project
- Run the following script to install npm modules:

  `npm install`

- Start the TypeScript watcher and lite server with next command:

  `npm start`

This script opens the web browser and navigates to the welcome page of the project.

Category service

I mentioned in `Chapter 5`, *Routing*, about the necessity to decouple the data from the presentation logic when implementing SPA. I partially realized it in the category and product views. The `CategoryListComponent` and `WelcomeComponent` use category returns from the `getCategories` function. Right now it is not suffering, but when we start getting and updating data from the server, we will need more functions. Better hide the implementation detail inside the single reusable data service class to use it in multiple components.

Let's refactor the category data acquisition business to a single service that provides categories, and share that service with all components that need them.

Rename the `category.ts` to `category.service.ts` to follow a name convention in which we spell the name of a service in lowercase followed by `.service`. If the service name is multi-word, we will spell the base filename in lower `dash-case`. Add an import statement to the top of the file:

```
import {Injectable} from '@angular/core';
```

Now create the `CategoryService` class and move the `categories` variable, `getCategories` and `getCategory` functions inside:

```
@Injectable()
export class CategoryService {
    categories: Category[] = [
        { id: '1', title: 'Bread & Bakery', imageL:
'http://placehold.it/1110x480', imageS: 'http://placehold.it/270x171',
desc: 'The best cupcakes, cookies, cakes, pies, cheesecakes, fresh bread,
biscotti, muffins, bagels, fresh coffee and more.' },
        { id: '2', title: 'Takeaway', imageL:
'http://placehold.it/1110x480', imageS: 'http://placehold.it/270x171',
desc: 'It's consistently excellent, dishes are superb and healthily cooked
with high quality ingredients.' },
        { id: '3', title: 'Dairy', imageL: 'http://placehold.it/1110x480',
imageS: 'http://placehold.it/270x171', desc: 'A dairy product is food
produced from the milk of mammals, primarily cows, water buffaloes, goats,
sheep, yaks, horses.' },
        { id: '4', title: 'Meat', imageL: 'http://placehold.it/1110x480',
imageS: 'http://placehold.it/270x171', desc: 'Only superior quality beef,
lamb, and pork.' },
        { id: '5', title: 'Seafood', imageL:
'http://placehold.it/1110x480', imageS: 'http://placehold.it/270x171',
desc: 'Great place to buy fresh seafood.' },
        { id: '6', title: 'Fruit & Veg', imageL:
```

```
'http://placehold.it/1110x480', imageS: 'http://placehold.it/270x171',
desc: 'A variety of fresh fruits and vegetables.' }
    ];

getCategories() {
    return this.categories;
}

getCategory(id: string): Category {
    for (let i = 0; i < this.categories.length; i++) {
        if (this.categories[i].id === id) {
            return this.categories[i];
        }
    }
    throw new CategoryNotFoundException(
        `Category ${id} not found`);
    }
}
```

Don't forget to add this to all references to categories property.

Injector provider for category service

We must register a service provider with the injector to tell Angular how to create the service. The best place to do that is in the providers property of a NgModule. We need only one instance of categories per application, so when we import the CategoryModule into the AppModule, Angular will register and create the singleton from the CategoryService class available across the whole application. Open the category.module.ts file, import the CategoryService and change @NgModule decorator with the following code:

```
import {CategoryService} from './category.service';

@NgModule({
    imports: [CommonModule, FormsModule, RouterModule],
    declarations: [CategoryListComponent, CategoryCardComponent,
CategorySlideComponent],
    exports: [CategoryListComponent, CategoryCardComponent,
CategorySlideComponent],
    providers: [CategoryService]
})
export class CategoryModule {}
```

Move to your web browser and open the browser console. We get a full bunch of issues, mostly about the wrong name of file `category.ts` was renamed to `category.service.ts`. We can easily fix that issue. Another problem is the use of the functions `getCategory` and `getCategories`. To fix that issue we need to import the `CategoryService`:

```
import {Category, CategoryService} from './category.service';
```

And inject it into constructors in all the necessary places such that:

```
export class CategoryListComponent {

    categories: Category[];

    constructor(private router: Router,
                private categoryService: CategoryService) {
this.categories = this.categoryService.getCategories();
    }

    filterProducts(category: Category) {
        this.router.navigate(['/products'],
            { queryParams: { category: category.id} });
    }
}
```

Move initialization of all variables inside the constructor for now, similar to `categories` in the preceding example.

Product service

Rename the `product.ts` to `product.service.ts`. Create the class `ProductService` and move the `products` variable, `getProducts` and `getProduct` functions into it:

```
export class ProductService {

    private products: Product[] = [
// ...
    ];
    getProducts(category?: string, search?: string) {
        if (category) {
            return this.products.filter((product: Product, index: number,
array: Product[]) => {
                return product.categoryId === category;
            });
        } else if (search) {
```

```
            let lowSearch = search.toLowerCase();
            return this.products.filter((product: Product, index: number,
array: Product[]) => {
                return product.title.toLowerCase().indexOf(lowSearch) !=
-1;
            });
        } else {
            return this.products;
        }
    }

    getProduct(id: string): Product {
        for (let i = 0; i < this.products.length; i++) {
            if (this.products[i].id === id) {
                return this.products[i];
            }
        }
        throw new ProductNotFoundException(`Product ${id} not found`);
    }
}
```

Fix the `import` in all classes to have references on old methods.

Injector provider for product service

We follow the same procedure for `ProductService` to register a service provider. Because we need only one instance of service per application, we can register it in the `ProductModule`. Open the `product.module.ts` file, import the `ProductService` and change the `@NgModule` decorator with the following code:

```
import {ProductService} from './product.service';

@NgModule({
    imports: [CommonModule, FormsModule, ReactiveFormsModule, RouterModule,
CategoryModule],
    declarations: [ProductListComponent, ProductCardComponent,
ProductSearchComponent, ProductGridComponent],
    exports: [ProductListComponent, ProductCardComponent,
ProductSearchComponent, ProductGridComponent],
    providers: [ProductService]
})
export class ProductModule {}
```

Now restart the application to see all of your products and categories again:

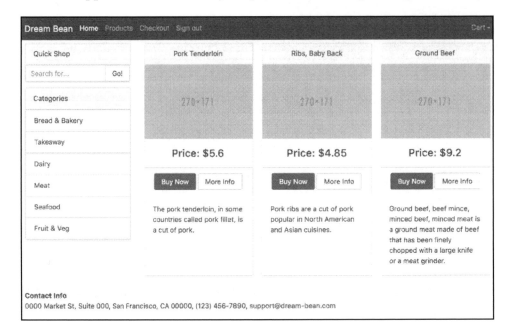

You can find the source code for this at `chapter_6/2.ecommerce-di`.

The shopping cart

A shopping cart is a piece of software that acts as an online store's catalog and allows users to select items for eventual purchase. It's known as a shopping basket. A shopping cart (or basket) allows a user to collect items while browsing an online catalog of products. The user should click on the **Buy Now** button to add the selected item to the cart. The total amount and number of items in the cart presents in the navigation bar component. The user is able to move to a checkout or view the cart to manage the number of purchased items.

The cart must store the items the user puts in the cart. The items should be:

- Fetchable to be able to display the cart content
- Updatable to be able to change the quantity of an item in the cart
- Removable

With this in mind, let's first create the basic cart functionality: adding, updating, and deleting items and defining a barebones item class and walk through the code usage.

Let's create the `cart` folder and `cart.service.ts` file inside. We will keep the model definition implemented as the `Cart` and the `CartItem` inside that file as well as the `CartService`.

The Cart model and CartItem

At the beginning, the `Cart` class needs an internal array for storing all the `items` in the cart:

```
export class Cart {
    count: number = 0;
    amount: number = 0;
    items: CartItem[] = [];
}
```

Next, it must `count` the number and keep the `amount` of all items. The `CartItem` is an interface defining the structure of data the cart can use:

```
import {Product} from '../product/product.service';

export interface CartItem {
    product: Product;
    count:   number;
    amount:  number;
}
```

The CartService

The `CartService` keeps the `cart` instance to make it available across the whole application:

```
cart: Cart = new Cart();
```

The `addProduct` method should add items to the cart:

```
addProduct(product: Product) {
    // Find CartItem in items
    let item: CartItem = this.findItem(product.id);
    // Check was it found?
    if (item) {
        // Item was found.
        // Increase the count of the same products
```

```
        item.count++;
        // Increase amount of the same products
        item.amount += product.price;
    } else {
        // Item was not found.
        // Create the cart item
        item = {
            product: product,
            count: 1,
            amount: product.price
        };
        // Add item to items
        this.cart.items.push(item);
    }
    // Increase count in the cart
    this.cart.count++;
    // Increase amount in the cart
    this.cart.amount += product.price;
}
```

The method takes one argument of type Product and tries to find the item containing the same one. The method needs to increment the number of products and increase the amount of the found cart item. Otherwise, it creates the new CartItem instance and assigns the product to it. After all, it is growing the total number of items and amount in the shopping cart.

Next, the removeProduct method of the class can be used to remove the product quickly from the cart:

```
removeProduct(product: Product) {
    // Find CartItem in items
    let item: CartItem = this.findItem(product.id);
    // Check is item found?
    if (item) {
        // Decrease the count
        item.count--;
        // Check was that the last product?
        if (!item.count) {
            // It was last product
            // Delete item from items
            this.remove(item);
        }
        // Decrease count in the cart
        this.cart.count--;
        // Decrease amount in the cart
        this.cart.amount -= product.price;
    }
```

```
}
```

The method takes one argument of product type and tries to find the item containing the same one. The method needs to decrement the number of goods associated with this item cart. It removes the cart item which includes no one product. In the end, it reduces the total number of items and amount in the shopping cart.

Method `removeItem` removes the particular item and reduces the total number of items and amount in the shopping cart:

```
removeItem(item: CartItem) {
    // Delete item from items
    this.remove(item);
    // Decrease count in the cart
    this.cart.count -= item.count;
    // Decrease amount in the cart
    this.cart.amount -= item.amount;
}
```

The following private method `findItem` helps to find `CartItem` by `Product` id:

```
private findItem(id: string): CartItem {
    for (let i = 0; i < this.cart.items.length; i++) {
        if (this.cart.items[i].product.id === id) {
            return this.cart.items[i];
        }
    }
    return null;
}
```

The last private method, `remove`, decreases the number of items in the cart:

```
private remove(item: CartItem) {
    // Find the index of cart item
    let indx: number = this.cart.items.indexOf(item);
    // Check was item found
    if (indx !== -1) {
        // Remove element from array
        this.cart.items.splice(indx, 1);
    }
}
```

The Cart menu component

The key aspect that I find must present on the shopping cart design is that, at first glance, the user should be able to find out how many items there are in the shopping cart. You need to keep your user informed about how many items are in the shopping cart so that users are aware of what they have added to the cart without having to use the dropdown.

Make sure shoppers can easily see the items in their cart and that they appear above the fold rather than on another page.

That is quite a significant UX design pattern. If you keep the shopping cart content somewhere in the sidebar or near the top right of your pages, you are removing extra steps in the checkout process and making it easier for shoppers to move throughout the site and keep track of items and order totals the whole time.

With this in mind, let's create the `cart-menu.component.ts` and `cart-menu.component.html`. Copy and paste the following code into the `cart-menu.component.ts` file:

```
import {Component, Input} from '@angular/core';

import {Cart, CartService} from './cart.service';

@Component({
    selector: 'db-cart-menu',
    templateUrl: 'app/cart/cart-menu.component.html'
})
export class CartMenuComponent {

    private cart: Cart;

    constructor(private cartService: CartService) {
        this.cart = this.cartService.cart;
```

```
        }
    }
```

The purpose of the local `cart` variable is to represent on view the content and update it with changes that happen after the user adds or removes the product to the cart.

We display the total number of items and amount in the label of the drop-down menu:

```
<ul class="nav navbar-nav float-xs-right">
    <li class="nav-item dropdown">
        <a class="nav-link dropdown-toggle" data-toggle="dropdown"
            href="#" role="button" aria-haspopup="true"
            aria-expanded="false">
            Cart: {{cart.amount | currency:'USD':true:'1.2-2'}}
                ({{cart.count}} items)
        </a>
        <div class="dropdown-menu dropdown-menu-right"
            aria-labelledby="cart">
        <!-- ... -->
```

Pay attention to the currency pipe with the following parameters:

- The first parameter is the ISO 4217 currency code, such as USD for the US dollar and EUR for the euro.
- * At the second place is a Boolean indicating whether to use the currency symbol (example $) or the currency code (example USD) in the output
- At the last place we add the digit info in the next format: `minIntegerDigits.minFractionDigits-maxFractionDigits`

I recommend using this pipe here and in all other places where you need to display the amount of currency.

We display the contents of the cart inside a Bootstrap 4 table:

```
<div class="table-responsive">
    <table class="table table-sm table-striped table-bordered
            table-cart">
        <tbody>
            <tr>
                <td class="font-weight-bold">Title</td>
                <td class="font-weight-bold">Price</td>
                <td class="font-weight-bold">Count</td>
                <td class="font-weight-bold">Amount</td>
            </tr>
            <tr *ngFor="let item of cart.items">
                <td>{{item.product.title}}</td>
```

```
            <td>{{item.product.price |
                    currency:'USD':true:'1.2-2'}}</td>
            <td>{{item.count}}</td>
            <td>{{item.amount |
                    currency:'USD':true:'1.2-2'}}</td>
        </tr>
    </tbody>
  </table>
</div>
```

At the bottom of the menu, we display the total amount and two buttons to navigate to `Cart` and `Checkout`:

```
<div class="row">
    <div class="col-md-12">
        <div class="total-cart float-xs-right">
            <b>Total:
                {{cart.amount | currency:'USD':true:'1.2-2'}}
            </b>
        </div>
    </div>
</div>
<div class="row">
    <div class="col-md-12">
        <a [routerLink]="['/cart']"
           class="btn btn-primary float-xs-right btn-cart">
            <i class="fa fa-shopping-cart" aria-hidden="true"></i>
            Cart
        </a>
        <a [routerLink]="['/checkout']"
           class="btn btn-success float-xs-right btn-cart">
            <i class="fa fa-credit-card" aria-hidden="true"></i>
            Checkout
        </a>
    </div>
</div>
```

Cart module

Let's add the `CartManuComponent` and `Cart Service` into the `CartModule` to make them easily accessible in the entire application:

```
import {NgModule} from '@angular/core';
import {CommonModule} from '@angular/common';
import {RouterModule} from '@angular/router';
```

```
import {CartMenuComponent} from './cart-menu.component';
import {CartService} from './cart.service';

@NgModule({
    imports: [CommonModule, RouterModule],
    declarations: [CartMenuComponent],
    exports: [CartMenuComponent],
    providers: [CartService]
})
export class CartModule {}
```

We need to add the `CartModule` into the `AppModule`:

```
//...
import { CartModule } from './cart/cart.module';
//...
@NgModule({
  imports: [
    BrowserModule, FormsModule, ReactiveFormsModule,
    routing, CartModule, CategoryModule, ProductModule],
  declarations: [AppComponent, NavbarComponent, FooterComponent,
    WelcomeComponent],
  bootstrap: [AppComponent]
})
export class AppModule { }
```

Update the Navbar

Open the `navbar.component.html` and find the cart placeholder:

```
<ul class="nav navbar-nav float-xs-right">
  <li class="nav-item dropdown">
    <a class="nav-link dropdown-toggle" data-toggle="dropdown"
       href="#" role="button" aria-haspopup="true"
       aria-expanded="false">Cart</a>
    <div class="dropdown-menu">
      <span>The Cart Placeholder</span>
    </div>
  </li>
</ul>
```

Change it to look more elegant:

```
<db-cart-menu></db-cart-menu>
```

Update the Cart via Service

And the last thing we must to do is inject the `CartService` into the `ProductGrid` component and start to listen to `addToCart` events. In the method with the same name we call the `addProduct` of `CartService` to add the selected goodie into the shopping cart:

```
addToCart(product:Product) {
    this.cartService.addProduct(product);
}
```

Now, try to click on **Buy Now** on different products and see changes happen in the navigation bar. Click the dropdown to display the shopping cart content:

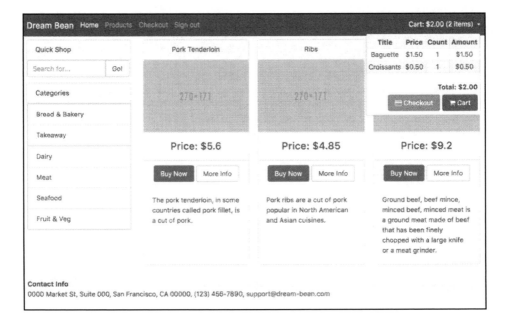

 You can find the source code at `chapter_6/3.ecommerce-cart`.

Summary

You will now be familiar with the dependency injection that Angular relies heavily on. As we've seen, we split our Angular code into visual components and services. Each of them depend upon one another, and dependency injection provides referential transparency. Dependency injection allows us to tell Angular what services our visual components depend on, and the framework will resolve these for us.

We created the classes for products and categories to hide the functionality into reusable services. Plus, we created the shopping cart component and service and wired the last to products, so the user can add the products to the cart.

In Chapter 7, *Working with Forms*, we will talk about how to use Angular 2 directives related to form creation and how to link a code based form component to the HTML form. Plus we will continue to build the project we started to develop in previous chapters.

7

Working with Forms

This chapter will show readers how to use Angular 2 directives related to form creation and how to use a code-based form component to the HTML form. The chapter will use Bootstrap 4 to enhance the look of the form and to indicate invalid input for our web application.

At the end of the chapter, you will have a solid understanding of:

- Bootstrap 4 forms
- Angular 2 form directives
- One-way and two-way data bindings
- How to add validation to a form
- Joining the pieces of our application

Let's start with the following steps:

1. Open the Terminal, create a folder called `ecommercem` and open it.
2. Copy the content of the project from the folder, `chapter_7/1.ecommerce-seed`, into the new project.
3. Run the following script to install NPM modules:

   `npm install`

4. Start the TypeScript watcher and lite server with the following command:

   `npm start`

This script opens the web browser and navigates to the welcome page of the project.

HTML form

An HTML form is a section of a web document containing:

- Text
- Images
- Markups
- Special elements such as controls, like checkboxes, radio buttons, and so on
- Labels on those controls that describe their purposes

The user modifies the controls by entering text or selecting the drop-down menu to complete the form and submits it to the backend for processing. Every control has a `name` attribute the form uses to collect a specific piece of data. Those names are important because:

- On the client side, it tells the browser which names to give each piece of data
- On the server side, it lets the server handle each piece of data by name

The form defines where and how to send the data to the server via `action` and `method` attributes accordingly. The form usually has a submit button to allow the user to send data to the server.

Bootstrap forms

Bootstrap 4 provides default style form controls and layout options to create the customs forms for consistent rendering across browsers and devices.

 For proper rendering, all inputs must have a `type` attribute.

Form controls

Bootstrap supports specific classes to customize the following form controls:

- The `form-group` class uses any group of form controls. You can use it with any block-level element such as `fieldset` or `div`.
- The `form-control` class uses textual inputs, select menus, and text areas.

- The `form-control-file` is the only one applicable to the file inputs.
- There are `form-check` and `formcheck-inline` classes we can use with checkboxes and radio buttons.

Form layouts

All forms by default are stacked vertically because Bootstrap 4 applies `display: block` and `width: 100%` to all form controls. We can use additional classes to vary this layout.

Standard form

Use the `form-group` class to create the form quickly:

```
<form>
  <div class="form-group">
    <label for="user_name">User Name</label>
    <input type="text" class="form-control" id="user_name">
  </div>
  <div class="form-group">
    <label for="password">Password</label>
    <input type="password" class="form-control" id="password">
  </div>
</form>
```

This class adds `margin-bottom` around a label and control for optimum spacing:

Inline form

Use the `form-inline` class if you need to lay out the form elements in a single horizontal row aligned to the left.

 The form aligns controls inline only in viewports wider than 768px.

Form controls behave differently because they receive `width:auto` instead of `width: 100%`. To provide the vertical alignment with all of them use the `display: inline-block`. You may need to manually address the width and alignment of individual controls:

```
<form  class="form-inline">
  <div class="form-group">
    <label for="user_name">User Name</label>
    <input type="text" class="form-control" id="user_name">
  </div>
  <div class="form-group">
    <label for="password">Password</label>
    <input type="password" class="form-control" id="password">
  </div>
</form>
```

 Each form control should have the pair `label` element.

I only added the `form-inline` class to the form element to lay out the element horizontally:

Hidden labels

You can hide away the labels in respect of placeholders for the standard and inline forms:

```
<form  class="form-inline">
  <div class="form-group">
    <label class="sr-only" for="user_name">User Name</label>
```

```
    <input type="text" class="form-control" id="user_name"
         placeholder="User Name">
  </div>
  <div class="form-group">
    <label class="sr-only" for="password">Password</label>
    <input type="password" class="form-control" id="password"
         placeholder="Password">
  </div>
</form>
```

We just add the `sr-only` class to each label:

Why can we not remove labels from the form to make them invisible? The answer to this question lies in the use of assistive technologies such as screen readers for people with limited abilities. The screen readers will render the form incorrectly if we do not include a label for every input. The Bootstrap authors intentionally designed the `sr-only` class to hide information from the layout of the rendering page only for screen readers.

Form control size

There are two extra sizes of form controls, in addition to the default one, that we can use to increase or decrease the size of the form:

- Use the `form-control-lg` to increase the size of input control
- Use the `form-control-sm` to decrease the size of input control

Help text

Sometimes we need to display the help text for associated form controls. Bootstrap 4 supports help text for standard and inline forms.

You can use the `form-text` class to create the block level help. It includes the `display: block` and adds some top margin for easy spacing from the preceding inputs:

```
<form>
  <div class="form-group">
    <label for="user_name">User Name</label>
    <input type="text" class="form-control" id="user_name">
```

```
    </div>
    <div class="form-group">
      <label for="password">Password</label>
      <input type="password" class="form-control" id="password">
      <p id="passwordHelpBlock" class="form-text text-muted">
        The password must be more than 8 characters long.
      </p>
    </div>
  </form>
```

Use the `text-muted` class with any typical inline element (like `span` or `small`) to create help text for inline forms:

```
<form  class="form-inline">
  <div class="form-group">
    <label for="user_name">User Name</label>
    <input type="text" class="form-control" id="user_name">
  </div>
  <div class="form-group">
    <label for="password">Password</label>
    <input type="password" class="form-control" id="password">
    <small id="passwordHelpInline" class="text-muted">
      Must be 8-20 characters long.
    </small>
  </div>
</form>
```

User Name		Password		Must be 8-20 characters long.

Form grid layout

We can use Bootstrap 4 grids to create more structured layouts for forms. Here are some guidelines:

- Wrap the form in an element with the `container` class

- Add the `row` class to `form-group`
- Use `col-*-*` classes to specify the width of labels and controls
- Add `col-form-label` class to all labels to vertically align them to corresponding controls

- Add `col-form-legend` to legend elements to help them appear similar to regular labels

Let's update our markup with grids:

```
<div class="container">
  <form>
    <div class="form-group row">
      <label for="user_name" class="col-sm-2 col-form-label">
        User Name
      </label>
      <div class="col-sm-10">
        <input type="text" class="form-control" id="user_name">
      </div>
    </div>
    <div class="form-group row">
      <label for="password" class="col-sm-2 col-form-label">
        Password
      </label>
      <div class="col-sm-10">
        <input type="password" class="form-control" id="password">
      </div>
    </div>
    <div class="form-group row">
      <label class="col-sm-2">Connection</label>
      <div class="col-sm-10">
        <div class="form-check">
          <label class="form-check-label">
            <input class="form-check-input" type="checkbox">
            Secure (SSL)
          </label>
        </div>
      </div>
    </div>
    <div class="form-group row">
      <div class="offset-sm-2 col-sm-10">
        <button type="submit" class="btn btn-primary">Sign in
        </button>
      </div>
    </div>
  </form>
```

```
</div>
```

Stacked checkboxes and radios

Bootstrap 4 improves the layout and behavior of checkboxes and radio buttons with the help of `form-check*` classes. There is only one class for both types to help vertically stack and space the sibling elements. The labels and inputs must have appropriate `form-check-label` and `form-check-input` classes to make that magic happens.

```
<div class="container">
  <form>
    <div class="form-group row">
    <label for="user_name" class="col-sm-2 col-form-label">
      User Name
    </label>
    <div class="col-sm-10">
      <input type="text" class="form-control" id="user_name">
      </div>
    </div>
    <div class="form-group row">
      <label for="password"
             class="col-sm-2 col-form-label">Password</label>
      <div class="col-sm-10">
        <input type="password" class="form-control" id="password">
      </div>
    </div>
    <fieldset class="form-group row">
      <legend class="col-form-legend col-sm-2">Language</legend>
      <div class="col-sm-10">
        <div class="form-check">
          <label class="form-check-label">
            <input class="form-check-input" type="radio"
                   name="language" id="lngEnglish" value="english"
                   checked>
          English
          </label>
        </div>
```

```
        <div class="form-check">
          <label class="form-check-label">
            <input class="form-check-input" type="radio"
                   name="language" id="lngFrench" value="french">
            French
          </label>
        </div>
        <div class="form-check disabled">
          <label class="form-check-label">
            <input class="form-check-input" type="radio"
                   name="language" id="lngSpain" value="spain"
                   disabled>
            Spain
          </label>
        </div>
      </div>
    </fieldset>
  </form>
</div>
```

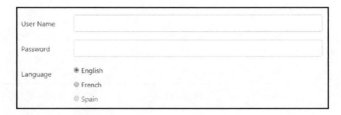

Inline checkboxes and radios

In scenarios when you need checkboxes or radio buttons to be layed out on a horizontal row you can:

- Add the `form-check-inline` class to the label element
- Add the `form-check-input` to the input

```
<form  class="form-inline">
  <div class="form-group">
    <label for="user_name">User Name</label>
    <input type="text" class="form-control" id="user_name">
  </div>
  <div class="form-group">
    <label for="password">Password</label>
    <input type="password" class="form-control" id="password">
    <small id="passwordHelpInline" class="text-muted">
```

```
          Must be 8-20 characters long.
      </small>
   </div>
   <div class="form-group">
      <label class="form-check-inline">
        <input class="form-check-input" type="radio" name="language"
               id="lngEnglish" value="english" checked>
          English
      </label>
      <label class="form-check-inline">
        <input class="form-check-input" type="radio" name="language"
               id="lngFrench" value="french">
          French
      </label>
      <label class="form-check-inline">
        <input class="form-check-input" type="radio" name="language"
               id="lngSpain" value="spain" disabled>
          Spain
      </label>
   </div>
</form>
```

Static control

In the cases when you need to display the plain text instead of input fields you can use the paragraph element marked with the `form-control-static` class:

```
<div class="container">
  <form>
    <div class="form-group row">
      <label for="user_name" class="col-sm-2 col-form-label">
        User Name
      </label>
      <div class="col-sm-10">
        <p class="form-control-static">Admin</p>
      </div>
    </div>
    <div class="form-group row">
      <label for="password" class="col-sm-2 col-form-label">
        Password
      </label>
```

```
        <div class="col-sm-10">
          <input type="password" class="form-control" id="password">
        </div>
      </div>
    </form>
  </div>
```

User Name	Admin
Password	

Disabled states

We can disable the input on one or many controls with an attribute of the same name:

```
<form>
  <div class="form-group">
    <label for="user_name">User Name</label>
    <input type="text" class="form-control" id="user_name"
           value="Admin" disabled>
  </div>
  <div class="form-group">
    <label for="password">Password</label>
    <input type="password" class="form-control" id="password">
    <p id="passwordHelpBlock" class="form-text text-muted">
      The password must be more than 8 characters long.
    </p>
  </div>
</form>
```

The disabled input field is shown lighter and with the `not-allowed` cursor:

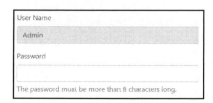

 Use custom JavaScript code to disable the anchor and fieldset because browsers such as IE 11 and below don't fully support this property.

Read-only inputs

To prevent modification of any input field you can use a read-only attribute:

```
<form>
  <div class="form-group">
    <label for="user_name">User Name</label>
    <input type="text" class="form-control" id="user_name"
           value="Admin" readonly>
  </div>
  <div class="form-group">
    <label for="password">Password</label>
    <input type="password" class="form-control" id="password">
    <p id="passwordHelpBlock" class="form-text text-muted">
      The password must be more than 8 characters long.
    </p>
  </div>
</form>
```

These fields appear lighter with the standard cursor:

Validation styles

Bootstrap supports three validation states and appropriate styles for the form controls:

- The has-success class defines the success state
- The has-danger class defines the danger state
- The has-warning class defines the warning state

We should apply those classes to the parent element, so all control-label, form-control, or text-muted elements will inherit the validation styles. We can use the feedback icons within the textual inputs such as form-control-success, form-control-warning, and form-control-danger. To give extra attention to validation, we can use contextual validation text with the help of form-control-feedback style. It adapts color to the parent has-* class:

```
<form>
    <div class="form-group has-success">
        <label class="control-label" for="username">Success
        </label>
        <input type="text" class="form-control
                form-control-success" id="username">
        <div class="form-control-feedback">That username's is
            ok.</div>
    </div>

    <div class="form-group has-warning">
        <label class="control-label" for="password">Warning
        </label>
        <input type="password" class="form-control
            form-control-warning" id="password">
        <div class="form-control-feedback">The password is
            weak</div>
    </div>

    <div class="form-group has-danger">
        <label class="control-label" for="card">Card</label>
        <input type="card" class="form-control
            form-control-danger"
            id="card">
        <div class="form-control-feedback">We accept only VISA and
            Master cards</div>
    </div>
</form>
```

Formless search

Look at the markup in the `product-search.component.html` file:

```
<div class="card">
    <div class="card-header">Quick Shop</div>
    <div class="input-group">
        <input #search type="text" class="form-control"
               placeholder="Search for...">
        <span class="input-group-btn">
            <button class="btn btn-secondary" type="button"
                    (click)="searchProduct(search.value)">Go!</button>
        </span>
    </div>
</div>
```

I didn't use the `form` tag here. Why? The answer is quite tricky. The form tag is required mostly for the following scenarios:

- You want to execute a non-AJAX request or post file to the server
- You need to programmatically capture the `submit` or `reset` events
- You want to add validation logic to the form

For others, we could abandon it. The logic behind the search field is to update URL with appropriate information without any request to the server. So this is why the search is formless.

The search form has one issue; the **Go** button is always enabled even when the search field is empty. This results in inappropriate search results. We need to add validation to fix this issue and we have two options here:

- Start listening to the key events from search field to manage the `enabled` property of the **Go** button
- Add validation and let Angular manage the `enabled` property of the **Go** button

Let's do both of them to see the difference.

User input from event object

The user interacts with the web page, modifying the controls, and this results in triggering the DOM events. We use event binding to listen to those events that update components and models with the help of some simple syntax:

```html
<div class="card">
    <div class="card-header">Quick Shop</div>
    <div class="input-group">
        <input #search type="text" class="form-control"
                placeholder="Search for..."
             (keyup)="searchChanged($event)">
        <span class="input-group-btn">
            <button class="btn btn-secondary" type="button"
                [disabled]="disabled"
                (click)="searchProduct(search.value)">Go!</button>
        </span>
    </div>
</div>
```

The shape of $event depends on which element raises the event. When the user types something on the input element it triggers the keyboard events and listens in the searchChanged method of the ProductSearchComponent:

```typescript
import {Component} from '@angular/core';
import {Router} from '@angular/router';

@Component({
    selector: 'db-product-search',
    templateUrl: 'app/product/product-search.component.html'
})
export class ProductSearchComponent {

    disabled: boolean = true;

    constructor(private router: Router) {}

    searchProduct(value: string) {
        this.router.navigate(['/products'], { queryParams: {
        search: value} });
    }

    searchChanged(event: KeyboardEvent) {
        // Get an input element
        let element:HTMLInputElement =
                    <HTMLInputElement>event.target;
        // Update the disabled property depends on value
```

```
            if (element.value) {
                this.disabled = false;
            } else {
                this.disabled = true;
            }
        }
    }
}
```

Firstly, we find the input element from the event `target` and change the `disabled` property of the component bound to the same name attribute of the `submit` button. By default, the disabled value equals true and the submit button is grayed out:

When the user inputs the text to search, the triggered events enable the button to update the URL:

User input from a template reference variable

We can use the `#search` template reference variable to get value directly from the input element like this:

```
<div class="card">
    <div class="card-header">Quick Shop</div>
    <div class="input-group">
        <input #search type="text" class="form-control"
            placeholder="Search for..."
            (keyup)="searchChanged(search.value)">
        <span class="input-group-btn">
            <button class="btn btn-secondary" type="button"
                [disabled]="disabled"
                (click)="searchProduct(search.value)">Go!</button>
        </span>
    </div>
</div>
```

The code of the `searchChanged` method becomes a bit smaller:

```
searchChanged(value: string) {
    // Update the disabled property depends on value
    if (value) {
        this.disabled = false;
    } else {
        this.disabled = true;
    }
}
```

> Opt to use the template reference variable to pass values instead of DOM events into the component listening methods.
> You can find the source code at `chapter_7/2.ecommerce-key-event-listenning`.

Product View

The product card component displayed in the products grid has a **More Info** button. When the user clicks the button, it navigates to the Product View where you can do the following:

- Display the product information
- Check the availability of the product
- Update the quantity of the product by clicking **Add to Cart** or **Remove from Cart**
- Return to the products list by clicking on **Continue Shopping**

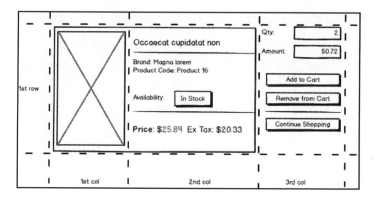

The wireframe of the Product View

Let's create the `product-view.component.html`. The content of this view is quite big, so I will explain it per columns.

Product image

In the first column, we show the image of the product. The product interface has reference to large images, so it is simple to present it on screen:

```
<div class="container">
    <div class="row">
      <div class="col-md-5">
      <img class="center-block product-img" src="{{product.imageL}}"
          alt="{{product.title}}">
      </div>
      <!-- ... -->
```

Here is what this column looks like:

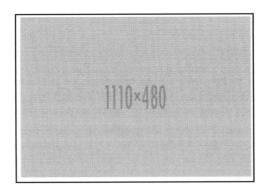

Product information

The second column keeps the information about the product. I decided to use a Bootstrap 4 card component to present the information on screen:

```
<div class="col-md-4">
    <div class="card">
        <div class="card-block">
            <h4 class="card-title">{{product.title}}</h4>
            <p class="card-text">{{product.desc}}</p>
        </div>
        <ul class="list-group list-group-flush">
            <li class="list-group-item">ID: {{product.id}}</li>
            <li class="list-group-item">Category:
                {{product.categoryId | categoryTitle}}</li>
        </ul>
        <div class="card-footer">
            <p class="card-text">Availability: In Stock</p>
```

```
            </div>
        </div>
        <div class="card" *ngIf="!product.isSpecial">
            <div class="card-block">
                <h4 class="card-title">Price:
                    {{product.price | currency:'USD':true:'1.2-2'}}</h4>
            </div>
        </div>
        <div class="card card-inverse card-danger"
             *ngIf="product.isSpecial">
            <div class="card-block">
                <h4 class="card-title">Price:
                    {{product.price | currency:'USD':true:'1.2-2'}}</h4>
            </div>
        </div>
    </div>
```

We have three cards here. The first one contains the product's general information such as the `title` and `description`. The following list keeps the product `id` and `category`. We use the `categoryTitle` pipe to print out the category title. At the end, we print out the availability information with the fake data. We will update this block in the next chapter, so leave it as it is for now.

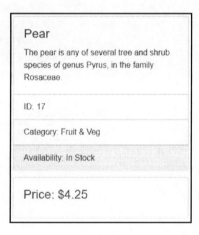

The second and third cards work against each other and present information depending on the value of the `isSpecial` property of the product. When this property is `true` we show the price in an altering color:

The CategoryTitle pipe

As was mentioned in `Chapter 4`, *Creating the Template*, the Angular Framework gives us pipes: a way to write display-value transformations that we can declare in templates. The pipe is a simple function that accepts an input value and returns a transformed value. In our case, we keep the category ID in the cart item, but we need to display the title of the category. For that reason we created the file `category.pipe.ts` with the following content:

```
import {Pipe, PipeTransform} from '@angular/core';
import {Category, CategoryService} from './category.service';

/*
 * Return category title of the value
 * Usage:
 *    value | categoryTitle
 * Example:
 *    {{ categoryId |  categoryTitle }}
 *    presume categoryId='1'
 *    result formats to 'Bread & Bakery'
*/
@Pipe({ name: 'categoryTitle' })
export class CategoryTitlePipe implements PipeTransform {

    constructor(private categoryService: CategoryService) { }
```

```
transform(value: string): string {
    let category: Category = this.categoryService.getCategory(value);
    return category ? category.title : '';
}
}
```

Plus, we updated the `CategoryModule` to declare and export the `CategoryTitlePipe`:

```
import {NgModule} from '@angular/core';
import {CommonModule} from '@angular/common';
import {RouterModule} from '@angular/router';

import {CategoryListComponent} from './category-list.component';
import {CategoryTitlePipe} from './category.pipe';
import {CategoryCardComponent} from './category-card.component';
import {CategorySlideComponent} from './category-slide.component';

import {CategoryService} from './category.service';

@NgModule({
    imports: [CommonModule, RouterModule],
    declarations: [CategoryListComponent, CategoryTitlePipe,
                   CategoryCardComponent, CategorySlideComponent],
    exports: [CategoryListComponent, CategoryTitlePipe,
              CategoryCardComponent, CategorySlideComponent],
    providers: [CategoryService]
})
export class CategoryModule {}
```

Now, the `CategoryTitlePipe` is available across the application.

Cart information in Product View

I used the Bootstrap 4 Form laid out inside the cart component in the last column to keep and manage information from the shopping cart as explained as follows.

Quantity and amount

The quantity and amount of the product are crucial for the user doing the shopping. To present them on the view, I bound the component properties of the same name to the template:

```
<div class="form-group row">
    <label for="first_name" class="col-xs-3 form-control-
label">Quantity</label>
```

```
        <div class="col-xs-9">
            <h4 class="form-control-static">{{quantity}}</h4>
        </div>
    </div>

    <div class="form-group row">
        <label for="last_name" class="col-xs-3 form-control-
label">Amount</label>
        <div class="col-xs-9">
            <h4 class="form-control-static">{{amount |
currency:'USD':true:'1.2-2'}}</h4>
        </div>
    </div>
```

Actions

The user uses **Add to Cart** and**Remove from Cart** buttons to increase and decrease the quantity of the product on the shopping cart. These buttons call the appropriate methods of the `CartService` to make the necessary changes in the shopping cart:

```
        <div class="form-group row">
            <div class="col-xs-12">
                <a class="btn btn-primary btn-block"
                    (click)="addToCart()">Add to Cart</a>
                <a class="btn btn-warning btn-block"
                    (click)="removeFromCart()">Remove from Cart</a>
            </div>
        </div>
        <div class="form-group row">
            <div class="col-xs-12">
                <a class="btn btn-secondary btn-block"
                    [routerLink]="['/products']">Continue Shopping</a>
            </div>
        </div>
    </form>
```

At the end, we have a **Continue Shopping** button to help the user navigate back to the Products View.

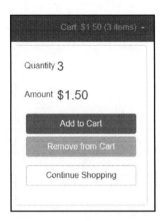

Every time a user adds or removes a product from the shopping cart, the changes happen in the Product View, which updates information in the Cart Menu present in the navigation bar.

Product View component

Now let's create `product-view.component.ts` with the following code:

```
import { Component } from '@angular/core';
import { ActivatedRoute } from '@angular/router';

import { Product, ProductService } from './product.service';
import { Cart, CartItem, CartService } from
    '../cart/cart.service';

@Component({
    selector: 'db-product-view',
    templateUrl: 'app/product/product-view.component.html'
})
export class ProductViewComponent {
    product: Product;
    cartItem: CartItem;

    get quantity(): number {
        return this.cartItem ? this.cartItem.count : 0;
    }

    get amount(): number {
        return this.cartItem ? this.cartItem.amount : 0;
    }
```

```
constructor(private route: ActivatedRoute,
            private productService: ProductService,
            private cartService: CartService) {
    this.route
        .params
        .subscribe(params => {
            // Get the product id
            let id: string = params['id'];
            // Return the product from ProductService
            this.product = this.productService.getProduct(id);
            // Return the cart item
            this.cartItem = this.cartService.findItem(id);
        });
}

addToCart() {
 this.cartItem = this.cartService.addProduct(this.product);
}

removeFromCart() {
 this.cartItem = this.cartService.removeProduct(this.product);
}
}
```

There are two properties, `product` and `cartItem`, available in `ProductViewComponent` to get information to the template. We use the `product` property to display information in the second column of the Product View. The `cartItem` property keeps the reference on the item in the shopping cart linked to the product:

```
export interface CartItem {
    product: Product;
    count: number;
    amount: number;
}
```

We need only show `count` and `amount` in the third column of the Product View but it is impossible without extra work:

The first problem is that we cannot show information from the `CartItem` until adding the product to the shopping cart. To solve it, we introduced the getter methods for `count` and `amount` properties:

```
get quantity(): number {
    return this.cartItem ? this.cartItem.count : 0;
}

get amount(): number {
```

```
        return this.cartItem ? this.cartItem.amount : 0;
    }
```

Another issue happens when the user adds a product to the shopping cart for the first time or removes the last one from it. As a solution, we need to reassign the `cartItem` from the shopping cart whenever we call the `addToCart` and `removeFromCart` methods:

```
addToCart() {
    this.cartItem = this.cartService.addProduct(this.product);
}

removeFromCart() {
    this.cartItem = this.cartService.removeProduct(this.product);
}
```

We use the `ActivatedRoute` service to retrieve the parameters for our route in the constructor. Since our parameters are provided as an `Observable`, we subscribe to them for the `id` parameter by name and tell `productService` and `cartService` to fetch appropriate information. We'll keep a reference to this `Subscription` so we can tidy things up later.

Adding ProductView to the ProductModule

Open the `product.module.ts` file to reference the `ProductView` there:

```
import {NgModule} from '@angular/core';
import {CommonModule} from '@angular/common';
import {RouterModule} from '@angular/router';

import {ProductListComponent} from './product-list.component';
import {ProductViewComponent} from './product-view.component';
import {ProductCardComponent} from './product-card.component';
import {ProductSearchComponent} from './product-search.component';
import {ProductGridComponent} from './product-grid.component';

import {ProductService} from './product.service';

import {CategoryModule} from './category/category.module';

@NgModule({
    imports: [CommonModule, RouterModule, CategoryModule],
    declarations: [ProductListComponent, ProductViewComponent,
        ProductCardComponent, ProductSearchComponent,
        ProductGridComponent],
    exports: [ProductListComponent, ProductViewComponent,
```

```
            ProductCardComponent, ProductSearchComponent,
            ProductGridComponent],
        providers: [ProductService]
})
export class ProductModule {}
```

The `ProductView` is now available in the entire application.

Product View route definition with a parameter

We must update the router configuration in the `app.routes.ts` so, when a user selects the product, Angular navigates to the `ProductViewComponent`:

```
/*
 * Angular Imports
 */
import {Routes, RouterModule} from '@angular/router';

/*
 * Components
 */
import {WelcomeComponent} from './welcome/welcome.component';
import {ProductListComponent} from
        './product/product-list.component';
import {ProductViewComponent} from
        './product/product-view.component';

/*
 * Routes
 */
const routes: Routes = [
  { path: '', redirectTo: 'welcome', pathMatch: 'full' },
  { path: 'welcome', component: WelcomeComponent },
  { path: 'products', component: ProductListComponent },
  { path: 'products/:id', component: ProductViewComponent },
];

/*
 * Routes Provider
 */
export const routing = RouterModule.forRoot(routes);
```

The id in the third route is a token for a route parameter. In a URL such as /product/123, the 123 is the value of the id parameter. The corresponding ProductViewComponent uses that value to find and present the product whose id equals 123.

Navigation to Product View

When the user clicks on the **More Info** button on the card in the Products View, the router uses information provided as an array to the routerLink to build the navigation URL to the Product View:

```
<div class="card-deck-wrapper">
    <div class="card-deck">
        <div class="card" *ngFor="let product of products">
            <div class="card-header text-xs-center">
                {{product.title}}
            </div>
            <img class="card-img-top center-block product-item"
                src="{{product.imageS}}" alt="{{product.title}}">
            <div class="card-block text-xs-center"
                [ngClass]="setClasses(product)">
                <h4 class="card-text">Price:
                    ${{product.price}}</h4>
            </div>
            <div class="card-footer text-xs-center">
                <button class="btn btn-primary"
                    (click)="buy(product)">Buy Now</button>
                <a class="btn btn-secondary"
                    [routerLink]="['/products', product.id]">
                        More Info
                </a>
            </div>
            <div class="card-block">
                <p class="card-text">{{product.desc}}</p>
            </div>
        </div>
    </div>
</div>
```

Here are how all three columns of the Product View look:

 You can find the source code at `chapter_7/3.ecommerce-product-view`.

Angular 2 forms

We didn't use Angular 2 forms in our project before, so now it's time to unveil those predominantly flexible tools. Based on the nature of the information of the web application requesting from the user, we can split it into static and dynamic forms:

- We use the template-driven approach to build static forms
- We use the model-driven approach to build dynamic forms

Forms setup

Before we use the new Angular 2 forms module, we need to install it. Open the Terminal window, navigate to the web project, and run the npm package manager with the following command:

```
$ npm install @angular/forms --save
```

Now, when the forms module is installed, we enable it during the application bootstrap. Open the `app.module.ts` file and update it with the following code:

```typescript
/*
 * Angular Imports
 */
import { NgModule } from '@angular/core';
import { BrowserModule } from '@angular/platform-browser';
import { FormsModule, ReactiveFormsModule } from '@angular/forms';
import { RouterModule } from '@angular/router';

/**
 * Modules
 */
import { CartModule } from './cart/cart.module';
import { CategoryModule } from './category/category.module';
import { ProductModule } from './product/product.module';

/*
 * Components
 */
import { AppComponent } from './app.component';
import { NavbarComponent } from './navbar/navbar.component';
import { FooterComponent } from './footer/footer.component';
import { WelcomeComponent } from './welcome/welcome.component';

/*
 * Routing
 */
import { routing } from './app.routes';

@NgModule({
  imports: [
    BrowserModule, FormsModule, ReactiveFormsModule,
    routing, CartModule, CategoryModule, ProductModule],
  declarations: [AppComponent, NavbarComponent, FooterComponent,
    WelcomeComponent],
  bootstrap: [AppComponent]
})
```

```
export class AppModule { }
```

We registered two different modules in `AppModule` because:

- The `FormsModule` is for template-driven forms
- The `ReactiveFormsModule` is for reactive or dynamic forms

We will discover both of them shortly.

Template-driven forms

This way is the simplest one to build forms and requires little to no application code. We create the form declaratively in the template with the help of built-in Angular 2 directives doing all the magic behind the scene for us. Let's talk about the Angular 2 specific directives we can use in the forms.

The NgForm directive

The `NgForm` directive creates a top-level `FormGroup` instance, providing information about the current state of the form, such as:

- The form value in JSON format
- The form validity state

Look at the directive definition of the class `FormGroupDirective` in the `form_group_directive.ts` from the source code of Angular 2:

```
@Directive({
  selector: '[formGroup]',
  providers: [formDirectiveProvider],
  host: {'(submit)': 'onSubmit()', '(reset)': 'onReset()'},
  exportAs: 'ngForm'
})
export class FormGroupDirective extends ControlContainer implements Form,
OnChanges { //
```

The property `exportAs` of the directive metadata exposes an instance of `FormGroupDirective` to the template via the name `ngForm` so in any template we can use the template variable referencing on it:

```
<form #myForm="ngForm">
```

```
        . . .
    </form>
```

The template variable `myForm` has access to the form value, so we can use the handle function to manage submitting values like this:

```
<form #myForm="ngForm" (ngSubmit)="handle(myForm.value)">
    . . .
</form>
```

The `ngSubmit` is an event signal where the user triggers a form submission.

The NgModel directive

The `NgModel` directive helps register form controls on a `NgForm` instance. We must specify the `name` attribute to every form control. With the combination of `ngModel` and `name` attributes, the form control will automatically appear in the `value` of the form:

```
<form #myForm="ngForm" (ngSubmit)="handle(myForm.value)">
    <label>User Name:</label>
    <input type="text" name="name" ngModel>
    <label>Password:</label>
    <input type="password" name="password" ngModel>

    <button type="submit">Submit</button>
</form>
```

Let's print out the `value` of the form in the `handle` function:

```
handle(value) {
    console.log(value);
}
```

The result is printed in JSON format:

```
{
  name: 'User',
  password: 'myPassword'
}
```

We can use the `ngModel` as an attribute directive with an expression to bind the existing model to the form controls. There are two ways we can approach this.

The **one-way binding** applies an existing value to the form control via property binding:

```
<form #myForm="ngForm" (ngSubmit)="handle(myForm.value)">
    <label>User Name:</label>
    <input type="text" name="name" [ngModel]="name">
    <label>Password:</label>
    <input type="password" name="password" [ngModel]="password">
    <label>Phone:</label>
    <input type="text" name="phone" [ngModel]="phone">
    <label>Email:</label>
    <input type="email" name="email" [ngModel]="email">
    <button type="submit">Submit</button>
</form>
```

In the `MyForm` class we have properties of the same name:

```
@Component({...})
export class MyForm {

    name: string = 'Admin';
    password: string;
    phone: string;
    email: string = 'admin@test.com';

    handle(value) {
        console.log(value);
    }
}
```

The **two-way binding** reflects changes on form control to an existing value of the property and vice versa:

```
<form #myForm="ngForm" (ngSubmit)="handle(myForm.value)">
    <label>User Name:</label>
    <input type="text" name="name" [(ngModel)]="name">
    <p>Hi {{name}}</p>
    <button type="submit">Submit</button>
</form>
```

Track change-state and validity with NgModel

Every time we manually or programmatically manipulate form controls, `NgModel` tracks the state changes that happen on them. Based on that information, `NgModel` updates the control with specific classes. We can use those classes to organize visual feedback to reflect the state of components:

- Class ng-untouched marks the control that was not visited yet
- Class ng-touched marks the visited control
- Class ng-pristine marks the control with the unchanged value
- Class ng-dirty marks the control with the changed value
- Class ng-invalid marks an invalid control
- Class ng-valid marks a valid control

So, we should be able to use the ng-valid or ng-invalid class for feedback to the user about invalid form control. Let's open the ecommerce.css file and add the following styles:

```css
.ng-valid[required], .ng-valid.required   {
  border-left: 2px solid green;
}

.ng-invalid:not(form)   {
  border-left: 2px solid red;
}
```

Now, all controls marked as required fields will show the green left borders while all invalid fields will have the red left borders.

The NgModelGroup directive

We can group the form controls into the control group. The form itself is a control group. It is possible to track the validity state of the controls in the group. Like the control uses a ngModel directive, the group utilizes a NgModelGroup directive:

```html
<form #myForm="ngForm" (ngSubmit)="handle(myForm.value)">
    <fieldset ngModelGroup="user">
        <label>User Name:</label>
        <input type="text" name="name" ngModel>
        <label>Password:</label>
        <input type="password" name="password" ngModel>
    </fieldset>
    <fieldset ngModelGroup="contact">
        <label>Phone:</label>
        <input type="text" name="phone" ngModel>
        <label>Email:</label>
        <input type="email" name="email" ngModel>
    </fieldset>
    <button type="submit">Submit</button>
</form>
```

We can use `fieldset` or `div` elements to group controls. With the help of `ngModelGroup`, we semantically group controls into `user` and `contact` information:

```
{
  user: {
    name: 'User',
    password: 'myPassword'
  },
  contact: {
    phone: '000-111-22-33',
    email: 'test@test.com'
  }
}
```

Model-driven forms

This approach helps to build forms without DOM requirements and makes them easy to test. It doesn't mean we don't need the templates. We need them in conjunction with the model-driven way. We are creating the form in a template and create the form model that represents the DOM structure. We can use two different APIs here:

- The low-level API based on `FormGroup` and `FormControl` classes
- The high-level API based on `FormBuilder` class

Any form is a `FormGroup`. Any `FormGroup` represents a set of `FormControls`. Let's imagine we have the following template:

```
<form>
    <label>User Name:</label>
    <input type="text" name="name">
    <label>Password:</label>
    <input type="password" name="password">
    <label>Phone:</label>
    <input type="text" name="phone">
    <label>Email:</label>
    <input type="email" name="email">
    <button type="submit">Submit</button>
</form>
```

Now create a model for our form:

```
import { Component } from '@angular/core';
import { FormGroup, FormControl } from '@angular/forms';

@Component({...})
```

```
export class MyForm {

  myForm:FormGroup = new FormGroup({
    name: new FormControl('Admin'),
    password: new FormControl(),
    contact: new FormGroup({
      phone: new FormControl(),
      email: new FormControl()
    })
  });
}
```

The myForm represents our form from the template. We create the FormControl for every field of the form and FormGroup for each group. In the first property, we assign the default value to the name. The FormGroup can contain another group and helps to create the hierarchy to replicate the DOM structure.

The FormGroup directive

Now we need to bind the model to the form elements with the help of an Angular 2 FormGroup directive. We need to assign the expression evaluations into the FormGroup instance:

```
<form [formGroup]="myForm">
  ...
</form>
```

The FormControlName directive

The next very important step is to associate the model properties with form elements. We use the FormControlName instead of the name attribute to register the controls:

```
import {Component} from '@angular/core';
import {FormControl, FormGroup, Validators} from '@angular/forms';

@Component({
  selector: 'logon-form',
  template: `
    <form [formGroup]="form" (ngSubmit)="onSubmit()">
      <div *ngIf="userName.invalid">Name is too short. </div>
      <input formControlName="userName" placeholder="User name">
      <input formControlName="password" placeholder="Password">
      <input formControlName="phone" placeholder="Phone">
      <input formControlName="email" placeholder="Email">
```

```
        <button type="submit">Submit</button>
      </form>`
})
export class LogonFormGroup {
  form = new FormGroup({
    userName: new FormControl('', Validators.minLength(2)),
    password: new FormControl('', Validators.minLength(5)),
    phone: new FormControl(''),
    email: new FormControl('')
  });

  get userName(): any { return this.form.get('userName'); }
  get password(): any { return this.form.get('password'); }

  constructor() {
    this.form.setValue({userName: 'admin', password: '12345', phone:
'123-123', email: 'mail@example.com'});
  }

  onSubmit(): void {
    console.log(this.form.value);
    // Will print {userName: 'admin', password: '12345',
    // phone: '123-123', email: 'main@example.com'}
  }
}
```

This directive keeps the `userName` of `FormControl` and `password` from `FormGroup` in sync with DOM elements of the same name. Any changes happen programmatically and the `FormGroup` properties will immediately be written into the DOM elements and vice versa. We use the `get` and `set` methods to access and update the form properties.

The FormGroupName directive

In cases when we have a group of controls, we can use the `FormGroupName` directive to associate a group of controls with a parent `FormGroupDirective` (formally a `FormGroup` selector). You should specify via the name attribute to which nested `FormGroup` element you would like to link, so it might be quite handy to organize a validation of sub-group elements separately:

```
import {Component} from '@angular/core';
import {FormControl, FormGroup, Validators} from '@angular/forms';

@Component({
  selector: 'logon-form',
  template: `
```

```
<form [formGroup]="form" (ngSubmit)="onSubmit()">
  <p *ngIf="userName.invalid">Name is invalid.</p>
  <input formControlName="userName" placeholder="User name">
  <input formControlName="password" placeholder="Password">
  <fieldset formGroupName="contact">
    <input formControlName="phone">
    <input formControlName="email">
  </fieldset>
  <button type="submit">Submit</button>
</form>`
})
export class LogonFormComponent {
  form = new FormGroup({
    userName: new FormControl('', Validators.minLength(2)),
    password: new FormControl('', Validators.minLength(5)),

    contact: new FormGroup({
      phone: new FormControl(''),
      email: new FormControl('')
    })
  });
  get userName(): any { return this.form.get(userName'); }
  get password(): any { return this.form.get('password'); }
  get phone(): any { return this.form.get('contact.phone'); }
  get email(): any { return this.form.get('contact.email'); }

  constructor() {
    this.form.setValue({userName: 'admin', password: '12345',
      phone: '123-123', email: 'mail@example.com'});
  }

  onSubmit() {
    console.log(this.form.value);
    // Will print: {userName: 'admin', password: '12345',
    // phone: '123-123', email: 'main@example.com'}
    console.log(this.form.status);
    // Will print: VALID
  }
}
```

We use the get method of the FormGroup to get access to properties. Individual controls are available via dot syntax as shown in the preceding code.

The FormBuilder class

The FormBuilder creates an AbstractControl form object from a user-specified configuration. So, instead of creating FormGroup, FormControl, and FormArray elements, we build the configuration to construct the model. We need only inject it in the constructor and call the group method to create the form group:

```
import {Component} from '@angular/core';
import {FormBuilder, FormGroup} from '@angular/forms';

@Component({...})
export class MyForm {
  myForm:FormGroup;

  constructor(private formBuilder: FormBuilder) {}

  ngOnInit() {
    this.myForm = this.formBuilder.group({
      name: [],
      password: ,
      contect: this.formBuilder.group({
        phone: [],
        email: []
      })
    });
  }
}
import {Component, Inject} from '@angular/core';
import {FormBuilder, FormGroup, Validators} from '@angular/forms';

@Component({
  selector: 'logon-form',
  template: `
    <form [formGroup]="form">
      <div formGroupName="name">
        <input formControlName="first" placeholder="First">
        <input formControlName="last" placeholder="Last">
      </div>
      <input formControlName="email" placeholder="Email">
      <button>Submit</button>
    </form>
    <form [formGroup]="form" (ngSubmit)="onSubmit()">
      <p *ngIf="userName.invalid">Name is invalid.</p>
      <input formControlName="userName" placeholder="User name">
      <input formControlName="password" placeholder="Password">
      <fieldset formGroupName="contact">
        <input formControlName="phone">
```

```
        <input formControlName="email">
      </fieldset>
      <button type="submit">Submit</button>
    </form>
    <p>Value: {{ form.value | json }}</p>
    <p>Validation status: {{ form.status }}</p>
  `
})
export class LogonFormComponent {
  form: FormGroup;
  constructor(@Inject(FormBuilder) fb: FormBuilder) {
    this.form = fb.group({
      userName: ['', Validators.minLength(2)],
      password: ['', Validators.minLength(5)],

      contact: fb.group({
        phone: [''],
        email: ['']
      })
    });
  }

  get userName(): any { return this.form.get(userName'); }
  get password(): any { return this.form.get('password'); }
  get phone(): any { return this.form.get('contact.phone'); }
  get email(): any { return this.form.get('contact.email'); }

  constructor() {
    this.form.setValue({userName: 'admin', password: '12345',
        phone: '123-123', email: 'mail@example.com'});
  }

  onSubmit() {
    console.log(this.form.value);
    // Will print: {userName: 'admin', password: '12345',
    // phone: '123-123', email: 'main@example.com'}
    console.log(this.form.status);
    // Will print: VALID
  }
}
```

As a result, we have a less verbose code.

A FormControl directive

At the beginning of this chapter, we talked about the formless search form. This form has only one element, and we don't need a `FormGroup` at all. Angular has a `FormControl` directive which doesn't have to be inside `FormGroup`. It only adds it to a single form control:

```
<div class="card">
    <div class="card-header">Quick Shop</div>
    <div class="input-group">
        <input #search type="text" class="form-control"
               placeholder="Search for..."
               [formControl]="seachControl">
        <span class="input-group-btn">
            <button class="btn btn-secondary" type="button"
                [disabled]="disabled"
                (click)="searchProduct(search.value)">Go!</button>
        </span>
    </div>
</div>
```

The updated version of the script looks like this:

```
import {Component} from '@angular/core';
import {Router} from '@angular/router';
import {FormControl} from '@angular/forms';

@Component({
    selector: 'db-product-search',
    templateUrl: 'app/product/product-search.component.html'
})
export class ProductSearchComponent {

    disabled: boolean = true;
    seachControl: FormControl;

    constructor(private router: Router) {}

    ngOnInit() {
        this.seachControl = new FormControl();
        this.seachControl.valueChanges.subscribe((value: string) => {
            this.searchChanged(value);
        });
    }

    searchProduct(value: string) {
        this.router.navigate(['/products'], { queryParams:
```

```
                                            { search: value} });
    }

    searchChanged(value: string) {
        // Update the disabled property depends on value
        if (value) {
            this.disabled = false;
        } else {
            this.disabled = true;
        }
    }
}
```

Built-in validators

I cannot image the form without validators. Angular 2 comes with several built-in validators we can use declaratively as directives or imperatively with `FormControl`, `FormGroup`, or `FormBuilder` classes. Here is a list of them:

- The form control with a `required` validator must have a non-empty value
- The form control with a `minLength` must have the value of the minimum length
- The form control with a `maxLength` must have the value of a maximum length
- The form control with a `pattern` must have the value to match the given regular expression

Here is an example of how to use all of them declaratively:

```
<form novalidate>
  <input type="text" name="name" ngModel required>
  <input type="password" name="password" ngModel minlength="6">
  <input type="text" name="city" ngModel maxlength="10">
  <input type="text" name="phone" ngModel
      pattern="^(\+\d{1,2}\s)?\(?\d{3}\)?[\s.-]\d{3}[\s.-]\d{4}$">
</form>
```

Bear in mind that the `novalidate` is not a part of Angular 2. It is an HTML5 Boolean form attribute. The form will not validate input fields on submission when it presents.

We can use the same validators imperatively with `FormGroup` and `FormControl`:

```
@Component({...})
export class MyForm {
  myForm: FormGroup;
```

```
ngOnInit() {
  this.myForm = new FormGroup({
    name: new FormControl('', Validators.required)),
    password: new FormControl('', Validators.minLength(6)),
    city: new FormControl('', Validators.maxLength(10)),
    phone: new FormControl('', Validators.pattern(
      '[^(\+\d{1,2}\s)?\(?\d{3}\)?[\s.-]\d{3}[\s.-]\d{4}$'))
  });
}
}
```

As mentioned, we can use the `FormBuilder` and less verbose code:

```
@Component({...})
export class MyForm {
  myForm: FormGroup;

  constructor(private fb: FormBuilder) {}

  ngOnInit() {
    this. myForm = this.fb.group({
      name: ['', Validators.required],
      password: ['', Validators.minLength(6)],
      city: ['', Validators.maxLength(10)],
      phone: ['', Validators.pattern(
        '[^(\+\d{1,2}\s)?\(?\d{3}\)?[\s.-]\d{3}[\s.-]\d{4}$')]
    });
  }
}
```

In both scenarios, we must use the `formGroup` directive to associate the `myForm` model with a form element in the DOM:

```
<form novalidate [formGroup]="myForm">
...
</form>
```

Creating a custom validator

Angular 2 has an interface `Validator` that can be implemented by classes that can act as validators:

```
export interface Validator {
    validate(c: AbstractControl): {
        return [key: string]: any
    };
```

```
    }
```

Let's create a function to validate the correctness of a ZIP code. Create the file
`zip.validator.ts` in the `shared` folder with the following code:

```
import {FormControl} from '@angular/forms';

export function validateZip(c: FormControl) {
  let ZIP_REGEXP:RegExp = new RegExp('[A-Za-z]{5}');

  return ZIP_REGEXP.test(c.value) ? null : {
    validateZip: {
      valid: false
    }
  };
}
```

The function `validateZip` expects the `FormControl` as an argument and must return an
error object if the value doesn't match the regular expression or null if the value is valid.
Now, we can import the `validateZip` function and use it in our class:

```
import {Component} from '@angular/core';
import {validateZip} from '../shared/zip.validator';
import {FormBuilder, FormGroup, Validators} from '@angular/forms';

@Component({...})
export class MyForm {
  form: FormGroup;

  constructor(private fb: FormBuilder) {}

  ngOnInit() {
    this.form = this.fb.group({
      name: ['', Validators.required],
      password: ['', Validators.minLength(6)],
      city: ['', Validators.maxLength(10)],
      zip: ['', validateZip]
    });
  }
}
```

Creating a custom validator directive

We can use Angular 2 built-in validators imperatively, or declaratively, with the help of some internal code to execute the validators on form controls. All built-in and custom validators must be registered in a multi-provider dependency token, NG_VALIDATORS. As you will remember from Chapter 6, *Dependency Injection,* the multi-property of the provider allows the injection of multiple values to the same token. Angular injects NG_VALIDATORS, instantiates the form, and performs validation on the form control. Let's create the custom validation directive we can use in template-driven forms. Open zip.valdator.ts and copy and paste the following code:

```
import {FormControl} from '@angular/forms';
import {Directive,forwardRef} from '@angular/core';
import {NG_VALIDATORS} from '@angular/forms';

export function validateZip(c: FormControl) {
  let ZIP_REGEXP:RegExp = new RegExp('[A-Za-z]{5}');

  return ZIP_REGEXP.test(c.value) ? null : {
    validateZip: {
      valid: false
    }
  };
}

@Directive({
  selector: '[validateZip][ngModel],[validateZip][formControl]',
  providers: [
    {provide: NG_VALIDATORS, useExisting: forwardRef(() =>
       ZipValidator), multi: true}
  ]
})
export class ZipValidator {

  validator: Function = validateZip;

  validate(c: FormControl) {
    return this.validator(c);
  }
}
```

And now in the form we can use ZipValidator as a directive:

```
<form novalidate>
  <input type="text" name="name" ngModel required>
  <input type="password" name="password" ngModel minlength="6">
  <input type="text" name="city" ngModel maxlength="10">
```

```
<input type="text" name="zip" ngModel validateZip>
</form>
```

Cart view

The cart view lists all items held in the user's shopping cart. It displays product details for each item and, from this page, a user can:

- Remove all goodies from his or her cart by clicking **Clear Cart**
- Update the quantity for any listed item
- Return to the products list by clicking on **Continue** shopping
- Proceed to checkout by clicking **Checkout**

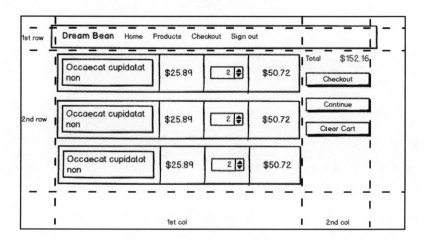

The wireframe of the cart view

The significant part of the cart view is formed with dynamic content laid out in the grid. Look at the first column of the wireframe. There are rows of similar data we can use to display, modify, and validate. For this purpose, we can use Angular static forms to present the content of the shopping cart on the view.

Let's create `cart-view.component.html`. In the first column, we need to print out information about products added to the shopping cart:

```
<div *ngIf="cart.count">
    <form #form="ngForm">
        <div class="table-responsive">
            <table class="table table-sm table-striped
                       table-bordered table-cart">
```

```
                    <tbody>
                        <tr>
                            <td class="font-weight-bold">Title</td>
                            <td class="font-weight-bold">Price</td>
                            <td class="font-weight-bold">Count</td>
                            <td class="font-weight-bold">Amount</td>
                        </tr>
                        <tr *ngFor="let item of cart.items">
                            <td>{{item.product.title}}</td>
                            <td>{{item.product.price |
                                currency:'USD':true:'1.2-2'}}</td>
                            <td>
                                <input type="number"
            name="{{item.product.id}}" min="1"
            [ngModel]="item.count"
            (ngModelChange)="item.count = update($event, item)">
                            </td>
                            <td>{{item.amount |
                                currency:'USD':true:'1.2-2'}}</td>
                        </tr>
                    </tbody>
                </table>
            </div>
        </form>
    </div>
    <div class="emty-cart" *ngIf="!cart.count">The cart is empty!</div>
```

We use the template-driven approach here and assign a form variable to the exposed ngForm. I split the double-way binding format into two statements:

- [ngModel]="item.count": This is used as property binding.
- (ngModelChange)="item.count = update($event, item)": This is used as event binding.

Every time a user updates the count value, this code calls the update method to add or remove products from the cart:

```
import {Component, Input} from '@angular/core';
import {Cart, CartItem, CartService} from './cart.service';

@Component({
    selector: 'db-cart-view',
    templateUrl: 'app/cart/cart-view.component.html'
})
export class CartViewComponent {

    private cart: Cart;
```

```
constructor(private cartService: CartService) {
    this.cart = this.cartService.cart;
}

clearCart() {
    this.cartService.clearCart();
}

update(value, item: CartItem) {
    let res = value - item.count;
    if (res > 0) {
        for (let i = 0; i < res; i++) {
            this.cartService.addProduct(item.product);
        }
    } else if (res < 0) {
        for (let i = 0; i < -res; i++) {
            this.cartService.removeProduct(item.product);
        }
    }
    return value;
}
}
```

Because we have a button, **Clear Cart**, we need to implement the method of the same name in CartService:

```
clearCart() {
    this.cart.items = [];
    this.cart.amount = 0;
    this.cart.count = 0;
}
```

Cart view route definition

I updated the router configuration in the app.routes.ts to reflect the changes necessary to apply to navigate to the CartViewComponent:

```
const routes: Routes = [
  { path: '', redirectTo: 'welcome', pathMatch: 'full' },
  { path: 'welcome', component: WelcomeComponent },
  { path: 'products', component: ProductListComponent },
  { path: 'products/:id', component: ProductViewComponent },
  { path: 'cart', component: CartViewComponent }
];
```

Navigation to cart view

When the user clicks on the **Cart** button in the markup of the Cart Menu, the router uses information from the link to navigate to the cart view:

```
<div class="row">
    <div class="col-md-12">
        <a [routerLink]="['/cart']"
           class="btn btn-primary pull-xs-right btn-cart">
            <i class="fa fa-shopping-cart" aria-hidden="true"></i>
            Cart
        </a>
        <a [routerLink]="['/checkout']"
           class="btn btn-success pull-xs-right btn-cart">
            <i class="fa fa-credit-card" aria-hidden="true"></i>
              Checkout
        </a>
    </div>
</div>
```

We need to update the `CartModule` to add the `CartViewComponent` into the declarations property of `NgModule`:

```
import {NgModule} from '@angular/core';
import {CommonModule} from '@angular/common';
import {FormsModule, ReactiveFormsModule} from '@angular/forms';
import {RouterModule} from '@angular/router';

import {CartMenuComponent} from './cart-menu.component';
import {CartViewComponent} from './cart-view.component';
import {CartService} from './cart.service';

@NgModule({
    imports: [CommonModule, FormsModule, ReactiveFormsModule,
RouterModule],
    declarations: [CartMenuComponent, CartViewComponent],
    exports: [CartMenuComponent, CartViewComponent],
    providers: [CartService]
})
export class CartModule {}
```

Here is the screenshot of the cart view:

Title	Price	Count	Amount
Baguette	$1.50	2	$3.00
Croissants	$0.50	2	$1.00
Pizza	$1.20	1	$1.20
Milk	$1.70	1	$1.70
Cream Cheese	$2.35	1	$2.35
Tuna	$3.45	1	$3.45
Salmon	$4.55	1	$4.55
Oysters	$7.80	1	$7.80
Scalops	$2.70	1	$2.70

Dream Bean Home Products Checkout Sign out — Cart: $27.75 (11 items)

Total **$27.75**

Checkout
Continue Shopping
Clear Cart

Contact Info
0000 Market St, Suite 000, San Francisco, CA 00000, (123) 456-7890, support@dream-bean.com

You can find the source code at `chapter_7/4.ecommerce-cart-view`.

The Checkout View

The Checkout View displays the customer details form, purchase conditions, and the order information. The customer should fill in the form, accept payment, and click on the **Submit** button to start the payment process.

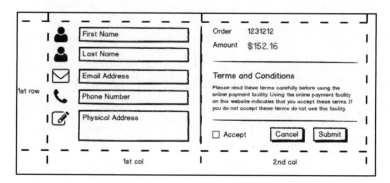

The wireframe of the Checkout View

Create the `checkout` folder and `checkout-view.component.ts` file:

```
import {Component, Input} from '@angular/core';
import {FormGroup, FormBuilder, Validators} from '@angular/forms';

import {Cart, CartItem, CartService} from '../cart/cart.service';

@Component({
    selector: 'db-checkout-view',
    templateUrl: 'app/checkout/checkout-view.component.html'
})
export class CheckoutViewComponent {

    private cart: Cart;
    form: FormGroup;

    constructor(private cartService: CartService,
                private fb: FormBuilder) {
        this.cart = this.cartService.cart;
    }

    ngOnInit() {
        this.form = this.fb.group({
            firstName: ['', Validators.required],
            lastName: ['', Validators.required],
            email: ['', Validators.required],
            phone: ['', Validators.required],
            address: []
        });
    }

    submit() {
        alert('Submitted');
        this.cartService.clearCart();
    }
}
```

I used the model-driven approach here to create the definition of the form. When the user clicks on the **Submit** button it shows the message and clears the shopping cart. Create the `checkout-view.component.html` and copy the following content there:

```
<form [formGroup]="form">
    <div class="form-group row">
        <label for="firstName"
               class="col-xs-2 col-form-label">First Name:</label>
        <div class="col-xs-10">
            <input class="form-control" type="text" value=""
                   id="firstName" formControlName="firstName">
```

```html
        <p [hidden]="form.controls.firstName.valid ||
                    form.controls.firstName.pristine"
                    class="form-text alert-danger">
            The First Name is required
        </p>
    </div>
</div>
<div class="form-group row">
    <label for="lastName" class="col-xs-2 col-form-label">
        Last Name:</label>
    <div class="col-xs-10">
        <input class="form-control" type="text" value=""
            id="lastName" formControlName="lastName">
            <p [hidden]="form.controls.lastName.valid ||
                        form.controls.lastName.pristine"
                        class="form-text alert-danger">
                The Last Name is required
            </p>
    </div>
</div>
<div class="form-group row">
    <label for="email"
        class="col-xs-2 col-form-label">Email:</label>
    <div class="col-xs-10">
        <input class="form-control" type="email" value=""
            id="email">
        <p [hidden]="form.controls.email.valid ||
                    form.controls.email.pristine"
                    class="form-text alert-danger">
            The Email is required
        </p>
    </div>
</div>
<div class="form-group row">
    <label for="phone"
        class="col-xs-2 col-form-label">Phone:</label>
    <div class="col-xs-10">
        <input class="form-control" type="phone" value=""
            id="phone">
        <p [hidden]="form.controls.phone.valid ||
                    form.controls.phone.pristine"
                    class="form-text alert-danger">
            The Phone is required
        </p>
    </div>
</div>
<div class="form-group row">
    <label for="address"
```

```
            class="col-xs-2 col-form-label">Address:</label>
        <div class="col-xs-10">
            <input class="form-control" type="text" value=""
                id="address">
        </div>
    </div>
</form>
```

We have several required fields, so when they are empty Angular 2, via `NgModel`, turns their bars red. That's OK to indicate the problem but not enough to say what exactly is wrong. We can use the validation error message to display if the control is invalid or was not touched. Look at the markup I copied from the preceding code:

```
<input class="form-control" type="text" value=""
        id="firstName" formControlName="firstName">
<p [hidden]="form.controls.firstName.valid ||
            form.controls.firstName.pristine"
            class="form-text alert-danger">
    The First Name is required
</p>
```

We read information about `FormControl` status directly from the form model. We check if the `firstName` field is valid or if it's pristine and show or hide the error message.

At the end, we bind the disabled property of the **Submit** button to the validity of the form, so the user will have the chance to send the data to the server only if all the fields of the form are valid:

```
<div class="col-xs-9">
    <button class="btn btn-primary" (click)="submit()"
        [disabled]="!form.valid">Submit</button>
    <button class="btn btn-secondary"
        [routerLink]="['/products']">Continue Shopping</button>
</div>
```

Checkout view route definition

Update the router configuration in the `app.routes.ts` to add the `CheckoutViewComponent`:

```
const routes: Routes = [
  { path: '', redirectTo: 'welcome', pathMatch: 'full' },
  { path: 'welcome', component: WelcomeComponent },
  { path: 'products', component: ProductListComponent },
  { path: 'products/:id', component: ProductViewComponent },
```

```
    { path: 'cart', component: CartViewComponent },
    { path: 'checkout', component: CheckoutViewComponent }
];
```

Navigation to Checkout View

When the user clicks on the **Checkout** button in the markup of the Cart Menu, the router navigates to the view:

```html
<div class="row">
    <div class="col-md-12">
        <a [routerLink]="['/cart']"
          class="btn btn-primary pull-xs-right btn-cart">
            <i class="fa fa-shopping-cart" aria-hidden="true"></i>
            Cart
        </a>
        <a [routerLink]="['/checkout']"
          class="btn btn-success pull-xs-right btn-cart">
            <i class="fa fa-credit-card" aria-hidden="true"></i>
              Checkout
        </a>
    </div>
</div>
```

The CheckoutViewComponent does not belongs to any module, so we need to add it to the AppModule:

```typescript
/*
 * Components
 */
import {AppComponent}  from './app.component';
import {NavbarComponent} from './navbar/navbar.component';
import {FooterComponent} from './footer/footer.component';
import {WelcomeComponent} from './welcome/welcome.component';
import {CheckoutViewComponent} from
'./checkout/checkout-view.component';

/*
 * Routing
 */
import {routing}  from './app.routes';

@NgModule({
  imports: [BrowserModule, FormsModule, ReactiveFormsModule,
            routing, CartModule, CategoryModule, ProductModule],
  declarations: [AppComponent, NavbarComponent, FooterComponent,
```

```
                    WelcomeComponent, CheckoutViewComponent],
    bootstrap: [AppComponent]
})
export class AppModule { }
```

Here is the screenshot of the Checkout View with validation error messages:

You can find the source code at `chapter_7/5.ecommerce-checkout-view`.

Summary

In this chapter, we discovered how to create forms with Bootstrap 4. We know that Bootstrap supports different layouts from simple to complex.

We investigated the Angular 2 forms module and can now create model-driven and template-driven forms.

We joined all the pieces of our application, and now it looks very nice.

In `Chapter 8`, *Advanced Components*, we will talk about the life cycle of a component and the methods that can be used at different stages of a component. This chapter also discusses how to create a multi-component application. As usual, we will continue to build the project we started to develop in previous chapters.

8

Advanced Components

This chapter describes the lifecycle of components and the methods that can be used at different stages of the lifecycle. In this chapter, we will analyze each stage of this cycle and we will learn how to make the most of the hook methods that are triggered when a component moves from one stage to another. This chapter also discusses how to create a multi-component application. Readers will be able to add more features to the app using Bootstrap.

At the end of the chapter, you will have a solid understanding of:

- Component lifecycle hooks interfaces
- Lifecycle hook methods
- Implementing hook interfaces
- Change detection
- Communication between components

Directives

The directive is the fundamental building block of Angular 2 and allows you to connect behavior to an element in the DOM. There are three kinds of directives:

- Attribute directives
- Structural directives
- Components

A directive is a class with an assigned `@Directive` decorator.

Attribute directives

The attribute directive usually changes the appearance or behavior of an element. We can change several styles or use it to render text bold or italic by binding to a property.

Structural directives

The structural directive changes the DOM layout by adding and removing other elements.

Components

The component is a directive with a template. Every component is made up of two parts:

- The class, where we define the application logic
- The view controlled by the component which interacts with it through an API of properties and methods

A component is a class with an assigned `@Component` decorator.

The directive lifecycle

To develop custom directives for any project, you should understand the basics of the Angular 2 directive lifecycle. A directive goes through a number of distinct stages between when it is created and when it is destroyed:

1. Instantiation
2. Initialization
3. Change detection and rendering
4. Content projection (only for components)
5. After view (only for components)
6. Destruction

The Angular lifecycle hooks

Angular offers directive lifecycle hooks that give us the ability to act when these key moments occur. We can implement one or more of the lifecycle hook interfaces in the Angular `core` library. Each interface has a single method whose name is the interface name prefixed with `ng`. Interfaces are optional for TypeScript and Angular calls the hook methods if they are defined.

> I recommend implementing the lifecycle hook interfaces to directive classes to benefit from strong typing and editor tooling.

Instantiation

The Injector creates the directive instance with the `new` keyword. Each directive may contain, at most, one constructor declaration. If a class contains no constructor declaration, an automatic constructor is provided. The primary purpose of the constructor is to create a new instance of an object and to set initial properties for it. Angular 2 uses constructor for dependency injection, so we can save references to dependent instances for later use:

```
export class CategoryListComponent {

    categories: Category[];

    constructor(private router: Router,
                private categoryService: CategoryService) {
        this.categories = this.categoryService.getCategories();
    }

    filterProducts(category: Category) {
        this.router.navigate(['/products'], {
          queryParams: { category: category.id}
        });
    }
}
```

In the preceding example, the class, `CategoryListComponent`, has a constructor with two parameters referencing on `Router` and `CategoryService`.

Initialization

There are data-bound input properties in every directive, and Angular saves the values of bounded properties at the initialization stage:

```
export class CategorySlideComponent {
    @Input() category: Category;
    @Output() select: EventEmitter<Category> =
        new EventEmitter<Category>();
}
```

The class `CategorySlideComponent` has a category-bounded to the property with the same name in the template.

We can implement `OnInit` and `OnChanges` interfaces to respond accordingly:

- Angular calls the `ngOnChanges` method when data-bound input property values change
- Angular calls the `ngOnInit` method after the first `ngOnChanges` and signals to us that the component has initialized

In the following code, we implement the `OnInit` interface to create the form controls and start listening to its value changes:

```
@Component({
    selector: 'db-product-search',
    templateUrl: 'app/product/product-search.component.html',
    changeDetection: ChangeDetectionStrategy.OnPush
})
export class ProductSearchComponent implements OnInit {

    disabled: boolean = true;
    seachControl: FormControl;

    constructor(private router: Router,
                private changeDetection: ChangeDetectorRef) {}

    ngOnInit() {
        this.seachControl = new FormControl();
        this.seachControl.valueChanges.subscribe((value: string)
            => {
            this.searchChanged(value);
            this.changeDetection.markForCheck();
        });
    }
    ...
```

}

Mostly we relying on the ngOnInit method for the following reasons:

- We need to perform an initialization after the constructor
- To finalize the component setup after Angular sets the input properties

This method is a perfect location for the heavy initialization logic to fetch data from the server or to update the internal state depending on input properties.

Change detection and rendering

This stage intentionally combines two important techniques that Angular 2 uses to bring life to the application. From one side, the change detection module of the framework looks after changes to the internal state of a program. It can detect changes in any data structure, from primitive to an array of objects. From the other side, the rendering part of Angular makes these changes visible in the DOM. Angular combines these two techniques in one stage to minimize the workload because rebuilding DOM trees is expensive.

NgZone service

Most of the time the application state changes because the following asynchronous tasks happen in the application:

- An event triggered by a user or application
- Directive and pipe properties change
- Callback functions calling from AJAX responses
- Callback functions calling from timers

Angular uses NgZone, an execution context from the Zone library, to hook into those asynchronous tasks to detect changes, error handling, and profiling. Zone can perform several significant operations whenever code enters or exits a zone such as:

- Starting or stopping a timer
- Saving a stack trace
- Overriding methods of execution code
- Association of data with individual zones, and so on

Every Angular application has a global zone object wrapping the executable code, but we can use the NgZone service for executing work inside or outside of the Angular zone as well. NgZone is a forked zone that extends the standard zone API and adds some additional functionality to the execution context. Angular uses NgZone to monkey-patch the global asynchronous operations such as setTimeout and addEventListener to update the DOM.

Change detection

Each directive in the Angular framework has a change detector, so we can define how change detection is performed. The hierarchical structure of directives brings change to the detector tree on the stage, so Angular always uses unidirectional data flow as a tool to deliver data from parents to children.

Most of the time, Angular's change detection occurs on properties and updates the view accordingly, independent of the structure of data:

```
@Component({
    selector: 'db-product-card',
    templateUrl: 'app/product/product-card.component.html'
})
export class ProductCardComponent {
    @Input() products: Product[];
    @Output() addToCart: EventEmitter<Product> =
        new EventEmitter<Product>();

    setClasses(product: Product) {
        return {
            'card-danger': product.isSpecial,
            'card-inverse': product.isSpecial
        };
    }

    buy(product: Product) {
      this.addToCart.emit(product);
    }
}
```

Property binding is used to supply data to a product, and event binding is used to inform other components of any updates, which it delegates to the store. The product is a reference to a real object with many fields:

```
export interface Product {
    // Unique Id
```

```
    id: string;
    // Ref on category belongs to
    categoryId: string;
    // The title
    title: string;
    // Price
    price: number;
    // Mark product with special price
    isSpecial: boolean;
    // Description
    desc: string;
    // Path to small image
    imageS: string;
    // Path to large image
    imageL: string;
}
```

Even though any field can be changed, the `product` reference itself stays the same. Angular will perform lots of check changes for properties of directives every time without performance degradation because the framework change detection system can execute hundreds and thousands of them within just a few milliseconds. Sometimes this massive change detection can be quite expensive so we can select a change detection strategy on a per-directive basis.

The internal state of a directive only depends on its input properties, so if these properties have not changed from one check to the next, then the directive doesn't need to be re-rendered. Bear in mind that all JavaScript objects are mutable, so change detection should check all input property fields to re-render a directive when necessary. If we use immutable structures, then change detection can be much faster. Let's have a look how that might happen.

Immutable objects

An immutable object can't change. It always has only one internal state, and if we want to make a change to such an object, we'll always get a new reference to that change.

Change detection strategy

Angular supports the following change detection strategies:

- The `Default` strategy means that the change detector will check the properties deeply per dirty check

- The `OnPush` strategy means that the change detector will check the changes of references on properties per dirty check

We can instruct Angular as to which change detection strategy it can use for specific directives via the `changeDetection` property of the decorator:

```
@Component({
    selector: 'db-product-card',
    templateUrl: 'app/product/product-card.component.html',
    changeDetection: ChangeDetectionStrategy.OnPush
})
export class ProductCardComponent {
...
}
```

The `OnPush` strategy will only work properly if all the values supplied to a directive via input properties are immutable.

 Don't use mutable values with the `OnPush` check detection strategy because it can take the Angular application into an inconsistent or unpredictable state.

Angular automatically triggers the change detector to check the directive in `OnPush` mode if any of the followings happen:

- When any directive input property changes
- Whenever a directive fires an event
- When any observable belonging to this directive fires an event

Triggering change detection programmatically

As mentioned earlier, every directive has a change detector that works automatically. In cases when we need to trigger the change detection programmatically we can use the `ChangeDetectionRef` class. We can call the `markForCheck` method of this class in the place where changes happen, so it marks the path from this directive to the root, to be checked for the next change detection run:

```
import {Component, ChangeDetectionStrategy, ChangeDetectorRef}
    from '@angular/core';
import {Router} from '@angular/router';
import {FormControl} from '@angular/forms';
```

```
@Component({
    selector: 'db-product-search',
    templateUrl: 'app/product/product-search.component.html',
    changeDetection: ChangeDetectionStrategy.OnPush
})
export class ProductSearchComponent {

    disabled: boolean = true;
    seachControl: FormControl;

    constructor(private router: Router,
                private changeDetection: ChangeDetectorRef) {}

    ngOnInit() {
        this.seachControl = new FormControl();
        this.seachControl.valueChanges.subscribe((value: string)
        => {
            this.searchChanged(value);
            this.changeDetection.markForCheck();
        });
    }

    searchProduct(value: string) {
        this.router.navigate(['/products'], {
          queryParams: { search: value}
        });
    }

    searchChanged(value: string) {
        // Update the disabled property depends on value
        if (value) {
            this.disabled = false;
        } else {
            this.disabled = true;
        }
    }
}
```

In the preceding code, we triggered change detection because the string value came from `searchControl` which is always immutable.

As we mentioned, we can implement OnChanges interfaces to detect changes to input the properties of a directive to respond accordingly on:

- Angular calls the ngOnChanges method when a data-bound input property value changes. Most of the time, we do not use this method, but if you need to change the internal state dependence on the input properties, that's the right place to do so.

In the following code, we use the OnChanges interface to look after changes that happen to the category input property:

```typescript
import {Component, Input, OnChanges, SimpleChanges}
    from '@angular/core';
import {Router} from '@angular/router';

import {Category} from './category.service';

@Component({
    selector: 'db-category-card',
    templateUrl: 'app/category/category-card.component.html'
})
export class CategoryCardComponent implements OnChanges {
    @Input() category: Category;

    constructor(private router: Router) {}

    ngOnChanges(changes: SimpleChanges): void {
        for (let propName in changes) {
            let change = changes[propName];
            let current  = JSON.stringify(change.currentValue);
            let previous = JSON.stringify(change.previousValue);
            console.log(`${propName}: currentValue = ${current},
                        previousValue = ${previous}`);
        }
    }

    filterProducts(category: Category) {
        this.router.navigate(['/products'], {
          queryParams: { category: category.id}
        });
    }
}
```

When the value assigns to the `category` the `ngOnChanges` method prints the following information:

```
category: currentValue = {"id":"1", "title":"Bread & Bakery",
"imageL":"http://placehold.it/1110x480",
"imageS":"http://placehold.it/270x171",  "desc":"The best cupcakes,
cookies, cakes, pies, cheesecakes, fresh bread, biscotti, muffins, bagels,
fresh coffee and more."}, previousValue = {}
```

The `SimpleChanges` class keeps the current and previous values of each changed property name, so we can iterate through and log them.

We can implement the `DoCheck` interface in our directive to detect and act upon changes that Angular doesn't catch on its own. Angular calls the `ngDoCheck` method during every change detection cycle. Please use this method with caution, because Angular calls it with enormous frequency, so an implementation must be very lightweight.

Content projection (only for components)

In general, the component is an HTML element and may have content such as text or markup. Angular 2 uses specific entry points marked with a `ng-content` tag to inject the content into the component template. This technique is known as a **content projection** and Angular uses Shadow DOM to achieve that.

Angular 2 takes advantages of web component standards and uses a set of the following technologies:

- Templates for structural DOM changes
- Shadow DOM for styles and DOM encapsulation

We used templates in our project, so now it's time to talk about how Angular uses Shadow DOM in different encapsulation types.

The Shadow DOM allows us to hide DOM logic behind other elements and apply styles in the scope of it. Everything inside the Shadow DOM is unavailable to other components, so we call it encapsulation. In fact, the Shadow DOM is a new technique, and not all web browsers support it, so Angular uses emulation to mimic how Shadow DOM behaves.

There are three encapsulation types in Angular:

- `ViewEncapsulation.None`: Angular doesn't use Shadow DOM and style encapsulation

- `ViewEncapsulation.Emulated`: Angular doesn't use Shadow DOM but emulates the style encapsulation
- `ViewEncapsulation.Native`: Angular uses Native Shadow DOM with all the benefits

We will use the `encapsulation` property of the `@Component` decorator to instruct Angular what encapsulation type to use.

Component styles

In Angular 2, we can apply styles for the whole document and for specific components. That change brings another level of granularity and helps organize more modular designs than regular style sheets. The component styles are different to any global styles. Any selector inside a component style is applied within the scope of this component and its children. The component styles bring the following benefits:

- We can use any name of CSS classes or selectors within the context of the component without fear of getting name conflicts with classes and selectors used in other parts of the application.
- The styles encapsulated in the component are invisible to the rest of the application and cannot be changed elsewhere. We can change or remove the component styles without affecting the styles of the whole application.
- Component styles can be taken to separate files and can co-locate with TypeScript and HTML codes, which makes the project code more structured and organized.

Special selectors

The component styles may include several special selectors. All of these came from the Shadow DOM world.

The :host pseudo-class

Any element that hosts the component calls the host. The only one way to target the styles of the host element from the hosted component is to use the `:host` pseudo-class selector:

```
:host {
  display: block;
  border: 1px solid black;
}
```

In the preceding code snippet, we changed the display and border styles in the parent's component template. In cases when we need to apply the host styles conditionally, use another selector as a parameter of the styles function form:

```
:host(.active) {
  border-width: 3px;
}
```

The preceding styles will apply to the host only when it has an active class.

The :host-context pseudo-class

Just imagine a situation where you are creating a theme for your web application and you would like to apply specific styles to your component, dependent on the presence or absence of other selectors. You could easily implement it with the help of the :host-context function:

```
:host-context(.theme-dark) p {
  background-color: gray;
}
```

The logic behind the preeding code is looking for a theme-dark CSS class in any ancestor from the component host element up to the document root and applying gray to the background-color style to all the paragraph elements inside the component.

The /deep/ selector

The styles of the component apply only to its template. If we need to apply them to all child elements then we need to use the /deep/ selector:

```
:host /deep/ h4 {
  font-weight: bold;
}
```

The /deep/ selector from the preceding code snippet will apply the bold to the font-weight style of all h4 header elements from the component through the child components tree down to all the child component views.

The /deep/ selector has an alias >>> we can use interchangeably for an emulated view encapsulation.

Non-view encapsulation

Angular doesn't use Shadow DOM and style encapsulation for this type. Let's imagine we have a `ParentComponent` in our project:

```
import {Component, Input, ViewEncapsulation} from '@angular/core';

@Component({
  selector: 'my-parent',
  template: `
  <div class="parent">
    <div class="parent__title">
     {{title}}
    </div>
    <div class="parent__content">
        <ng-content></ng-content>
    </div>
  </div>`,
  styles: [`
    .parent {
      background: green;
      color: white;
    }
  `],
  encapsulation: ViewEncapsulation.None
})
export class ParentComponent {
  @Input() title: string;
}
```

In the code of an `AppComponent`, we have the following:

```
import { Component } from '@angular/core';

@Component({
  selector: 'my-app',
  template: `
  <my-parent >
    <my-child></my-child>
  </my-parent>`
})
export class AppComponent { }
```

The `ParentComponent` has its own style and it could override it with another component because it will be applied to the document head later:

```
<head>
  ...
  <style>
    .parent {
      background: green;
      color: white;
    }
  </style>
  <style>.child[_ngcontent-ced-3] {
    background: red;
    color: yellow;
  }</style>
</head>
```

Angular generates the following HTML code which runs in the browser:

```
<my-app>
  <my-parent  ng-reflect->
    <div class="parent">
      <div class="parent__title">
       Parent
      </div>
      <div class="parent__content">
        <my-child _nghost-fhc-3="">
          <div _ngcontent-fhc-3="" class="child">
            Child
          </div>
        </my-child>
      </div>
    </div>
  </my-parent>
</my-app>
```

There is no Shadow DOM involvement, and the application applied styles to the entire document. Angular replaced `ng-content` with the contents of the child component.

Emulated view encapsulation

The emulated view is the default view encapsulation which Angular uses to create components. Angular doesn't use Shadow DOM but emulates the style encapsulation. Let's change the value of the `encapsulation` property to see the difference. Here is the style Angular generates for the emulated view encapsulation:

```
<head>
  ...
  <style>.parent[_ngcontent-xdn-2] {
    background: green;
    color: white;
  }</style><style>.child[_ngcontent-xdn-3] {
    background: red;
    color: yellow;
  }</style>
</head>
```

The style of the parent component looks different and belongs to a specific element. This is how Angular emulates the style encapsulation:

```
<my-app>
    <my-parent  _nghost-xdn-2=""
                ng-reflect->
        <div _ngcontent-xdn-2="" class="parent">
            <div _ngcontent-xdn-2="" class="parent__title">
                Parent
            </div>
            <div _ngcontent-xdn-2="" class="parent__content">
                <my-child _nghost-xdn-3="">
                    <div _ngcontent-xdn-3="" class="child">
                        Child
                    </div>
                </my-child>
            </div>
        </div>
    </my-parent>
</my-app>
```

The markup part of the page looks very similar to the non-view encapsulation.

Native view encapsulation

The native view is one of the simplest encapsulations. It uses the native Shadow DOM to encapsulate content and style. Angular doesn't need to generate any styles for the parent component:

```
<head>
  ...
  <style>.child[_ngcontent-sgt-3] {
      background: red;
      color: yellow;
    }</style>
</head>
```

Now, the styles for the parent component are unavailable for other applications as well as the markup code:

```
<my-app>
  <my-parent  ng-reflect->
    #shadow-root
      <style>.child[_ngcontent-sgt-3] {
        background: red;
        color: yellow;
      }</style>
      <style>.parent {
        background: green;
        color: white;
      }</style>
      <div class="parent">
        <div class="parent__title">
          Parent
        </div>
        <div class="parent__content">
            <my-child _nghost-sgt-3="">
                <div _ngcontent-sgt-3="" class="child">
                    Child
                </div>
            </my-child>
        </div>
      </div>
  </my-parent>
</my-app>
```

If we need to project more than one child content, we can use `ng-content` with a dedicated `select` attribute:

```
import {Component, Input, ViewEncapsulation} from '@angular/core';

@Component({
  selector: 'my-parent',
  template: `
  <div class="parent">
    <div class="parent__title">
     {{title}}
    </div>
    <div class="parent__content">
        <ng-content></ng-content>
    </div>
    <div class="parent__content">
        <ng-content select=".another"></ng-content>
    </div>
  </div>`,
  styles: [`
    .parent {
      background: green;
      color: white;
    }
  `],
  encapsulation: ViewEncapsulation.Native
})
export class ParentComponent {
  @Input() title: string;
}
```

Bear in mind that the `select` attribute expects string values that Angular can use in the `document.querySelector`. In the application component, we have something similar:

```
import { Component } from '@angular/core';

@Component({
  selector: 'my-app',
  template: `
  <my-parent >
    <my-child></my-child>
    <my-child class="another"></my-child>
  </my-parent>`
})
export class AppComponent { }
```

Here is the resulting markup generated by Angular:

```html
<div class="parent">
    <div class="parent__title">
        Parent
    </div>
    <div class="parent__content">
        <my-child _nghost-cni-3="">
            <div _ngcontent-cni-3="" class="child">
                Child
            </div>
        </my-child>
    </div>
    <div class="parent__content">
        <my-child class="another" _nghost-cni-3="">
            <div _ngcontent-cni-3="" class="child">
                Child
            </div>
        </my-child>
    </div>
</div>
```

     You can find the source code at `chapter_8/1.view-encapsulation`.

Now, we know that content projection is the way Angular imports HTML content from outside of the component and inserts it into the designed part of the template. When Angular projects the external content into a component it calls the hook methods of the `AfterContentInit` and `AfterContentChecked` interfaces:

- After Angular projects the external content into its view and the content has been initialized, it calls the `ngAfterContentInit` method
- After Angular checks the bindings of the external content that it has projected into its view, it calls the `ngAfterContentChecked` hook method

We can use any of those to manipulate properties of the content's elements. To organize access to one or many content elements, we must take the parent component's property and decorate it with `@ContentChild` or `@ContentChildren`. Angular uses parameters passing into the decorator to select the content's elements:

- If the parameter is a type, Angular will find an element bounded to a directive or a component with the same type
- If the parameter is a string, Angular will interpret it as a selector to find corresponding elements

Angular sets the value of the decorated property before calling the `ngAfterContentInit` method so that we can access it within the method. Later, when Angular checks and updates the content elements, it calls `ngAfterContentChecked` to inform us that the containing elements were updated. Let's have a look at how can we use it. Here is the child component we will use as a content of the parent component:

```
import {Component, Input} from '@angular/core';

@Component({
  selector: 'my-child',
  template: `
  <div class="child">
    Child is {{status}}
  </div>`,
  styles: [`
    .child {
      background: red;
      color: yellow;
    }
  `]
})
export class ChildComponent {
  @Input() status: string = 'Not Ready';
}
```

We will look at the `status` property of the child component and print out the values on the console from the parent component:

```
import {Component, Input, AfterContentInit, AfterContentChecked,
    ContentChild} from '@angular/core';

import {ChildComponent} from './child.component';

@Component({
  selector: 'my-parent',
  template: `
```

```
<div class="parent">
  <div class="parent__title">
   {{title}}
  </div>
  <div class="parent__content">
      <ng-content></ng-content>
  </div>
</div>`,
styles: [`
  .parent {
    background: green;
    color: white;
  }
`]
})
export class ParentComponent implements
            AfterContentInit, AfterContentChecked {
  @Input() title: string;

  // Query for a CONTENT child of type ChildComponent`
  @ContentChild(ChildComponent) contentChild: ChildComponent;
  ngAfterContentInit() {
    // contentChild is set after the content has been initialized
    console.log('AfterContentInit. Child is',
                this.contentChild.status);
    this.title = 'Parent';
  }

  ngAfterContentChecked() {
    console.log('AfterContentChecked. Child is',
                this.contentChild.status);
    // contentChild is updated after the content has been checked
    if (this.contentChild.status == 'Ready') {
      console.log('AfterContentChecked (no change)');
    } else {
      this.contentChild.status = 'Ready';
    }
  }
}
```

Let's combine them together inside the application component template:

```
import { Component } from '@angular/core';

@Component({
  selector: 'my-app',
  template: `
  <my-parent >
```

```
      <my-child></my-child>
    </my-parent>`
})
export class AppComponent { }
```

Now, run the application and we will get the following login console:

```
AfterContentInit. Child is Not Ready
AfterContentChecked. Child is Not Ready
AfterContentChecked. Child is Ready
AfterContentChecked (no change)
```

You can find the source code for this at `chapter_8/2.after-content`.

After view (only for components)

When Angular finishes the initialization of the component's view and its children's views, it calls the methods of the two hook interfaces, `AfterViewInit` and `AfterViewChecked`. We can use the moment of initialization to update or manipulate view elements:

- Angular calls the `ngAfterViewInit` method when it finishes initialization of the component's view and its children's view
- Angular calls the `ngAfterViewChecked` method after every check on the bindings of the component's view and the view of its children's view

We can use either of these to manipulate view elements. To organize access to one or many view elements, we must have the property in the parent component and decorate it with `@ViewChild` or `@ViewChildren`. Angular uses parameters passing into the decorator to select view elements:

- If the parameter is a type, Angular will find an element bounded to a directive or a component with the same type
- If the parameter is a string, Angular will interpret it as a selector to find corresponding elements

Angular sets the value of the decorated property before calling the `ngAfterViewInit` method. Later, after every check and update of the view elements, it calls `ngAfterViewChecked` to inform us that the viewing elements were updated. Let's have a look at how we can use it. Here is the child component we will use in the template of the parent component:

```
import {Component, Input} from '@angular/core';

@Component({
  selector: 'my-child',
  template: `
  <div class="child">
    Child is {{status}}
  </div>`,
  styles: [`
    .child {
      background: red;
      color: yellow;
    }
  `]
})
export class ChildComponent {
  @Input() status: string = 'Not Ready';
}
```

We are watching the `status` property of the child component and will print out the values on the console from parent component:

```
import {Component, Input, AfterViewInit, AfterViewChecked,
        ViewChild, ChangeDetectionStrategy} from '@angular/core';

import {ChildComponent} from './child.component';

@Component({
  selector: 'my-parent',
  changeDetection: ChangeDetectionStrategy.OnPush,
  template: `
  <div class="parent">
    <div class="parent__title">
      {{title}}
    </div>
    <div class="parent__content">
      <my-child></my-child>
    </div>
  </div>`,
  styles: [`
    .parent {
```

```
          background: green;
          color: white;
        }
    `]
})
export class ParentComponent implements
                AfterViewInit, AfterViewChecked {
    @Input() title: string;

    // Query for a VIEW child of type `ChildComponent`
    @ViewChild(ChildComponent) viewChild: ChildComponent;

    ngAfterViewInit() {
      // viewChild is set after the view has been initialized
      console.log('AfterViewInit. Child is', this.viewChild.status);
      this.title = 'Parent';
    }

    ngAfterViewChecked() {
      console.log('AfterViewChecked. Child is',
                  this.viewChild.status);
      // viewChild is updated after the view has been checked
      if (this.viewChild.status == 'Ready') {
        console.log('AfterViewChecked (no change)');
      } else {
        this.viewChild.status = 'Ready';
      }
    }
}
```

Bear in mind that we use `OnPush` change detection in this code to prevent cycling invocation of the `ngAfterViewChecked` method. Here is the application component template:

```
import { Component } from '@angular/core';

@Component({
  selector: 'my-app',
  template: `
  <my-parent >
  </my-parent>`
})
export class AppComponent { }
```

Now, run application and we will get the following login console:

```
AfterViewInit. Child is Not Ready
AfterViewChecked. Child is Not Ready
```

```
AfterViewChecked. Child is Ready
AfterViewChecked (no change)
```

You can find the source code for this at the `chapter_8/3.after-view`.

Parent to child communications

Organizing the communication between parent and child components is not trivial, so let's talk about different techniques we can use to achieve that.

Parent to child communication via input binding

Every directive may have one or more input properties. We can bind any property of a child component with static string or the parent component variables to organize communication between them. Here is the child component:

```
import {Component, Input, Output, EventEmitter, OnInit }
        from '@angular/core';

@Component({
  selector: 'my-child',
  template: `
  <div class="child">
    {{desc}} belongs to {{parent}} with {{emoji}}
  </div>`,
  styles: [`
    .child {
      background: red;
      color: yellow;
    }
  `]
})
export class ChildComponent {
  @Input() desc: string;
  @Input('owner') parent: string;
  private _emoji: string;  @Input() set emoji(value: string) {
    this._emoji = value || 'happy';
  }
  get emoji(): string {
    return this._emoji;
```

```
    }

@Output() status: EventEmitter<string> =
            new EventEmitter<string>();

  ngOnInit(): void {
    this.status.emit('Ready');
  }
}
```

It has three input properties marked with @Input decorators:

- The property desc is decorated by its natural name
- The property parent is decorated with an alias name so that the parent component will see it by name owner
- The property emoji is a combination of getter/setter methods so that we can add some logic to assign values to a private variable

It has one output property status to communicate from child to parent. I intentionally added an OnInit hook interface so that we can send a message back to the parent after the creation of a child. Here is the parent component:

```
import {Component, Input} from '@angular/core';

@Component({
  selector: 'my-parent',
  template: `
  <div class="parent">
    <div class="parent__title">
     {{title}}. Child is {{status}}
    </div>
    <div class="parent__content">
        <my-child [desc]="'Child'"
                  [owner]="title"
                  [emoji]="'pleasure'"
                  (status)="onStatus($event)" ></my-child>
    </div>
  </div>`,
  styles: [`
    .parent {
      background: green;
      color: white;
    }
  `]
})
export class ParentComponent {
```

```
@Input() title: string;
status: string;

onStatus(value: string) {
  this.status = value;
}
}
```

The parent component sets all the input properties of the child and listens to the `status` event in the `onStatus` method. After creation, the child component emits the status event and the parent component prints that information close to the title.

Parent. Child is Ready
Child belongs to Parent with pleasure

You can find the source code for this at `chapter_8/4.parent-child-input-binding`.

Parent to child communication via a local variable

The parent element has no access to properties or methods of the child component. We can create a template reference variable within the parent template to organize access to child component class members:

```
import {Component, Input} from '@angular/core';

@Component({
  selector: 'my-parent',
  template: `
  <div class="parent" [ngInit]="child.setDesc('You are mine')">
    <div class="parent__title">
      {{title}}
    </div>
    <div class="parent__content">
        <my-child #child></my-child>
    </div>
  </div>`,
  styles: [`
    .parent {
      background: green;
      color: white;
    }
```

```
  `]
})
export class ParentComponent {
  @Input() title: string;
}
```

In the preceding parent component, we created the `child` local template variable and used it within the `NgInit` directive to call the `setDesc` method of the child component:

```
import {Component, Input} from '@angular/core';

@Component({
  selector: 'my-child',
  template: `
  <div class="child">
    {{desc}}
  </div>`,
  styles: [`
    .child {
      background: red;
      color: yellow;
    }
  `]
})
export class ChildComponent {
  @Input() desc: string;

  setDesc(value: string) {
    this.desc = value;
  }
}
```

There is a `NgInit` directive we used to initialize the `desc` property of the child component:

```
import {Directive, Input} from '@angular/core';

@Directive({
  selector: '[ngInit]'
})
export class NgInit {
  @Input() ngInit;

  ngOnInit() {
    if(this.ngInit) {
      this.ngInit();
    }
  }
}
```

You can find the source code for this at
`chapter_8/5.parent-child-local-variable`.

Parent-child communication via a call to ViewChild

When we need to have access to the child component from the parent we can use
`AfterViewInit` and `AfterViewChecked` hooks. Angular calls them after it creates the
child views of a component. Here is the child component:

```
import {Component, Input} from '@angular/core';

@Component({
  selector: 'my-child',
  template: `
  <div class="child">
    {{desc}}
  </div>`,
  styles: [`
    .child {
      background: red;
      color: yellow;
    }
  `]
})
export class ChildComponent {
  @Input() desc: string;
}
```

The parent component imports the necessary classes and implements the `AfterViewInit`
interface:

```
import {Component, Input, AfterViewInit, ViewChild}
  from '@angular/core';

import {ChildComponent} from './child.component';

@Component({
  selector: 'my-parent',
  template: `
  <div class="parent">
    <div class="parent__title">
```

```
      {{title}}
    </div>
    <div class="parent__content">
        <my-child></my-child>
    </div>
  </div>`,
  styles: [`
    .parent {
      background: green;
      color: white;
    }
  `]
})
export class ParentComponent implements AfterViewInit {
  @Input() title: string;

  @ViewChild(ChildComponent)
  private child: ChildComponent;
  ngAfterViewInit()
  {
    this.child.desc = "You are mine";
  }
}
```

We are injecting the child component into the parent with the help of the `@ViewChild` decorator introduced previously. The `AfterViewInit` interface is very important in this scenario because the `child` component is unavailable until the Angular displays the parent view and calls the `ngAfterViewInit` method.

 You can find the source code for this at `chapter_8/6.parent-child-viewchild`.

Parent-child communication via a service

Another possible way to organize parent-child communication is via a common service. We assign the service to a parent component and lock the scope of the service instance between this parent component and its children. No single component outside of this subtree will have access to the service or their communications. Here, the child component has access to the service injectable via the constructor:

```
import {Component, Input, OnDestroy} from '@angular/core';
import {Subscription} from 'rxjs/Subscription';
import {CommonService} from './common.service';
```

```
@Component({
  selector: 'my-child',
  template: `
  <div class="child">
    {{desc}}
  </div>`,
  styles: [`
    .child {
      background: red;
      color: yellow;
    }
  `]
})
export class ChildComponent implements OnDestroy {
  @Input() desc: string;

  subscription: Subscription;

  constructor(private common: CommonService) {
    this.subscription = this.common.childQueue.subscribe(
      message => {
        this.desc = message;
      }
    );
  }

  ngOnDestroy() {
    // Clean after yourself
    this.subscription.unsubscribe();
  }
}
```

We run a subscription on messages coming from the parent component in the constructor. Please be careful of the OnDestroy interface at implementation. The code in the ngOnDestroy method is a memory-leak guard step. The parent component has a CommonService registered as a provider and injected through the constructor:

```
import {Component, Input, OnInit} from '@angular/core';
import {CommonService} from './common.service';

@Component({
  selector: 'my-parent',
  template: `
  <div class="parent">
    <div class="parent__title">
      {{title}}
    </div>
    <div class="parent__content">
```

```
        <my-child></my-child>
    </div>
  </div>`,
  styles: [`
    .parent {
      background: green;
      color: white;
    }
  `],
  providers: [CommonService]
})
export class ParentComponent implements OnInit {
  @Input() title: string;

  constructor(private common: CommonService) {
    this.common.parentQueue.subscribe(
      message => {
        this.title = message;
      }
    );
  }

  ngOnInit() {
    this.common.toChild("You are mine");
  }
}
```

We don't need the memory-leak guard step here because the parent component controls the lifetime of the registered provider.

You can find the source code for this at `chapter_8/7.parent-child-service`.

Destroying

This stage is the last one whilst a directive still exists. We can implement the `OnDestroy` interface to catch this moment:

- Angular calls the `ngOnDestroy` method before destroying the directive
- Angular adds cleanup logic to this method to unsubscribe observables and detach event handlers to avoid memory leaks

We can notify another component (parent or sibling) about the fact that the directive will disappear soon. We must free allocated resources, unsubscribe from observables and DOM event listeners, and unregister all callbacks from services.

Summary

In this chapter, we discovered the lifecycle of components and the methods that can be used at different stages of them. We learned that Angular has interfaces with hook methods and how to make the most of the hook methods that are triggered when a component moves from one stage to another.

We unveiled how Angular change detection works and how we can manage it. We discussed how to organize communication between components.

In Chapter 9, *Communication and Data Persistence*, we will work at HTTP requests and store data on the Firebase platform. We will learn how to use the built-in HTTP library to work with endpoints. Also, we will learn how to use observables to work with data. At the end of the chapter, we will learn how to work with Firebase as the persistence layer of the app. As usual, we will continue to build the project that we started to develop in previous chapters.

9

Communication and Data Persistence

This chapter is about working with HTTP requests and storing data on the server. We will learn how to use the built-in HTTP library to work with endpoints. Also, we will learn how to use **Observables** to work with data. At the end of the chapter, we will learn how to work with Firebase as the persistence layer of the app. As usual, we will continue to build the project we started to develop in previous chapters.

At the end of the chapter, you will have a solid understanding of the following:

- HttpModule
- Creating connections
- Observables
- Installing Firebase tools
- Connecting to Firebase

Let's begin:

1. Open the Terminal, create the folder `ecommerce`, and move into the folder.
2. Copy the contents of the project from the folder `chapter_9/1.ecommerce-seed` into the new project.
3. Run the following script to install the npm modules:

   npm install

4. Start the TypeScript watcher and lite server with the following command:

   npm start

This script opens the web browser and navigates to the welcome page of the project.

Client to server communication

The web browsers and servers function as a **client-server system**. In general, the web server keeps the data and shares it with any number of web browsers on request. The web browsers and servers must have a common language, and they must follow rules so that both know what to expect. The language and rules of communication are defined in communications protocols. The **Transmission Control Protocol** (**TCP**) is a standard that defines how to establish and maintain a network conversation via which application programs can exchange data. TCP works with the **Internet Protocol** (**IP**), which defines how computers send packets of data to each other. Together, TCP and IP are the basic rules defining the Internet. The web browsers and servers communicate via **TCP/IP** stack. To send data over a TCP/IP network requires four steps or layers:

- The **Application layer** encodes the data being sent. It does not care about how the data gets between two points, and it knows very little about the status of the network. Applications pass data to the next layer in the TCP/IP stack and then continue to perform other functions until a reply is received.
- The **Transport layer** splits the data into manageable chunks, and adds port number information. The Transport Layer uses port numbers for addressing, which range from 1 to 65,535. Port numbers from 0 to 1,023 are called **well-known ports**. The numbers below 256 are reserved for public services that run on the Application layer.
- The **Internet layer** adds IP addresses stating where the data is from and where it is going. It's the *glue* that holds networking together. It permits the sending, receiving, and routing of data.
- The **Link layer** adds **Media Access Control** (**MAC**) address information to specify which hardware device the message came from, and which hardware device the message is going to. The MAC address is fixed at the time the interface was manufactured and cannot be changed.

All client-server protocols operate in the Application layer. Application-layer protocol states the basic communication patterns. For the data exchange format to be formalized, the server implements an **Application Program Interface** (**API**), such as a web service. The API is an abstraction layer for resources like databases and custom software. The **Hypertext Transfer Protocol** (**HTTP**) is the Application-layer protocol that implements the **World Wide Web** (**WWW**). While the web itself has many different facets, the primary purpose of HTTP is to transfer hypertext documents and other files from web servers to web clients.

Web API

The interaction between web clients and servers' assets happens via the defined interface called the **Web API**. It is a server architectural approach providing programmable interfaces to a set of services serving different types of consumers. The Web API is typically defined as a set of HTTP request and response messages. In general, the structure of the reply message is represented in an **Extensible Markup Language** (**XML**) or **JavaScript Object Notation** (**JSON**) format.

In the epoch of Web 1.0, the Web API was synonymous for **Simple Object Access Protocol** (**SOAP**) based web services and **Service-Oriented Architecture** (**SOA**). In Web 2.0, this term is moving towards **Representational State Transfer** (**REST**) style web resources and **Resource-Oriented Architecture** (**ROA**).

REST

REST is an architectural style of the World Wide Web and is used for design networked applications. There is not a standard or W3C recommendation for REST. The term REST was introduced and defined in 2000 by *Roy Fielding* in his doctoral dissertation. Later, he used REST to design HTTP 1.1 and **Uniform Resource Identifiers** (**URIs**).

REST as a programming approach is:

- *Platform-independent* so that the server can be installed on Linux, Windows, and so on
- *Language-independent*, so we can use C#, Java, JavaScript, and so on
- Standards-based and can run on top of HTTP standards

REST uses simple HTTP protocol to make calls between clients and servers rather than using a complicated mechanism such as a **Remote Procedure Call** (**RPC**), **Common Object Request Broker Architecture** (**CORBA**), or **SOAP**. Any application calls RESTful makes conforms to the constraints of REST:

- The **client-server constraint** means that the client and server are separated so that they may be replaced and developed independently
- The client and server communication is based on **stateless constraint**, so there is no client context stored on the server between requests and each request contains all the information necessary to service the request
- The **cacheable constraint** defines whether the server responses must implicitly or explicitly mark themselves as cacheable, or not

- To comply with **layer systems constraints**, the client and server use the layered architecture to improve the overall system capability and scalability
- The server can follow the **code on demand optional constraints** to customize the functionality of the client by the transfer of executable code such as JavaScript

RESTful applications use HTTP requests for all four **CRUD** (**Create, Read, Update,** and **Delete**) operations. REST doesn't include security, encryption, session management, and so on but we can build them on the top of HTTP.

Let's have a look at a typical endpoint we used to read the product: `http://localhost:9000/product/123`.

There is just a URL sent to the server using a simple HTTP GET request. The `product` here is the resource in the URL. There is a standard convention in REST design to use nouns to identify resources. REST can handle more complex requests, like:
`http://localhost:3000/products?category=1`.

If necessary, we can utilize the HTTP `POST` method to send long parameters or binaries inside the POST body.

REST response formats

For most of the time, the server responds with XML, **Comma-Separated Values** (**CSV**), or JSON formats in REST. The choice depends on the format's advantages:

- XML is easily expandable and type safe
- CSV is very compact
- JSON is easy to parse

REST and AJAX

We use the **Asynchronous JavaScript and XML** (**AJAX**) client-side technique to create asynchronous web applications. AJAX uses `XMLHttpRequest` objects to send requests to the server to dynamically change the web page. The AJAX and REST requests are similar.

REST API design guidelines

What is the next step we need to take to create the proper REST API? That question has no simple answer, and since there's no one widely adopted standard that works in all cases I recommend we get the answer from well-known sources such as Microsoft REST API Guidelines, available at: `https://github.com/Microsoft/api-guidelines`.

The HttpModule

So far, we have developed only the frontend of our application and it is therefore pretty useless. We need somewhere to store our products and categories so that we can fetch them later on. To do this, we're going to connect to a server, which is going to house a RESTful API that serves up JSON.

Out of the box, Angular 2 includes `HttpModule` to organize some low-level methods of fetching and posting our data.

To use the new `HttpModule` in our project, we have to import it as a separate add-on module called `@angular/http`, shipped in a separate script file as part of the Angular npm package. We import the `@angular/http` in the `systemjs.config.js` file configured `SystemJS` to load that library when we need it:

```
var ngPackageNames = [
    'common',
    'compiler',
    'core',
    'forms',
    'http',
    'platform-browser',
    'platform-browser-dynamic',
    'router',
    'router-deprecated',
    'upgrade',
];
```

Our application will access `HttpModule` services from anywhere in the application, so we should register them by adding the `HttModule` to the list of `imports` of the `AppModule`. After the bootstrap, all the `HttpModule` services become available to the root level of `AppComponent`:

```
import {NgModule} from '@angular/core';
import {BrowserModule} from '@angular/platform-browser';
import {FormsModule, ReactiveFormsModule} from '@angular/forms';
```

```
import {HttpModule} from '@angular/http';

/**
 * Modules
 */
import {CartModule} from './cart/cart.module';
import {CategoryModule} from './category/category.module';
import {ProductModule} from './product/product.module';

/*
 * Components
 */
import {AppComponent}  from './app.component';
import {NavbarComponent} from './navbar/navbar.component';
import {FooterComponent} from './footer/footer.component';
import {WelcomeComponent} from './welcome/welcome.component';
import {CheckoutViewComponent} from
'./checkout/checkout-view.component';

/*
 * Routing
 */
import {routing}  from './app.routes';

@NgModule({
   imports: [HttpModule, BrowserModule, FormsModule,
             ReactiveFormsModule, routing, CartModule,
             CategoryModule, ProductModule],
   declarations: [AppComponent, NavbarComponent, FooterComponent,
                  WelcomeComponent, CheckoutViewComponent],
   bootstrap: [AppComponent]
})
export class AppModule { }
```

The in-memory Web API

Because we don't have a real web server that can handle our requests, we will use a mock service to mimic the behavior of the real one. That approach has the following advantages:

- It rapidly stubs out API designs and new endpoints. **Service mocking** gives you the ability to use **Test Driven Development** (**TDD**).
- It shares APIs between team members. We won't have downtime whilst the frontend team waits for the other team to finish. This approach makes the financial argument for mocking unusually high.

- It takes control of simulated responses and performance conditions. We can use mocks to create a proof of concept, as a wireframe, or as a demo, so they can be very cost efficient to use.

It has disadvantages that we should know about:

- We have to do double the work and sometimes this can mean quite a lot
- It has deployment constraints if you need to deploy it somewhere
- The mocking code is subject to bugs
- The mock is only a representation of what it is mocking, and it can misrepresent the real service

The in-memory Web API is an optional service in the `angular-in-memory-web-api` library. It's not part of Angular 2, so we need to install it as a separate npm package and register for module loading by `SystemJS` inside the `systemjs.config.js` file:

```
// map tells the System loader where to look for things
var map = {
    'app':        'app',
    'rxjs':       'node_modules/rxjs',
    'angular-in-memory-web-api':
                   'node_modules/angular-in-memory-web-api',
    '@angular': 'node_modules/@angular'
};


// packages tells the System loader how to load when no filename
// and/or no extension
var packages = {
    'app':  { main: 'main.js',  defaultExtension: 'js' },
    'rxjs': { defaultExtension: 'js' },
    'angular-in-memory-web-api':
            { main: 'index.js', defaultExtension: 'js' },
};
```

Next, we need to create an `InMemoryDataService` class which implements `InMemoryDbService`, to create an in-memory database:

```
import {InMemoryDbService} from 'angular-in-memory-web-api';

import {Category} from './category/category.service';
import {Product} from './product/product.service';

export class InMemoryDataService implements InMemoryDbService {
  createDb() {
    let categories: Category[] = [
```

```
            { id: '1', title: 'Bread & Bakery',
              imageL: 'http://placehold.it/1110x480',
              imageS: 'http://placehold.it/270x171',
              desc: 'The best cupcakes, cookies, cakes, pies,
                    cheesecakes, fresh bread, biscotti, muffins,
                    bagels, fresh coffee and more.' },
            { id: '2', title: 'Takeaway',
              imageL: 'http://placehold.it/1110x480',
              imageS: 'http://placehold.it/270x171',
              desc: 'It's consistently excellent, dishes are superb
                    and healthily cooked with high quality
                    ingredients.' },
                        // ...
    ];

        let products: Product[] = [
            // Bakery
            { id: '1', categoryId: '1', title: 'Baguette',
              price: 1.5, isSpecial: false,
              imageL: 'http://placehold.it/1110x480',
              imageS: 'http://placehold.it/270x171',
              desc: 'Great eaten fresh from oven. Used to make sub
              sandwiches, etc.' },
            { id: '2', categoryId: '1', title: 'Croissants',
              price: 0.5, isSpecial: true,
              imageL: 'http://placehold.it/1110x480',
              imageS: 'http://placehold.it/270x171',
              desc: 'A croissant is a buttery, flaky,
                    viennoiserie-pastry named for its well-known
                    crescent shape.' },
            //
        ];
        return {
          categories,
          products
        };
    }
  }
```

The `createDb` method should create a *database* object hash whose keys are collection names and whose values are arrays of the group objects. It is safe to call it again because it returns new arrays with new objects. That allows `InMemoryBackendService` to morph the arrays and objects without touching the source data. I moved the datasets from `ProductService` and `CategoryService` in this file.

Analogous with the `HttModule`, we are importing the `InMemoryWebApiModule` and `InMemoryDataService` into the list of `imports` of the `AppModule`. They replace the default `Http` client backend within in-memory Web API alternative services:

```
import {HttpModule} from '@angular/http';
// Imports for loading & configuring the in-memory web api
import {InMemoryWebApiModule} from 'angular-in-memory-web-api';
import {InMemoryDataService}  from './in-memory-data.service';
And finally, we need to link the InMemoryWebApiModule to use the
InMemoryDataService:
@NgModule({
  imports: [HttpModule,
            InMemoryWebApiModule.forRoot(InMemoryDataService),
            BrowserModule, FormsModule, ReactiveFormsModule,
```

The method `forRoot` prepares the in-memory Web API in the root application module to create an in-memory database in the moment of bootstrapping. It has a second parameter of `InMemoryBackendConfigArgs` type and keeps `InMemoryBackend` configuration options such as delay (in milliseconds) to simulate latency, host for this service, and so on.

Now everything is ready to change both `ProductService` and `CategoryService` to start them using an `HTTP` service.

The HTTP client

The Angular **HTTP client** communicates with a server via AJAX requests using an HTTP protocol. Components of our project will never talk directly to HTTP client services. We delegate data access to service classes. Let's update the imports in `ProductService` as shown in the following:

```
import {Injectable} from '@angular/core';
import {Headers, Http, Response} from '@angular/http';
import 'rxjs/add/operator/toPromise';
```

Next, fetch the products with the `Http` service:

```
getProducts(category?:string, search?:string):Promise<Product[]> {
  let url = this.productsUrl;
  if (category) {
    url += `/?categoryId=${category}`;
  } else if (search) {
    url += `/?title=${search}`;
  }
  return this.http
```

```
      .get (url)
      .toPromise()
      .then ((response:Response) => response.json().data as Product[])
      .catch (this.handleError);
  }
```

As you see, we are using a standard HTTP GET request to fetch the set of products. The `InMemoryWebApiModule` quite cleverly understands the query parameters in the requested URL. Here, the `ProductGridComponent` utilizes the `ProductService` to display our grid of products on the web page:

```
@Component ({
    selector: 'db-product-grid',
    templateUrl: 'app/product/product-grid.component.html'
})
export class ProductGridComponent implements OnInit {
    products: any = [];

    constructor(private route: ActivatedRoute,
                private productService: ProductService,
                private cartService: CartService) {}

    ngOnInit(): void {
        this.route
            .queryParams
            .subscribe (params => {
                let category: string = params['category'];
                let search: string = params['search'];
                // Clear view before request
                this.products = [];
                // Return filtered data from getProducts function
                this.productService.getProducts(category, search)
                .then((products: Product[]) => {
                    // Transform products to appropriate data
                    // to display
                    this.products = this.transform(products);
                });
            });
    }
    //
}
```

The `products` property here is just an array of products. We use a simple `NgFor` directive to iterate through them:

```
<db-product-card *ngFor="let row of products"
    [products]="row" (addToCart)="addToCart($event)">
</db-product-card>
```

The source code changes in `CategoryService` a bit differently because of the nature of the categories data. The set of categories is static, so we don't need to fetch them every time and can keep them in the cache inside `CategoryService`:

```
@Injectable()
export class CategoryService {
    // URL to Categories web api
    private categoriesUrl = 'app/categories';
    // We keep categories in cache variable
    private categories: Category[] = [];

    constructor(private http: Http) {}

    getCategories(): Promise<Category[]> {
      return this.http
          .get(this.categoriesUrl)
          .toPromise()
          .then((response: Response) => {
             this.categories = response.json().data as Category[];
             return this.categories;
          })
          .catch(this.handleError);
    }

    getCategory(id: string): Category {
        for (let i = 0; i < this.categories.length; i++) {
            if (this.categories[i].id === id) {
                return this.categories[i];
            }
        }
        return null;
    }

    private handleError(error: any): Promise<any> {
        window.alert(`An error occurred: ${error}`);
        return Promise.reject(error.message || error);
    }
}
```

In the `getCategory` method, we can easily find the category by ID because we simply fetch it from the cache.

The HTTP Promises

Carefully look at how we return the data from an HTTP GET request. We use the toPromise method just after the get method of the Http class:

```
getCategories(): Promise<Category[]> {
    return this.http
        .get(this.categoriesUrl)
        .toPromise()
        .then((response: Response) => {
            this.categories = response.json().data as Category[];
            return this.categories;
        })
        .catch(this.handleError);
}
```

So, why do we need this method and what exactly does it do?

Almost all the Http service methods return a RxJS Observable. Observables are a powerful way to manage asynchronous data flows. To convert a RxJS Observable into a Promise, we use the toPromise operator. It just fetches a single chunk of data and returns it immediately. Before using the toPromise operator, we need to import it from RxJS implicitly because the library is quite extensive and we should include only those features that we need:

```
import 'rxjs/add/operator/toPromise';
```

Let's talk about Observable and why Http uses them everywhere.

 You can find the source code for this at chapter_9/2.ecommerce-promise.

RxJS library

The **RxJS** is a project actively developing by Microsoft in collaboration with many open source developers. There is a set of libraries organized as an API for asynchronous and event-based programming. We use Observables to represent the asynchronous data streams. There are many operators to query and Schedulers to parameterize the concurrency in them. In short–the RxJS is a combination of Observer and Iterator patterns and functional programming.

Before use we can import all core modules:

```
import * as Rx from 'rxjs/Rx';
```

Better import only necessary functionality if you care about the size of your application:

```
import { Observable } from 'rxjs/Observable';
import 'rxjs/add/operator/map';

Observable.of(1,2,3).map(x => x * x); // Result: [1, 4, 9]
```

The RxJs is huge, and I suggest to refer to the official website to learn more: `http://reactivex.io`

Observables versus promises

In our days the **Observables** are a proposed feature for JavaScript version ES2016 (ES7), so we use the RxJS as the polyfill library to bring them into the project until the next new version of JavaScript is released. Angular 2 has basic support for Observables and we use RxJS to extend this functionality. Promises and Observables bring the abstractions that help us deal with the asynchronous nature of our applications with several key differences:

- Observables emit multiple values over time, in contrast to Promises which can return only one value or error
- Observables are treated like arrays and allow us to use operators, collection-like methods to manipulate values
- Observables can be cancelled
- Observables can be retried with one of the retry operators

So we use `toPromise` specially to convert the stream of data from a request into a single value. Do we really need that? I've made some changes in the project to show you how easy it is to use Observables in Angular 2 applications. Just have a look at the modified version of `ProductService`:

```
getProducts(category?:string,search?:string):Observable<Product[]>{
  let url = this.productsUrl;
  if (category) {
    url += `/?categoryId=${category}`;
  } else if (search) {
    url += `/?title=${search}`;
  }
  return this.http
    .get(url)
```

```
        .map((response:Response) => response.json().data as Product[])
        .catch(this.handleError);
}

getProduct(id: string): Observable<Product> {
    return this.http
        .get(this.productsUrl + `/${id}`)
        .map((response: Response) => response.json().data as Product)
        .catch(this.handleError);
}
```

We use several transformation operators from the RxJS package in the preceding code, so don't forget to import them from the package. There are many operators in RxJS helping us to organize different sorts of transformations:

- The `map` operator transforms the items by applying a function to each of them.
- The `flatMap`, `concatMap`, and `flatMapIterable` operators transform the items into Observables or Iterables and flatten them into one.
- The `switchMap` operator transforms the items into Observables. The items emitted from the most-recently transformed Observable will be mirrored.
- The `scan` operator sequentially applies a function to each emitted item to emit only successive values.
- The `groupBy` operator helps divide and organize Observables by key to emit the groups of items from the original one.
- The `buffer` operator combines emitted items into bundles. It emits bundles instead of emitting one item at a time.
- The **cast** casts all items from the source Observable into a particular type before reemitting them.

RxJS is really big and I recommend starting to learn more about it from the official website: `https://github.com/Reactive-Extensions/RxJS`.

When successful a request returns an instance of the `Response` class. The response data is in JSON string format, so we must parse that string into JavaScript objects which we do by calling the `json` method of the `Response` class. As usual, we should deal with errors because we have to be prepared for something to go wrong, as it surely will. We catch errors by calling the `handleError` method of our class. Bear in mind, we must transform the error into a user-friendly message, and return it in a new, failed observable via `Observable.throw`:

```
private handleError(error: any): Promise<any> {
    window.alert(`An error occurred: ${error}`);
    return Promise.reject(error.message || error);
```

```
}
```

There are two different techniques to display Observable data on the web page. The first approach is organizing a subscription of Observable data as implemented in:

```
ProductViewComponent:
@Component({
    selector: 'db-product-view',
    templateUrl: 'app/product/product-view.component.html'
})
export class ProductViewComponent implements OnInit {

    product: Product;

    constructor(private route: ActivatedRoute,
                private productService: ProductService,
                private cartService: CartService) { }
    ngOnInit(): void {
        this.route
            .params
            .subscribe(params => {
                // Get the product id
                let id: string = params['id'];
                // Return the product from ProductService
                this.productService.getProduct(id)
                    .subscribe((product:Product) =>
                        this.product = product);
                // Return the cart item
                this.cartItem = this.cartService.findItem(id);
            });
    }
  }
}
```

We subscribed to all changes that happen in `ProductService` and immediately assign them to the `product` property, so Angular delivers them into the template.

Another approach is to forward the Observable result to the template as implemented in:

```
ProductGridComponent:
@Component({
    selector: 'db-product-grid',
    templateUrl: 'app/product/product-grid.component.html'
})
export class ProductGridComponent implements OnInit {
    products: Observable<Product[]>;

    constructor(private route: ActivatedRoute,
```

```
                private productService: ProductService,
                private cartService: CartService) {}

        ngOnInit(): void {
            this.route
                .queryParams
                .debounceTime(300) // wait for 300ms pause in events
                .subscribe(params => {
                    let category: string = params['category'];
                    let search: string = params['search'];
                    this.products = this.productService
                                    .getProducts(category, search)
                                    .map(this.transform);
                });
        }
        //
    }
```

We then forward the Observable result to the template via the `product` property where the `async` pipe in the `NgFor` handles the subscription:

```
<db-product-card *ngFor="let row of products | async"
        [products]="row" (addToCart)="addToCart($event)">
</db-product-card>
```

Sometimes, we may need to start one request, then cancel it and make a different request before the server has responded to the first one. It is complicated to implement such a sequence with Promises, so let's have a look how Observables can help us.

Observables in search-by-title

We have a feature to search products by title. The user types the title and then presses the **Go** button to request data from the server. We can improve the user experience here, so that when the user types a title into the search box, we will make repeated HTTP requests for products filtered by title. Look at the updated markup of `ProductSearchComponent`:

```
<div class="card">
    <div class="card-header">Quick Shop</div>
    <input #search type="text" class="form-control"
            placeholder="Search for..."
            (keyup)="searchProduct(search.value)">
</div>
```

We removed the **Go** button. An input element gathers the search title from the user and calls the `searchProduct` method after each `keyup` event. The `searchProduct` method updates the query parameters of the URL:

```
@Component({
    selector: 'db-product-search',
    templateUrl: 'app/product/product-search.component.html'
})
export class ProductSearchComponent {

    constructor(private router: Router) {}

    searchProduct(value: string) {
      this.router.navigate(['/products'], {
        queryParams: { search: value} });
    }
}
```

The `ProductGridComponent` listens to the stream of query parameters change in the `route` and manipulates the stream before it reaches the `productService`:

```
ngOnInit(): void {
    this.route
        .queryParams
        .debounceTime(300) // wait for 300ms pause in events
        .distinctUntilChanged() // only changed values pass
        .subscribe(params => {
            let category: string = params['category'];
            let search: string = params['search'];
            this.products = this.productService
                            .getProducts(category, search)
                            .map(this.transform);
        });
}
```

In the preceding code, we wait for the user to stop typing for at least 300 milliseconds with the `debounceTime` operator. Only changed search values make it through to the service via the `distinctUntilChanged` operator. Later, we fetch category and search query parameters and request products from `productService`.

We can quickly start the server and open our web application in the browser to check that all works as expected. From that point, we can demonstrate our project to colleagues or stakeholders as a proof of concept that we will use in future development.

Next, we need a real database and hosting server to finish development and test everything in the real environment. Let's use Firebase to store and sync our data in real time and deliver web content faster.

You can find the source code for this at `chapter_9/3.ecommerce-promise`.

Introduction to Firebase

Firebase is a *Realtime NoSQL JSON Database*. Any piece of data is accessible by URL. Firebase contains SDK for different platforms, such as JavaScript for the Web, IOS, Android, and so on. It includes authentication baked inside core libraries, so we can quickly authenticate users directly from clients via OAuth provided by GitHub, Google, Twitter, and Facebook. It also supports anonymous and password authentication. Firebase provides a hosting service for static assets through the Firebase Console or CLI. Firebase uses web sockets to update data on all connected clients in real time.

If you've never used Firebase before you need to register an account first. Open your web browser and navigate to `https://firebase.google.com/`. Click on **SIGN IN** and use your Google account to set up your Firebase account.

Creating a Firebase project

We are planning to use the Firebase SDK library to access and store data. However, before that, we need to add Firebase to our web application. We'll need a Firebase project, the Firebase SDK, and a short snippet of initialization code that has a few details about our project. Click **Go to console** or open the **Firebase Console** from the following address: `https://firebase.google.com/console`.

Click on the **Create New Project** button and add a project name and your country of origin:

In less than a minute, we will have access to the Firebase relative database, authentication, storage, and so on.

Installing Firebase CLI tools

We will use the Firebase CLI tools to manage, view, and deploy our project to Firebase from a Terminal. Let's open the Terminal, navigate to our project, and run the following command:

```
npm install -g firebase-tools
```

After installation, we will have a globally available Firebase command. Now, we can sign into Firebase from the Terminal. Remember you must already have set up a Google account to proceed:

```
firebase login
```

This command establishes connection to your remote Firebase account and grants access to our projects:

If you interested in knowing what commands the Firebase CLI supports, please go to the official website: `https://firebase.google.com/docs/cli/`.

Initializing a project directory

We will use the Firebase CLI to perform many trivial tasks, such as running the local server or for deployment. Before using it, we need to initialize a project directory for the folder which will contain the `firebase.json` file. Usually we use the root folder of the Angular project as the Firebase project directory. Open the Terminal, navigate to the root folder of our project and execute the following command:

```
firebase init
```

This command will guide you through setting up the project directory. If necessary, you can run this command again safely.

Please answer `Yes` to the question: `Configure as a single-page app (rewrite all URLs to /index.html)?` The Firebase CLI creates the `rewrites` settings inside the `firebase.json` file. We use a rewrite because we want to show the same content for multiple URLs. This is applicable for our application because we configured the Angular Component Router using the default HTML 5 `pushState` strategy. It produces URLs that are easier for users to understand and it preserves the option to do server-side rendering later.

Importing data into Firebase

Before use, we need to import our data into the Firebase database. Open the Firebase console, find your project and click to move it in:

Find the **Database** menu item on the sidebar and click it. That brings the Firebase Realtime Database instance onto the stage. Click the context menu button on the right side and, from the drop-down menu, choose **Import JSON**. I prepared the `firebase.import.json` file for import, so just select it from the root folder of our project and click on **Import**:

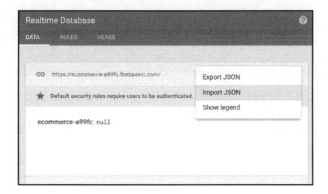

The Firebase Realtime Database stores the data as JSON objects. It looks like a cloud-hosted JSON tree. In contradistinction to an SQL database, there are no tables or records. Each data incorporated to the JSON tree becomes a node in the existing JSON structure with an associated key. We can provide our own keys, such as `category` or `product` IDs, or Firebase can provide them for us in a moment when we save data with a POST request.

The keys must be UTF-8 encoded and cannot be longer than 768 bytes. They can't contain ., $, #, [,], /, or ASCII control characters such as 0-31 or 127.

The data structure of the Dream Bean website is quite simple and contains only two entities with a product to category relationship. The Firebase Realtime Database supports nesting data up to 32 levels deep, and the first temptation is to add `category` into `product`, but be careful doing that because, when you retrieve data later, Firebase will return the product and all of its child nodes as well. Plus, we will have trouble when we try to grant someone read or write access to nodes. The best solution here is denormalize our data to keep the structure as flat as possible. We can follow these recommendations:

- Split data into separate paths
- Add an index or key to your data
- Use an index or key to fetch relational data

At the beginning stage, we deliberately added `categoryId` into the product entity to quickly and efficiently fetch data by index:

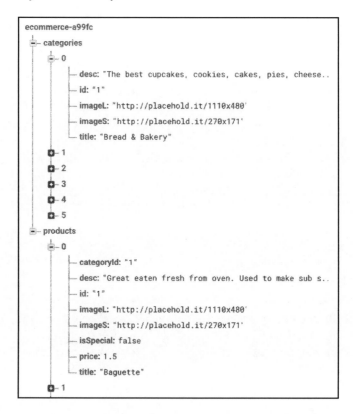

The Firebase database rules

Firebase always creates default rules for each new database:

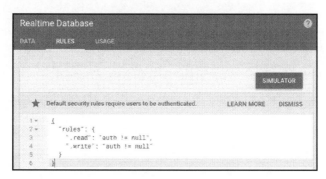

The rules of the Firebase Realtime Database are quite flexible and expression based. We can use JavaScript-like language to define:

- The structure of data
- The data indexes
- Secure data with the Firebase Authentication service

By default, the database rules require Firebase authentication and grant full read and write permissions only to authenticated users, so it isn't accessible to everyone. We will change the rules to organize read access to everyone but keep write access to authenticated users. Rules can be configured in two different ways. The easiest way to create an immediate effect is to use the Firebase console, so let's open it, select the **Database** menu from the side bar and choose the **Rules** tab. You should see the text area with the current rules. You can manually change them or copy the following rules and paste them into the text area:

```
{
  "rules": {
    ".read": true,
    ".write": "auth != null"
  }
}
```

Click **Publish** to apply the new rules on the database. Another way to manage database rules is to create a special JSON file, so the Firebase CLI will use this file when we deploy our project into Firebase. Open the Terminal, navigate into our project and run the following command:

```
firebase init
```

Now, choose the **Database: Deploy Firebase Realtime Database Rules** option. Leave the default answer to all the questions:

Open the `database.rules.json` and update it:

```
{
  "rules": {
    ".read": true,
    ".write": "auth != null"
  }
}
```

Now, once the data's been imported into the database, its time to connect our project to it.

Connecting to Firebase

To organize communication, we need the **AngularFire2** library to integrate Firebase Realtime observers and authentication with Angular2.

Installing AngularFire2 and Firebase

First of all, install the AngularFire2 and Firebase SDK libraries as npm modules:

```
npm install -save angularfire2 firebase
```

The next step is to install Typescript 2 locally because AngularFire2 depends on it:

```
npm install -save-dev typescript@2.0.0
```

Now, update the `systemjs.config.js` file with those two libraries because they need to be mapped with `SystemJS` for module loading:

```
// map tells the System loader where to look for things
var map = {
    'app':          'app',
    'rxjs':         'node_modules/rxjs',
    '@angular':     'node_modules/@angular',
    'firebase':     'node_modules/firebase',
    'angularfire2': 'node_modules/angularfire2'
  };

// packages tells the System loader how to load
// when no filename and/or no extension
var packages = {
 'app':          {main: 'main.js',  defaultExtension: 'js'},
 'rxjs':         {defaultExtension: 'js'},
 'firebase':     {main: 'firebase.js', defaultExtension: 'js'},
 'angularfire2': {main: 'angularfire2.js', defaultExtension: 'js'}
};
```

The AngularFire2 and Firebase setup

We need to set up the AngularFire2 module and Firebase configuration before use. Open the `app.module.ts` file and import the `AngularFireModule`. Now open the web browser, navigate to the Firebase console, and select your project (if it was not already open). Next, click on the **Add Firebase to your app** link:

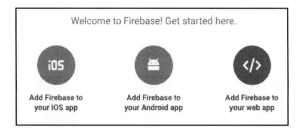

Firebase creates the initialization code snippet, which we will use in our application:

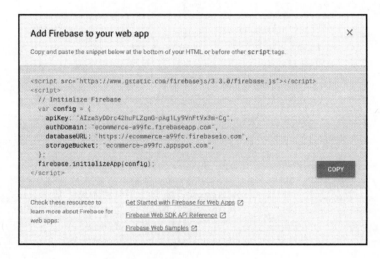

Select the initialization configuration and copy to the clipboard. Switch back to our project and paste it so our code will look like the following:

```
/*
 * Angular Firebase
 */
import {AngularFireModule} from 'angularfire2';
// Initialize Firebase
export var firebaseConfig = {
  apiKey: "AIzaSyDDrc42huFLZqnG-pAg1Ly9VnFtVx3m-Cg",
  authDomain: "ecommerce-a99fc.firebaseapp.com",
  databaseURL: "https://ecommerce-a99fc.firebaseio.com",
  storageBucket: "ecommerce-a99fc.appspot.com",
};

@NgModule({
  imports: [HttpModule,
            AngularFireModule.initializeApp(firebaseConfig),
            BrowserModule, FormsModule, ReactiveFormsModule,
```

```
            routing, CartModule, CategoryModule, ProductModule],
   declarations: [AppComponent, NavbarComponent, FooterComponent,
                  WelcomeComponent, CheckoutViewComponent],
   bootstrap: [AppComponent]
})
export class AppModule { }
```

We are ready to use Firebase in our project.

Getting categories from Firebase

AngularFire2 syncs data as lists with the help of `FirebaseListObservable`, so open the `category.service.ts` file and import it:

```
import {Injectable} from '@angular/core';
import {AngularFire, FirebaseListObservable} from 'angularfire2';
import {Observable} from 'rxjs/Observable';
import 'rxjs/add/operator/catch';
//
@Injectable()
export class CategoryService {
    // URL to Categories Firebase api
    private categoriesUrl = 'categories';
    // We keep categories in cache variable
    private categories: Category[] = [];

  constructor(private af: AngularFire) {}

    getCategories(): Observable<Category[]> {
        return this.af.database
            .list(this.categoriesUrl)
            .catch(this.handleError);
    }

    getCategory(id: string): Category {
        for (let i = 0; i < this.categories.length; i++) {
            if (this.categories[i].id === id) {
                return this.categories[i];
            }
        }
        return null;
    }

    //
}
```

We inject the `AngularFire` service into the constructor. It creates the `FirebaseListObservable` through the `AngularFire.database` service, as we call it in the `getCategories` method with the relative URL.

Getting products from Firebase

It's a different story for fetching data for the products. It is not enough to have only one URL, we need to use query parameters. The list method of the `AngularFire.database` service has a second parameter object that we can use to specify the query parameters:

```
import {Injectable} from '@angular/core';
import {AngularFire, FirebaseListObservable} from 'angularfire2';
import {Observable} from 'rxjs/Observable';
import 'rxjs/add/operator/catch';
import 'rxjs/add/observable/empty';
//...
export class ProductService {

    // URL to Products web api
    private productsUrl = 'products';

    constructor(private af: AngularFire) {}

    getProducts(category?: string, search?: string):
            Observable<Product[]> {
        if (category || search) {
            let query = <any>{};
            if (category) {
                query.orderByChild = 'categoryId';
                query.equalTo = category;
            } else {
                query.orderByChild = 'title';
                query.startAt = search.toUpperCase();
                query.endAt = query.startAt + '\uf8ff';
            }
            return this.af.database
                .list(this.productsUrl, {
                    query: query
                })
                .catch(this.handleError);
        } else {
            return Observable.empty();
        }
    }
}
```

```
getProduct(id: string): Observable<Product> {
    return this.af.database
        .object(this.productsUrl + `/${id}`)
        .catch(this.handleError);
}
//...
}
```

We use Firebase Realtime Database queries to retrieve data based on various factors selectively. To construct a query for `products`, we start by specifying how we want the data to be ordered using one of the ordering functions:

- The `orderByChild` retrieves ordered nodes by a child key
- The `orderByKey` retrieves ordered nodes by their keys
- The `orderByValue` retrieves ordered nodes by the value of their children
- The `orderByPriority` retrieves ordered nodes by priority value

The result of the `orderByChild` function for a specified child key will be ordered as follows:

- Children with a null value
- Children with a false Boolean value
- Children with a true Boolean value
- Children with a numeric value sorted in ascending order
- Children with a string sorted lexicographically in ascending order
- Children with objects sorted lexicographically by key name in ascending order

 The Firebase database keys can only be strings.

The result of the `orderByKey` function will be returned in ascending order by key name as follows:

- Children with a key that can be parsed as a 32-bit integer come first and are sorted in ascending order
- Children with a string value key come next and are sorted in ascending order lexicographically

The result of the `orderByValue` function will be ordered by its value.

The Firebase database priority values can only be numbers and strings.

The result of the `orderByPriority` function will be the ordering of children, and is determined by their priority and key as follows:

- Children with no priorities are sorted by key
- Children with a number are sorted numerically
- Children with a string are sorted lexicographically
- Children who have the same priority are sorted by key

After we've decided how the retrieved data should be ordered, we can use the limit or range methods to conduct complex queries:

- The `limitToFirst` creates a query limited to the first set number of children
- The `limitToLast` creates a query limited to the last set number of children
- The `startAt` creates a query with a particular starting point
- The `endAt` creates a query with a specific ending point
- The `equalTo` creates a query with a particular matching value

We use the `limitToFirst` and `limitToLast` queries to set a maximum number of children the Firebase will return. Using `startAt` and `endAt` queries helps us to choose the arbitrary starting and ending points in the JSON tree. The `equalTo` query filters data based on **exact matching**.

When we select the category we create a query based on a combination, `orderByChild` and `equalTo`, because we know the exact value of `categoryId` to filter:

```
let query = <any>{};
query.orderByChild = 'categoryId';
query.equalTo = category;
return this.af.database
    .list(this.productsUrl, {
        query: query
    })
    .catch(this.handleError);
```

When the user searches by inputting the title, we use a combination of `orderByChild`, `startAt`, and `endAt`:

```
let query = <any>{};
```

```
query.orderByChild = 'title';
query.startAt = search.toUpperCase();
query.endAt = query.startAt + '\uf8ff';
return this.af.database
    .list(this.productsUrl, {
        query: query
    })
    .catch(this.handleError);
```

The \uf8ff character used in the preceding query helps us create a trick. It's a very high value in the Unicode range, and because it's after most regular characters in Unicode, the query matches all values that start with the user's input value.

Deploying the application to Firebase

Our application has only static content, and that means that we can deploy it to Firebase Hosting. We can do this with a single command:

```
firebase deploy
```

The Firebase CLI deploys our web application to the domain:
https://<your-firebase-app>.firebaseapp.com.

We can manage and rollback deployments from the Firebase console:

You can find the source code for this chapter at
`chapter_9/4.ecommerce-firebase`.

Summary

In this chapter, we discovered what data persistence is, and how important it is in client to server communications. We started with a brief tour of the Web APIs before diving deeper into REST to provide a reminder of the main principles of both.

We looked at Angular 2's departure from the `HttpModule` and we discussed how to use it to organize client to server communications. As a bonus, we learnt that we can use the in-memory web API to create proofs of concept, wireframes, or demos.

Observables are a proposed feature for JavaScript version ES2016 (ES7), and we talked about the RxJS polyfill library used in Angular 2 with Observables to help us deal with the asynchronous nature of our applications.

Firebase is a real-time no-SQL JSON database which keeps any piece of data accessible by URL. Firebase contains SDK for different platforms, such JavaScript for the Web, IOS, and Android. We demonstrated how to use it as a persistence layer of our application.

In Chapter 10, *Advanced Angular Techniques*, we will secure our data with the help of the Firebase platform. We will learn how to install `ng2-bootstrap` and how this will enable us to create directives in an easier way. Finally, we will end by building the project we started to develop in previous chapters.

10
Advanced Angular Techniques

This chapter is about advanced Angular techniques. We will learn about how to create client-side authentication, and how to test it on Firebase. We will introduce Webpack to manage modules and their dependencies and transform static assets to build bundles. We will learn how to install `ng2-bootstrap` and how it will enable readers to create an application in an easier way. Finally, we will finish building the project we started to develop in previous chapters.

At the end of the chapter, you will have a solid understanding of:

- Webpack
- Firebase authentication
- The `ng2-bootstrap` components
- Angular CLI
- JIT versus AOT compilation

Let's begin:

1. Open the Terminal, create the folder `ecommerce`, and move in to it
2. Copy the contents of the project from the `chapter_10/1.ecommerce-seed` folder into the new project
3. Run the following script to install `npm` modules:

   ```
   npm install
   ```

4. Start the TypeScript watcher and lite server with the next command:

   ```
   npm start
   ```

This script opens the web browser and navigates to the welcome page of the project.

Webpack

Until now, we've used SystemJS to dynamically load the modules in our application. Now we will start using Webpack's approach to compare it with SystemJS. Our code is growing dramatically along with the chapters of this book, and we must decide what strategy we will use to load the modules shaping our web application. Webpack comes with core functionality and supports many bundle strategies out of the box or with extensions using specific loaders and plugins. It traverses through the required statements of the project to generate the bundles we have defined. We can use plugins for specific tasks such as minification, localization, and so on. Here is a small list of supported features:

- The **hot module reloading** instantly updates Angular 2 components without refresh
- Load bundles as you need them via the **lazy loading** mechanism
- Separate application code on bundles
- Use **hashing** to cache bundles of your web application efficiently in the browser
- Generate **source maps** for bundles to easily debug minified versions of bundles, and so on

Webpack migration

Of course, using Webpack require a little commitment of time, but we get all of the benefits of managing separate dependencies and performance improvements. I've prepared a detailed migration plan to move from SystemJS to Webpack painlessly.

Installing Webpack CLI

Before using it, we must install Webpack globally. Run the following command in the Terminal to make the command available:

```
npm install -g webpack
```

Updating packages

We've used the `lite-server` to serve our application until now. Webpack has its own `webpack-dev-server`, a little Node.js Express server to serve bundles via Webpack middleware. The `webpack-dev-server` is a separate npm package, so we need to update `devDependencies` in the `package.json` accordingly:

```
"devDependencies": {
    "typescript": "^2.0.0",
    "typings": "^1.0.5",

    "ts-loader": "^0.8.2",
    "webpack": "^1.12.2",
    "webpack-dev-server": "^1.12.1"
}
```

The `webpack-dev-server` will serve the files in the current directory, unless we configure it. Change the `scripts` section in the `package.json` as defined in the following code:

```
"scripts": {
    "start": "webpack-dev-server",
    "build": "webpack",
    "postinstall": "typings install"
}
```

Updating TypeScript configuration

From one side, Webpack is a module bundler, and it uses CommonJS or AMD formats to resolve dependencies between modules. From the other side, the Typescript compiler supports several module code generations. We need to choose one module format compatible for both, so I've decided to use the CommonJS as it's much more convenient. Please open the `tsconfig.json` file and update it with the following:

```
{
  "compilerOptions": {
    "target": "es5",
    "module": "commonjs",
    "moduleResolution": "node",
    "sourceMap": true,
    "emitDecoratorMetadata": true,
    "experimentalDecorators": true,
    "removeComments": false,
    "noImplicitAny": false
  }
}
```

Now, it's time to install all necessary `npm` modules and `typings`. Open the Terminal and run the following command:

```
npm install
```

Creating Webpack configuration file

There are two ways to configure Webpack:

- Via CLI when Webpack reads a file `webpack.config.js` or we specify it as a `--config` option
- Via Node.js API where we pass the configuration object as a parameter

The first approach is more convenient for us, so let's create the `webpack.config.js` file. A configuration file in Webpack is a CommonJS module. We put all of our configuration, loaders, and other specific information relating to the build, into this file. There are two main properties each configuration file must have:

- The entry point for one or many bundles.
- The output affecting the results of the compilation which tells Webpack how to write compiled files to disk. There is only one output property, even if we have multiple entry points.

Let's add the following content into the `webpack.config.js` file:

```
module.exports = {
    entry: "./app/main",
    output: {
        path: __dirname,
        filename: "./dist/bundle.js"
    },
    resolve: {
        extensions: ['', '.js', '.ts']
    },
    devServer: {
        historyApiFallback: true,
        open: true,
        watch: true,
        inline: true,
        colors: true,
        port: 9000
    },
    module: {
        loaders: [{
```

```
        test: /\.ts/, loaders: ['ts-loader'],
          exclude: /node_modules/
    }]
  }
};
```

We will use the `main.js` file in the app folder as an entry point. We are planning to save the results of the compilation into the `bundle.js` file under the `dist` directory. The `__dirname` is the name of the directory that the currently executing script resides in. I added the array of `extensions` that Webpack will use to `resolve` the modules.

Webpack can only handle JavaScript natively, so we need to add the `ts-loader` into the `loaders` to process TypeScript files. **Loaders** allow us to preprocess files as we request them. Loaders can be chained together and they are always applied right to left. We can specify loaders in the module `request` but if we want to avoid repetitiveness, there is a better method. Just add them into the Webpack configuration file and specify how to apply them to the different file types. Webpack uses the `test` property of the loader to find the specific files and transform their content respectively. We can add extra conditions to find the files via `include` and `exclude` conditional properties. The condition is always tested against an absolute path and can be one of the following:

- A regular expression
- A string with a path
- A function getting the path as a parameter and returning a Boolean result
- An array of one of the above combined with `and`

And last but not least is the development server configuration. We can configure the `webpack-dev-server` via CLI, but a more elegant way is to add the `devServer` section into the `webpack.config.js` file where we can put all the properties the server needs:

- The `historyApiFallback` helps in using the HTML5 history API
- The `open` flag just opens the backend server URL in the web browser
- The `watch` flag tells runtime to watch the source files and recompile bundles whenever they are changed
- The `inline` flag embeds the `webpack-dev-server` runtime into the bundle
- The `colors` option adds some colors to the output
- The `port` contains the backend server URL port number
- The `host` keeps the server URL host

Let's test how Webpack builds the project with the following command:

```
npm run build
```

Webpack should create the `bundle.js` file inside the `dist` folder.

Updating the markup

The next thing to do is to update the `index.html` file. We need to delete all code belonging to SystemJS and insert the new code:

```html
<html>
  <head>
    <title>The Dream Bean Grocery Store</title>
    <base href="/">
    <meta charset="UTF-8">
    <meta name="viewport"
          content="width=device-width, initial-scale=1">
    <link rel="stylesheet"
          href="node_modules/bootstrap/dist/css/bootstrap.css">
    <link rel="stylesheet"
href="https://maxcdn.bootstrapcdn.com/font-awesome/4.6.3/css/font-awesome.min.css">
    <link rel="stylesheet" href="assets/ecommerce.css">
  </head>

  <body>
    <my-app>Loading...</my-app>
  </body>

  <script src="node_modules/zone.js/dist/zone.js"></script>
  <script src="node_modules/reflect-metadata/Reflect.js"></script>

  <script src="node_modules/jquery/dist/jquery.min.js"></script>
  <script
      src="node_modules/tether/dist/js/tether.min.js"></script>
  <script
      src="node_modules/bootstrap/dist/js/bootstrap.js"></script>

  <script src="dist/bundle.js"></script>
</html>
```

Now we are ready to start the `webpack-dev-server` server. Open the Terminal and run the following command:

```
npm start
```

Webpack opens the web browser and navigates to the following web address: `http://localhost:9000`.

 You can find the source code for this at `chapter_10/2.ecommerce-webpack`.

Preparing our project for production

We can use the project as it is but it's better to make some changes to improve the build pipeline so we can produce it ready to deploy the project structure. Let's create a source folder and move our source code, styles, and template files inside. I would like to include all my resources into the bundles and show you the full potential usage of Webpack via plugins.

The three main entries

The code of our project is still far from production status. We've left references on our JavaScript resources inside the `index.html` file, plus we need to consider how to load style files, Angular 2, and other third-party modules. The plan is quite simple: we need to split all dependencies into their own bundles:

- The `main` file will keep references on our application
- The `polyfill` file contains references on all necessary polyfills
- The `vendor` file contains all the vendors we use

One of the benefits of this approach is that we can add and remove polyfills and vendors independently of our code, so we don't need to recompile it.

Webpack plugins

Webpack has a set of built-in plugins. We need to add them into the `plugins` property in the Webpack configuration file. Webpack splits plugins by groups such as configuration, output, optimize, dependency injection, localization, debugging, and others. You can find the list of built-in Webpack plugins here: `https://webpack.github.io/docs/list-of-plugins.html`.

The DefinePlugin

It's obvious that we need to separate development and production configurations because they have different global constants and behaviors. This plugin allows us to create global constants configurable at compile time and available across all other plugins:

```
const NODE_ENV = process.env.NODE_ENV;
//...
config.plugins = [
  new DefinePlugin({
    'process.env.NODE_ENV': JSON.stringify(NODE_ENV)
  }),
  //...
];
```

Now the `process.env.NODE_ENV` is available in the global scope and the following code in `main.ts` file will work:

```
if (process.env.NODE_ENV === 'production') {
  enableProdMode();
}
```

The ProvidePlugin

The Bootstrap module requires several third-party libraries, such as *jQuery* and *Tether* , to be included in our application. We will use the `ProvidePlugin` to automatically load those modules and make them available in Bootstrap:

```
new ProvidePlugin({
    jQuery: 'jquery',
    $: 'jquery',
    jquery: 'jquery',
    "Tether": 'tether',
    "window.Tether": "tether"
})
```

The ProgressPlugin

We use this plugin to show the progress of compilation in the Terminal.

The LoaderOptionsPlugin

This plugin allows us to add options to some specific loaders:

```
new LoaderOptionsPlugin({
    debug: false,
    minimize: ENV_PRODUCTION
})
```

If you develop your own loader, you can activate the debug mode for it to set it to equals true. In our case, we use the ENV_PRODUCTION global constant to activate loaders into minimize mode only for production.

The CommonsChunkPlugin

Webpack has an opt-in feature helping to split the code into chunks and load them on demand. Furthermore, we need to define split points and Webpack will take care of everything, such as dependencies, output, and runtime stuff:

```
new CommonsChunkPlugin({
  name: ['vendor', 'polyfills'],
  minChunks: Infinity
})
```

In our project, I've explicitly isolated the vendor and polyfills files in their bundles. The minChunks option is the minimum number of chunks which need to contain a module before it can move to common chunks. It can contain a number, callback function, or the Infinity keyword. Passing the Infinity creates a common chunk without moving the modules into it.

The UglifyJsPlugin

This plugin minimizes all the JavaScript output of chunks:

```
new UglifyJsPlugin({
  comments: false,
  compress: {
    dead_code: true, // eslint-disable-line camelcase
    screw_ie8: true, // eslint-disable-line camelcase
    unused: true,
    warnings: false
  },
  mangle: {
    screw_ie8: true  // eslint-disable-line camelcase
```

```
    }
  })
```

We use it only for production, where it deletes the comments, and compresses and mangles variables names in JavaScript files.

The following are several third-party plugins I've used in our project. All of them must be installed as separate npm modules:

The extract-text-webpack-plugin

I imported the style file of our project in the `main.ts` file as follows:

```
/**
 * Import styles
 */
import './assets/ecommerce.scss';
```

Webpack will include the code for the `ecommerce.scss` file in the `bundle.js` file. That solution worked perfectly for development, but I would like to keep the styles as a separate file in production for the following reasons:

- The CSS is not a part of JavaScript bundle
- The CSS bundle requests in parallel to the JavaScript bundle
- The CSS is cached separately
- Runtime is faster because of less code and DOM operations

The `ExtractTextPlugin` must be added into two places:

- In the loader to extract the CSS file
- In the plugin to specify the resulting filename and the necessary behavior of the compiler:

```
config.module.loaders.push({
  test: /\.scss$/,
  loader: ExtractTextPlugin
          .extract('css?-autoprefixer!postcss!sass'),
  include: path.resolve('src/assets/ecommerce.scss')
});
config.plugins.push(
    new ExtractTextPlugin('styles.[contenthash].css')
)
```

After compilation we will have style and source map files ready for production.

The webpack-md5-hash plugin

Whenever Webpack compiles resources into bundles, it calculates the hash sum of each bundle and uses this number as a chunkhash string in the names of files:

```
[chunkhash].[id].chunk.js
```

I prefer to use the Md5 based hash generator plugin to replace a standard Webpack chunkhash with Md5 for our project.

The html-webpack-plugin

As we've said, Webpack calculates and generates the hash for filenames of bundles every time, so we must somehow update that information in our index.html file. The html-webpack-plugin helps make this process painless and adds all HTML generated bundles to an application quickly:

```
new HtmlWebpackPlugin({
    chunkSortMode: 'dependency',
    filename: 'index.html',
    hash: false,
    inject: 'body',
    template: './src/index.html'
})
```

I used the index.html from the source file as a template that the plugin will use to generate the final HTML file inside the dist folder. We can inject generated JavaScript bundles into the head, but usually, we add them to the bottom of the page, just before closing the body tag. This plugin will add the chunks bundles by order of dependencies. The format of the template is based on the **Embedded JavaScript** (**EJS**) templating system, so we can pass values into the plugin, and it will retrieve them directly into the HTML.

Loaders

The newest version of the project uses a wider number of loaders. Loaders, like modules, can be installed via npm. We use loaders to teach Webpack new functionality. You can find the list of Webpack loaders here: https://webpack.github.io/docs/list-of-loaders.html.

Loader naming conventions and search order

Usually, loaders are named as `<context-name>-loader` for easily referencing them in configuration by their full or short name. You can change the loaders' naming convention and precedence search order via the `moduleTemplates` property of `resolveLoader` in the Webpack configuration:

```
["*-webpack-loader", "*-web-loader", "*-loader", "*"]
```

The bootstrap-loader

The `bootstrap-loader` loads the Bootstrap styles and scripts in the Webpack bundle. By default, it's preconfigured to load Bootstrap 3. We can use a special configuration file, `.bootstraprc`, to tweak many details of the loading process. The `bootstrapVersion` option tells the loader which major version of Bootstrap to load. Authors of the plugin recommend using the default configuration as a starting point to prevent unwanted upgrades or mistakes. You can write it in YAML or JSON formats. You can find the full documentation on the official website: `https://github.com/shakacode/bootstrap-loader`.

The css-loader

The `css-loader` can download CSS files as a part of bundle. It resolves and interprets the `imports` and `url` statements as a `require`:

```
url(image.png) => require("./image.png")
```

By default, the `css-loader` minimizes the CSS files if specified to do so by the module system. The web address of the project on GitHub is `https://github.com/webpack/css-loader`.

The file-loader

The `file-loader` copies the file in the output folder and returns the public URL:

```
var url = require("file!./file.png");
```

It processes the content of the file to sum the MD5 hash and uses it as a filename of the resulting file:

```
/public-path/0dcbbaa701328a3c262cfd45869e351f.png
```

You can configure a custom filename template via query parameters such as `name`, `ext`, `path`, `hash`:

```
require("file?name=js/[hash].script.[ext]!./javascript.js");
// => js/0dcbbaa701328a3c262cfd45869e351f.script.js
```

You can find documentation on the official website: `https://github.com/webpack/file-loader`.

The postcss-loader

Over 200 PostCSS plugins exist to solve global CSS problems, to use future CSS today, or to improve the readability of CSS files. The official list of plugins to discover can be found at: `http://postcss.parts/`.

The `postcss-loader` uses PostCSS JS plugins to transform styles:

```
const autoprefixer = require('autoprefixer');
//...
config.module.loaders.push({
    test: /\.scss$/,
    loader:
      ExtractTextPlugin.extract('css?-autoprefixer!postcss!sass'),
    include: path.resolve('src/assets/ecommerce.scss')
});
```

You can find full documentation about how to use it here: `https://github.com/postcss/postcss-loader`.

The raw-loader

This loader just reads the file content and returns it as a string:

```
var fileContent = require("raw!./file.txt");
// => returns file.txt content as string
```

Check the official website here: `https://github.com/webpack/raw-loader`.

The resolve-url-loader

Usually, we use this file in conjunction with other loaders. It resolves relative paths in the `url` statement based on the original source file:

```
var css = require('!css!resolve-url!./file.css');
```

Follow the link on the official website: `https://github.com/bholloway/resolve-url-loader`.

The sass-loader

It loads the SASS file for processing:

```
var css = require("!raw!sass!./file.scss");
// returns compiled css code from file.scss, resolves Sass imports
```

Find full documentation here: `https://github.com/jtangelder/sass-loader`.

The style-loader

You can forget about adding CSS files into HTML files manually with the help of the style-loader. It adds CSS to the DOM by injecting the style tag. It can be very useful for development, but I recommend you extract the contents of CSS into a separate file or bundle if you build for production. The web address for full information is: `https://github.com/webpack/style-loader`.

The ts-loader

You must install TypeScript before using this loader. It loads the TypeScript files and runs the compile:

```
module.exports.module = {
    loaders: [
        // all files with a `.ts` or `.tsx` extension
        // will be handled by `ts-loader`
        { test: /\.tsx?$/, loader: 'ts-loader' }
    ]
}
```

Visit the official website for more information: `https://github.com/TypeStrong/ts-load`
`er`.

The url-loader

This loader is similar to file loader, but it just returns a data URL, if the file size is smaller than the limit:

```
require("url?limit=10000!./file.png");
// => DataUrl if "file.png" is smaller that 10kb
```

Find more information here: `https://github.com/webpack/url-loader`.

 You can find the source code at `chapter_10/3.ecommerce-webpack-advanced`.

User authentication

Authentication is a process of providing identity to the user. Without that, we can't provide the user specific services to grant permission to the user's data. It's a high risk to security sensitive information such as credit card details, so we need to save the user data securely.

Adding authentication in the application

Firebase brings easy authentication, so we can integrate it with any existing login server or clear cloud-based solutions. It supports third-party authentication from GitHub, Google, Twitter, and Facebook as well as built-in authentication via e-mail. Each provider has their own steps to set it up. I will use the **password authentication provider**, but you can add others at any time. Please find the official documentation from the following web page: `htt`
`ps://firebase.google.com/docs/auth`.

Enabling authentication provider

When we created the instance of our web application, Firebase disabled all providers, so we need to enable one before use. Open the web browser, navigate to the Firebase console, and go into our application. Click on the **Auth** menu item on the left sidebar:

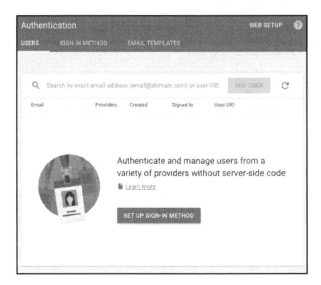

Click on **SET UP SIGN-IN METHOD** to enter. Click on **Email/Password** and activate the provider in the popup dialog:

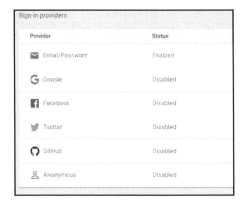

The following **OAuth redirect domains** section keeps only those domains that we whitelisted to initiate authentication for our application:

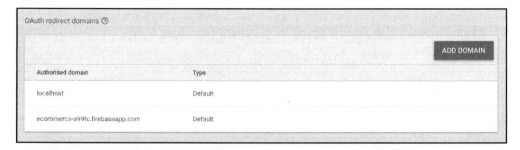

When we registered our application, Firebase added the following origins:

- The `localhost` so that we can develop and test locally
- The `https://<your-project-id>.firebaseapp.com` so that we can use Firebase hosting

If you plan to host your application in other authorized origins, you need to add all of them to enable authentication from their domains here.

AngularFirebase2 authentication

The **AngularFire2 authentication** works without configuration, but it's good practice to configure it before use. The best place to do that is the `app.module.ts` file file where we defined the `AppModule`:

```
/*
 * Angular Firebase
 */
import {AngularFireModule, AuthProviders, AuthMethods}
    from 'angularfire2';
import * as firebase from 'firebase';

// Initialize Firebase
export var firebaseConfig = {
  apiKey: "AIzaSyDDrc42huFLZqnG-pAg1Ly9VnFtVx3m-Cg",
  authDomain: "ecommerce-a99fc.firebaseapp.com",
  databaseURL: "https://ecommerce-a99fc.firebaseio.com",
  storageBucket: "ecommerce-a99fc.appspot.com",
};
// Initialize Firebase Authentication
```

```
const firebaseAuthConfig = {  provider: AuthProviders.Password,  method:
AuthMethods.Redirect}

@NgModule({
  imports: [HttpModule,
            AngularFireModule.initializeApp(firebaseConfig,
firebaseAuthConfig),
            BrowserModule, FormsModule, ReactiveFormsModule,
            routing, CartModule, CategoryModule, ProductModule],
    declarations: [AppComponent, NavbarComponent, FooterComponent,
               WelcomeComponent, CheckoutViewComponent],
    bootstrap: [AppComponent]
})
export class AppModule { }
```

In the `firebaseAuthConfig`, we indicated that we use password authentication and Firebase will redirect to the login page for sign-in. Create the `auth` folder and `auth.service.ts` file inside it.

Authentication service

The `AuthService` is an adapter class that hides implementation details of how Firebase authenticates the user. It uses the `FirebaseAuth` class to do all the work for us:

```
constructor(public auth$: FirebaseAuth) {
    auth$.subscribe((state: FirebaseAuthState) => {
        this.authState = state;
    });
}
```

Some components of our application need to know the authentication status of the user in real time, so I subscribed to listening to the `FirebaseAuthState` events from the `FirebaseAuth` service. Our class consists of two main methods to manage authentication of the user:

```
signIn(email: string, password: string):
    firebase.Promise<FirebaseAuthState> {
    return this.auth$.login({
        email: email,
        password: password
    }, {
        provider: AuthProviders.Password,
        method: AuthMethods.Password,
    });
}
```

```
signOut(): void {
    this.auth$.logout();
}
```

The `signIn` method expects user credentials, such as an e-mail and password, to log in and returns the `FirebaseAuthState` in a Firebase promise. The `signOut` helps us to log out from the application

The SignInComponent

Create the `sign-in.component.ts` file to keep the code of **SignInComponent**. It is a form where the user inputs his or her credentials and clicks on **Sign In** to pass the e-mail and password into the authentication service. It listens to the response that Firebase returns to redirect the user to the welcome page:

```
onSubmit(values:any): void {
    this.submitted = true;
    this.auth.signIn(values.email, values.password)
        .then(() => this.postSignIn())
        .catch((error) => {
            this.error = 'Username or password is incorrect';
            this.submitted = false;
        });
}

private postSignIn(): void {
    this.router.navigate(['/welcome']);
}
```

The code shows an error message if the e-mail and password combination is incorrect. To protect the routes of the application from unauthorized users, we will use the Angular 2 feature called Guards.

Angular Guards

The Angular 2 router provides a feature called **Guard** that returns either `Observable<boolean>`, `Promise<boolean>`, or `boolean` to allow it to activate, deactivate, or load a component. It can be registered in dependency injection as a function or class. The class registration has benefits if we need dependency injection capabilities. To register the Guard as a class, we need to implement one of the interfaces provided by Angular.

There are four Angular Guards interfaces:

- The `CanActivate` Guard checks if a route can be activated

- The `CanActivateChild` Guard checks if the children routes of a particular route can be activated

- The `CanDeactivate` Guard checks if a route can be deactivated

- The `CanLoad` Guard checks if a module can be loaded

Because our Guard code will use the authentication service, I created the `auth.guard.ts` file and the `AuthGuard` as a class that implements the `CanActivate` interface:

```
export class AuthGuard implements CanActivate {

    constructor(private auth: AuthService, private router: Router)
    { }

    canActivate(): Observable<boolean>|boolean {
      return this.auth.auth$.map((authState: FirebaseAuthState)=>{
          if (authState) {
              return true;
          } else {
              this.router.navigateByUrl('/login');
              return false;
          }
      }).first();
    }
}
```

The Angular router will call the `canActivate` method of the interface to decide if a route can be activated by listening to the `FirebaseAuthState` event. If a user is successfully authenticated the method returns `true`, then the component registered in the route will be activated. If not, it returns `false` and redirects the user to the login page.

Logout in Navbar

I think it's a good idea if our users have the option to sign-out from a web application. We should inject the authentication service into the `Navbar` component and create the logout method to call it to sign-out the user:

```
export class NavbarComponent {
  constructor(private authService: AuthService,
             private router: Router) { }
```

```
logout() {
  this.authService.signOut();
  this.router.navigateByUrl("/login");
  }
}
```

As you'll remember, we have an `authenticated` property in `AuthService` which changes the state when the user signs in or out of the application. We will use it to manage the appearance of the **Sign Out** and **Cart** components in the markup:

```
<div class="collapse navbar-toggleable-xs"
  id="exCollapsingNavbar">
  <a class="navbar-brand" href="">Dream Bean</a>

  <div class="nav navbar-nav">
    <a class="nav-item nav-link" (click)="logout()"
       *ngIf="authService.authenticated">Sign out</a>
  </div>

  <db-cart-menu *ngIf="authService.authenticated"></db-cart-menu>
</div>
```

When the user is signed-in to the application, those two components becomes visible.

Updating the Firebase database rules

Now, when we secure our application on the client side, we must change the Firebase database rules so that only authenticated users have access to the data:

```
{
  "rules": {
    ".read": "auth != null",
    ".write": "auth != null",
    "products": {
      ".indexOn": ["categoryId", "title"]
    }
  }
}
```

Time to play

Open the Terminal and run the following command to make a production build:

```
npm run build
```

After successfully doing this, we can deploy our application onto Firebase hosting:

```
firebase login
firebase deploy
```

Open a web browser and navigate to the web application:
`https://<your-project-id>.firebaseapp.com`.

Any combination of e-mail and password brings the exception authorization message on the screen:

Our application doesn't have a registration form so that we can add the *test user* directly into the Firebase via console. Open the Firebase console and navigate to our application. Click on the **Auth** link on left sidebar to open the **Authentication** page:

Click on **Add User** to open the popup dialog:

Add an Email/Password user

Email

admin@dreambean.com

Password

123456

CANCEL   ADD USER

Fill in the blank fields and click **Add User**. Now that we have the registered test user we can go back to our application and use the e-mail and password to successfully sign-in.

You can find the source code for this at `chapter_10/ 4.ecommerce-firebase-auth`.

The ng2-bootstrap

There is the `ng2-bootstrap` library which has no dependencies on jQuery and Bootstrap JavaScript files. It has a set of native Angular 2 directives for Bootstrap versions 3 and 4, so it costs nothing to try it out. For more information about how to use different components please go to the official website: `https://valor-software.com/ng2-bootstrap/index-bs 4.html`.

Firstly, we will clean the project out of the bootstrap-centric modules:

```
npm uninstall –save bootstrap bootstrap-loader jquery tether
```

Then, remove Bootstrap 4 modules from the `vendors.js` file:

```
// Bootstrap 4
import "jquery";
import "bootstrap-loader";
```

Now, we are ready to install, so open the Terminal and install `ng2-bootstrap`:

```
npm install ng2-bootstrap --save
```

The `ng2-bootstrap` module must be imported into `AppModule`. After installation, `ng2-bootstrap` supports Bootstrap version 3, so it's necessary to set the theme to Bootstrap 4 before use:

```
import {Ng2BootstrapModule, Ng2BootstrapConfig, Ng2BootstrapTheme}        from
'ng2-bootstrap';
Ng2BootstrapConfig.theme = Ng2BootstrapTheme.BS4;

@NgModule({
  imports: [
    AngularFireModule.initializeApp(firebaseConfig,
      firebaseAuthConfig), AuthModule,
    BrowserModule, FormsModule, ReactiveFormsModule,
    routing, CartModule, CategoryModule, ProductModule,
      Ng2BootstrapModule],
  declarations: [AppComponent, NavbarComponent, FooterComponent,
    WelcomeComponent, CheckoutViewComponent],
  bootstrap: [AppComponent]
})
export class AppModule { }
```

Finally, we will add the link on Bootstrap 4 CSS referencing on CDN inside the index.html:

```
<link rel="stylesheet"
href="https://maxcdn.bootstrapcdn.com/bootstrap/4.0.0-alpha.2/css/bootstrap
.min.css" crossorigin="anonymous">
```

The migration plan is clear enough: find all the places where we can use ng2-bootstrap and change the Bootstrap 4 based code to the appropriate components.

Updating the slideshow on the welcome page

On the welcome page, we use the slideshow component for cycling through images as a carousel. ng2-bootstrap has a native component carousel doing the same thing. The main benefit of using the new component is writing less markup code:

```
<carousel>
  <slide *ngFor="let category of slideCategories; let i=index"
        [active]="category.active">
    <db-category-slide [category]="category"></db-category-slide>
  </slide>
</carousel>
```

The carousel has the following properties we can use to manage the slideshow:

- The `interval` property is an amount of time in milliseconds to delay between automatically cycling an item. By default, this amount equals 5,000. If you change it to `false`, the carousel will not automatically cycle.
- The `noTransition` property will disable transition between slides. It is `false` by default.
- The `noPause` property will disable pausing on the carousel mouse hover. It's `false` by default.
- The `noWrap` property will prevent continuous cycling. By default, it's set to `false`.

Update the drop-down cart in Navbar

We use the drop-down component in Navbar to display the user's cart information. Let's update this component on analog from `ng2-bootstrap`.

First of all, we need import the `DropdownModule` into the `CartModule`:

```
import {DropdownModule} from 'ng2-bootstrap';

@NgModule({
    imports: [CommonModule, FormsModule, ReactiveFormsModule,
            RouterModule, DropdownModule],
    declarations: [CartItemCountComponent, CartMenuComponent,
            CartViewComponent],
    exports: [CartMenuComponent, CartViewComponent,
            CartItemCountComponent],
    providers: [CartService]
})
export class CartModule {}
```

After that, open the `cart-menu.component.html` and update the markup code wrapping the cart's content:

```html
<div class="nav navbar-nav float-xs-right">
    <div class="nav-item">
        <div dropdown>
            <a href class="nav-link" id="cart-dropdown"
                dropdownToggle>
                Cart: {{cart.amount | currency:'USD':true:
                        '1.2-2'}} ({{cart.count}} items)
            </a>
```

```
                  <div class="dropdown-menu dropdown-menu-right"
                      dropdownMenu aria-labelledby="cart-dropdown">
                    <!-- cart content -->
                  </div>
              </div>
          </div>
      </div>
```

Any `ng2-bootstrap` drop-down based solution should include the following component:

- A drop-down root element marked with a `dropdown` directive
- An optional toggle element marked as `dropdownToggle`
- A drop-down menu holding the content marked with `dropdownMenu`

We can use the `isOpen` property to manage the opened state of a dropdown.

 You can find the source code for this at `chapter_10/5.ecommerce-ng2-bootstrap`.

Angular CLI

Now you have some knowledge about how to create a web application with SystemJS or Webpack and you understand that this is not a trivial process. Remember that all of the configurations belonging to different module loaders is too complicated and sometimes you will spend too much time on routine tasks. We've managed everything by ourselves until now, but it would be worth adding the Angular CLI to the scaffold to handle tedious tasks and build Angular applications.

The following command will install the Angular CLI:

```
npm install -g angular-cli
```

Run the following command to get the use commands:

```
ng --help
```

We will create the new Angular project with the following command:

```
ng new ecommerce
```

After several minutes you will be ready to start the Angular 2 project with the installed NPM modules. Move into the project folder and start the development server:

```
cd ecommerce
ng serve
```

Now open `localhost:4200` in the web browser. The Angular CLI follows the recommended application structure and style guide when generating the source code and folders. We followed the same principles when we developed our project so that we can smoothly move the code from the previous project into the new one.

Stop the server and install the following modules:

```
npm i angularfire2 firebase @types/request ng2-bootstrap
```

Find the `angular-cli.json` file in the root of the project and make the following changes in `styles` and `scripts` to add references on our `ecommerce.scss` style and `ng2-bootstrap` bundle:

```
"styles": [
  "assets/ecommerce.scss"
],
"scripts": [
  "../node_modules/ng2-bootstrap/bundles/ng2-bootstrap.umd.js"
],
```

Copy the `database.rules.json`, `firebase.json`, and `firebase.import.json` files from the previous project, so we can use Firebase CLI to deploy our project to the host.

Delete all files from the `src/app` folder except for the `index.ts` file. Copy all the files from the `src/app` folder of the previous project into the new one.

Now run the development server, and open or refresh the `localhost:4200` in the web browser to see how our project is back online.

From now, you can generate new components, routes, services, and pipes with a simple command as well as run tests and builds. Please check the official website of Angular CLI to get more information: `https://cli.angular.io`.

Just-in-time compilation

My big concern is the size of our application. Look at the stats Webpack usually prints at the time of building the chunk files:

```
            Asset      Size  Chunks              Chunk Names
    main.bundle.js   3.84 MB    0, 3  [emitted]  main
  styles.bundle.js   11.1 kB    1, 3  [emitted]  styles
 scripts.bundle.js    254 kB    2, 3  [emitted]  scripts
         inline.js   5.53 kB       3  [emitted]  inline
          main.map   4.18 MB    0, 3  [emitted]  main
        styles.map   16.1 kB    1, 3  [emitted]  styles
       scripts.map    299 kB    2, 3  [emitted]  scripts
        inline.map   5.59 kB       3  [emitted]  inline
        index.html  799 bytes        [emitted]
Child html-webpack-plugin for "index.html":
            Asset    Size  Chunks         Chunk Names
       index.html  3.08 kB       0
webpack: bundle is now VALID.
```

The bundle files are more than 4 Mbytes. Why is the application so huge?

When the application loads in the browser, Angular compiles it at runtime using the **Just-In-Time (JIT)** compiler. That compiler is the part of the code we load whenever we bootstrap the application. Note, we used this approach for building our project based on SystemJS or Webpack module loaders. That solution has the following drawbacks:

- Performance penalty, because code always compiles before use
- Rendering penalty, because each view is compiling before display
- Size penalty, because the code includes JIT compile
- Code quality penalty, because JIT compilation discovers errors at runtime

We can solve many of those issues if we start using the **Ahead-Of-Time (AOT)** compilation.

AOT compilation

In an AOT approach, we compile all resources upfront, so we don't need to download the compiler into a web browser. This has the following benefits:

- Smaller application size, because the code doesn't include the compiler
- Blazing rendering, because the browser code and templates are precompiled
- Fewer resource requests, because the styles and templates are compiled into the code
- Better template bindings error detection at the moment of compilation

- Fever possibilities for injection attack, because the web browser doesn't need to evaluate precompiled templates and components

So, how can we use this fantastic approach? The answer is very simple: use Angular CLI. It supports AOT out of the box, so we need only add the following commands into the scripts of `package.json`:

```
"scripts": {
  "start": "ng serve",
  "lint": "tslint "src/**/*.ts"",
  "test": "ng test",
  "pree2e": "webdriver-manager update",
  "e2e": "protractor",
  "prod:build": "ng build --prod --aot",   "prod:serve": "ng serve --prod --aot"
},
```

Save the changes, open the Terminal and run AOT build:

```
npm run prod:build
```

The size of the bundle files after `gzip` compression are less than 400 Kbytes:

Asset	Size	Chunks		Chunk Names
styles.7486365d13c6487a030e.bundle.map	32.3 kB	1, 3	[emitted]	styles
main.db3924218d853c0d28cd.bundle.js	1.37 MB	0, 3	[emitted]	main
scripts.84d279fe3f7a3de7ea6c.bundle.js	254 kB	2, 3	[emitted]	scripts
inline.js	1.47 kB	3	[emitted]	inline
main.db3924218d853c0d28cd.bundle.map	7.85 MB	0, 3	[emitted]	main
styles.7486365d13c6487a030e.bundle.js	4.87 kB	1, 3	[emitted]	styles
scripts.84d279fe3f7a3de7ea6c.bundle.map	531 kB	2, 3	[emitted]	scripts
inline.d41d8cd98f00b204e980.bundle.map	13.5 kB	3	[emitted]	inline
scripts.84d279fe3f7a3de7ea6c.bundle.js.gz	41.5 kB		[emitted]	
main.db3924218d853c0d28cd.bundle.js.gz	331 kB		[emitted]	
index.html	862 bytes		[emitted]	

You may start the development server with AOT and check the resulting size of the application your web browser:

```
npm run prod:serve
```

You can find the source code at `chapter_10/6.ecommerce-aot-compilation`.

Summary

In this chapter, we learned how to create a client-side solution for account management and authentication, and how to test it on Firebase. We introduced Webpack and migrated our application from SystemJS. We know that it traverses through the required statements of the project to generate the bundles we have defined. Later we rediscovered our project and made more changes to use Webpack plugins. We now know that Webpack has a set of built-in plugins we can split by groups, such as configuration, output, optimize, dependency injection, localization, debugging, and others.

We learned that authentication is a process of providing identity to the user, and without that, we can't provide user specific services to grant permission to the user's data. We learned that Firebase brings easy authentication with any existing login server or uses a clear cloud-based solution. It supports third-party authentication from GitHub, Google, Twitter, and Facebook as well as built-in authentication via e-mail. Now we know that the AngularFire2 authentication works without configuration.

The `ng2-bootstrap` library has a set of native Angular 2 directives for Bootstrap versions 3 and 4 and it has no dependencies on jQuery and Bootstrap JavaScript files. We quickly integrated it into our project.

The Angular CLI helps to easy create an application, generate components, routes, services, and pipes out of the box. It supports the Ahead-Of-Time compilation to dramatically decrease the size of the application and improve the performance and security.

Finally, we ended by building the project we started to develop in previous chapters.

Index

M

Media Access Control (MAC) 314
Media Queries 48
microsyntax 152
modern web application 163

N

naming convention 131
Nav component 74
nav-stacked class 77
nav-tabs class 76
Navbars
  about 78
  colors, managing 80, 81
  containers 81, 82, 83
  content 79, 80
  content alignment 86
  Responsive Navbar 83
  responsive utilities 84
navigation component
  about 132, 133
  decorators 133, 134
  NavItem object 135, 136
  tree of components 135
navigation
  dropdowns, adding 77
navs 74
ng2-bootstrap
  drop-down cart, updating in Navbar 371
  reference 369
  slideshow, updating on welcome page 370
NgClass directive 149
NgFor directive 152, 153
NgStyle directive 150
NgSwitch directive 151
NguIf directive 150, 151
NgZone service 283, 284

O

Observables
  about 313
  in search-by-title 328
  versus promises 326
one-way binding

NgModel directive 256

P

Panel 48
parent to child communication
  about 303
  via input binding 303
  via local variable 305
  via service 308, 309
  via to call a ViewChild 307, 308
password authentication provider 361
pills 76
pipe operator 139, 140
postcss-loader
  reference 359
PostCSS.parts
  reference 359
Prepros
  reference 50
product card 181, 182
product service
  about 212
  injector provider 213
Product View
  about 241
  adding, to ProductModule 249
  cart info 245
  CategoryTitle pipe 244
  component 247, 249
  image, displaying 242
  information 242, 244
  navigation 251
  route definition, with parameter 250
production project
  entries 353
  loaders 357
  preparing 353
  Webpack plugins 353
products grid component
  about 183
  AllModule, updating 189
  card columns 184
  card desk 185
  card groups 183
  products module 189

Made in the USA
Middletown, DE
08 April 2017